≋ Hounslow

PLEASE DO NOT REMOVE THIS CARD

**Hounslow Library
Treaty Road Hounslow
01-570 0622**

This book should be returned by the latest date stamped on the card. If you wish to keep it longer you may renew it by post, telephone (once only) or by calling at the library. Please quote card number, author, title, class number and date due for return.

Fines will be charged on overdue books.

LONDON BOROUGH OF HOUNSLOW

D0349311

Peace and the
Strategy Conflict

Peace and the Strategy Conflict

WILLIAM R. KINTNER

A Foreign Policy Research Institute Book

FREDERICK A. PRAEGER, *Publishers*
New York · Washington · London

FREDERICK A. PRAEGER, PUBLISHERS
111 Fourth Avenue, New York, N.Y. 10003, U.S.A.
77–79 Charlotte Street, London W.1, England

Published in the United States of America in 1967
by Frederick A. Praeger, Inc., Publishers
© 1967 by the Foreign Policy Research Institute, University of Pennsylvania

Library of Congress Catalog Card Number: 67-20486

Printed in the United States of America

Acknowledgments

A book of this kind results from the work of many minds. At least vicariously, I have benefited from the insights and constructs developed by American, European, Soviet, and Chinese strategists. I have also gained from studying the informative theories of those who believe that peace can best be assured by arms control and disarmament and by the creation of new international institutions or the strengthening of those that now exist.

I have profited from the wise counsel and assistance of many experienced, disciplined minds, among them my colleagues at the Foreign Policy Research Institute. The guidance, support, and stimulation of the Institute's director, Robert Strausz-Hupé, were invaluable. I am grateful for the constructive criticism and suggestions of James E. Dougherty, Robert Pfaltzgraff, Jr., David Schwartz, Robert Crane, and Robert Herber. Benson Adams, who has an unusual aptitude for searching analysis, was my principal research assistant throughout the preparation of this book. Other research assistants of the Institute who participated in various stages of this study were John Tierney, Ross K. Baker, Robert H. Mills, David Williams, and Carol Lee Hurley.

Particular acknowledgment is made of the substantial intellectual stimulation I have received over the years from conversations about strategy with Richard B. Foster. The imaginative help of William R. Davey and Anne Jonas is also reflected in the book.

Among the many individuals who participated in conferences or otherwise contributed to the study are Dandridge Cole, Francis Hoeber, Brigadier General Henry Huglin, USAF (Ret.), Brigadier General William F. Ryan, USAF (Ret.), Thomas Schelling, Edward Teller, Alvin Cottrell, Anthony J. Wiener, and Thomas Wolfe.

The help of many officers of the United States Air Force is deeply appreciated; regrettably they, as well as other personnel now serving in various departments of the government, must remain anonymous.

For editorial advice, I am indebted to Robert Strausz-Hupé, Robert Pfaltzgraff, Jr., Robert C. Herber, Patricia Wirt, Brenda Rosenbaum, Margaret M. Capotrio, Trevor Depuy, and particularly Robin di Campi.

Only those who have lived through the "nth" draft know how much this book owes to the unfailing industry and secretarial assistance of Kay E. Christiansen, Linda K. Compter, Elaine E. Eisenmann, Diana M. Fillmore, Rachel Halterman, Christine F. Mynaugh, Marilyn T. Popp, Sherry Brosius, Betty Brown, and Marcia Rose.

I wish also to acknowledge permission to quote from the following:

Urie Bronfenbrenner, "Allowing for Soviet Perceptions," *International Conflict and Behavioral Science,* edited by Roger Fisher (New York: Basic Books, 1964).

Bulletin of Atomic Scientists, April, 1962. (Statements made by Peter L. Kapitza.)

"Strategies and Realities," by J. I. Coffey, reprinted from *Proceedings* by permission; copyright © 1966 U.S. Naval Institute.

"Producing Change in an Adversary," by Morton Deutsch, Chapter 8 of *International Conflict and Behavioral Science,* edited by Roger Fisher, Basic Books, Inc., Publishers, New York, 1964.

"Is Russia Winning the Arms Race?," from a copyrighted article in *U.S. News and World Report,* February 6, 1967.

Herman Kahn, "Arms Control and Current Arms Environment," *The Prospects for Arms Control,* edited by James E. Dougherty, with John F. Lehman, Jr. (New York: Mcfadden-Bartell, 1965).

Konrad Lorenz, *On Aggression* (New York: Harcourt, Brace & World, Inc., 1963).

Oleg Penkovskiy, *The Penkovskiy Papers,* translated by Peter Deriabin (New York: Doubleday & Co., 1965).

"Power and Policy Problems in the Defense of the West," *Proceedings of the Asilomar National Strategy Seminar,* Asilomar Conference Grounds, Monterey Peninsula, California. April 25–30, 1960.

Anatol Rapoport, "The Sources of Anguish," *Bulletin of Atomic Scientists,* December, 1965.

Lewis F. Richardson, "Mathematics of War and Foreign Politics," *The World of Mathematics,* edited by James R. Newman (New York: Simon and Schuster, 1956).

Thomas C. Schelling, *The Strategy of Conflict* (Harvard University Press, 1960).

Arthur M. Schlesinger, Jr., *A Thousand Days* (Boston: Houghton Mifflin Co., 1965).

J. David Singer, "The Political Science of Human Conflict," in *The Nature of Human Conflict,* Elton B. McNeil, Editor, © 1965. Reprinted by permission of Prentice-Hall, Inc., Englewood Cliffs, N.J.

"Soviet and American Foreign Policy Attitudes: Content Analysis of Elite Articulations," *Journal of Conflict Resolution,* December, 1964.

Jeremy Stone, *Containing the Arms Race* (M.I.T. Press: Cambridge, Mass., 1966).

Jeremy J. Stone, "The Anti-Missile Folly," *The New Leader,* January 2, 1967.

John Strachey, "The Challenge of Democracy," *The Great Ideas Today.* (Encyclopaedia Britannica, Inc., William Benton, Publisher, 1965, reprinted with the permission of the *Encounter,* London.)

Robert Strausz-Hupé, "The Real Communist Threat," *International Affairs,* October, 1965.

Edward Teller, "Planning for Peace," *Orbis,* Summer, 1966.

L. J. M. van den Buch, "Strategic Concepts of the Russian High Command," *NATO's Fifteen Nations,* December, 1965–January, 1966.

Letter to subscribers of *Disarmament and Arms Control* from Wayland Young, editor, March 21, 1966.

Foreword

In a century marked by incessant conflict, the cry for peace is almost universal. Yet, rarely has there been so much confusion and debate over the conditions of peace: How do we keep the peace? And with whom should we make peace? In the United States, the controversy mounts with each passing year of this nuclear age. And those who clamor the loudest for peace seem to be least able to discern the links between peace, values, and power.

There is growing confusion in our own country over which nation or nations threaten world peace as well as the security of this nation. Fewer than four years after the Soviet Union introduced missiles armed with nuclear warheads into Cuba, Secretary of Defense Robert S. McNamara, in his 1966 statement concerning the U.S. military posture, advised the United States Congress that "the focus of the U.S. defense problem has shifted perceptibly toward the Far East."

Apparently, the Soviet Union, although constantly building on its already impressive military capabilities, is regarded by some U.S. officials as far less of a long-range threat to the United States and world peace than is more backward and much weaker Communist China. As a rule, those responsible for U.S. security plan defense on the basis of information about the capabilities of potential adversaries. Some leaders now seem to assume that Soviet intentions have so changed that Soviet capabilities can be disregarded. Yet there is no shred of hard evidence that the Soviets are ready to reach agreement with the United States on any crucial issue. Nonetheless, we are asked to believe that the Soviet Union, now a "have" nation, seeks only to preserve its economic and technological base and has lost its ideological and expansionist ardor. We are told that the oft-pro-

ix

claimed Soviet slogan "peaceful coexistence" has become the core
and principle of Soviet foreign policy.

Isn't there an organic relationship among repeatedly affirmed Soviet Communist revolutionary goals, reiterated Soviet intentions to
achieve strategic superiority, and a steadily growing Soviet strategic
arsenal? If words have any meaning, there is. Yet, those who believe
themselves more adept at reading the minds of Soviet leaders regard
this view as outside the "mainstream" of realistic thinking.

Evidence gathered about Soviet technological gains and increased
production of a range of advanced weapons is rarely exposed to public scrutiny if such evidence runs counter to the official U.S. assessment of Soviet intentions. Many Americans find it hard to believe
that there is, in the words of André Beaufre, "a peacetime strategy at
the operational level . . . primarily concerned with the production
of new equipment to outdate that of an opponent," and that until
this strategy has been "accorded its rightful place in the strategic
pyramid, it will not be conducted efficiently." The proper conduct of
this strategy may prove to be the best way to preserve the peace. Its
improper conduct could upset whatever little stability remains in the
international order.

Each of the diverging paths toward peace currently being advocated for the United States has far-reaching implications. The problem is an enormously complex one—as complex as the sum of all the
ramifications of human society on this globe. Many intelligent and
well-intentioned men, deeply committed to the preservation of American values, find themselves at opposite poles on this issue.

A growing number of informed people believe that nuclear weapons no longer possess political or military utility except to deter a
general war. Allegedly, deterrence is achieved by the very existence
of nuclear weapons, and any approach to international relations that
envisages a continued role for nuclear power is deemed obsolete. But
we are living in a period of dynamic equilibrium, one in which political and technological variables do not stand still. This equilibrium
can be unexpectedly upset. If, in the future, an expansionist nation
should develop unique means to make nuclear power exploitable,
the U.S. deterrent and, with it, international stability will prove to
have been the good fortune of a passing season.

My view is that the strategic nuclear superiority of the United

States has been, and can continue to be, the major contribution to whatever tenuous stability the world enjoys. Yet, according to the available public evidence, it appears that the measures and programs adopted by the Defense Department to ensure future U.S. strategic advantage are no longer adequate, particularly in light of the sustained Soviet drive to reverse the strategic balance of power. In surveying the utility and reality of American nuclear power in the nine chapters of this book, I have suggested what needs to be done to close a missile gap far more serious than that debated in 1960.

Should the United States use its strategic nuclear superiority as a guardian of world peace or abandon it on the ground that power advantage is the major obstacle to peace? In the evolution of United States–Soviet strategy wrought by the advent of nuclear weapons, the Cuban missile crisis has been considered the watershed. Since then, the United States appears to have been moving away from the margin of strategic superiority it enjoyed over the Soviet Union. The Soviets, in contrast, have evidenced a continuing quest for superiority over their main rival, primarily by exploiting science and technology for military purposes. The strategic assets and liabilities of the United States, the Soviet Union, and Communist China spur the global power confrontation. The Soviets, however, face the unique dilemma of how to divide the West and neutralize the power of the United States before the growing threat of Communist China rivets Soviet attention to the East. Meanwhile, the retention of strategic superiority by the United States may depend on whether it regards its relations with the Soviet Union as revolving on nuclear cooperation or competition. In the face of external threat, the U.S. goal to ameliorate the arms race seems at odds with the need to maintain strategic superiority. Since the character of U.S. relations with its NATO allies in Western Europe may open or close the door to future Soviet gains, the question of NATO vis-à-vis a U.S.–Soviet *détente* will influence U.S. strategic trends in important ways.

For the present, U.S. strategic superiority is indispensable to the preservation of peace. Most Americans would agree with Polybius that "peace, with justice and honor, is the fairest, most profitable possession, but with disgrace and shameful cowardice it is infamous and harmful." It is my hope that this book will advance the pursuit of peace with justice and honor, not only for Americans, but for our allies and ultimately for peoples everywhere.

Contents

Peace and the Strategy Conflict

1

Competitive Paths Toward Peace

An intense intellectual conflict is being waged in the halls of academe and in the offices of the Department of State, on the floors of Congress and on the E-ring of the Pentagon. The dispute concerns the search for peace—what path the United States should pursue and whether the United States should keep a strategic superiority over the Soviet Union.

Strategic superiority has been the ultimate support of U.S. foreign policy in the last decade. For the near future, it is the ultimate guarantee of our own and the Free World's security and the best insurance against nuclear war. Conversely, U.S. failure to maintain superiority would be the strongest possible inducement for the Communists to accelerate aggression at whatever level of conflict seems to them most advantageous.

A few years ago, this thesis seemed self-evident to most Americans. Yet within the past several years, a significant trend of thought has been running toward the unilateral abandonment of U.S. strategic superiority on grounds that this nation's power lead is the major barrier to peace. Now the thesis is being challenged on many grounds, but particularly because of a fear of nuclear weapons magnified by the increasing membership in the nuclear club. Although the survival of strategic superiority as a national policy is far from certain, it is a decision that will determine the standing of the United States in the world of the 1970's.

Measuring Strategic Superiority

Throughout the Cold War, the United States has maintained strategic superiority over the Soviet Union by committing her resources, judgment, and will. That superiority has been a result of many things: a purposeful policy, a calculating choice of weapons,

3

and a systematic search for military-technological advantage. Superiority never has been, nor can be, a simple sum of constants (although the U.S. has been favored by an advantage of numbers in effective offensive delivery systems). Weapons, logistics, or economic resources by themselves cannot assure strategic superiority. History has so often recorded the defeat of "superior" powers by "inferior" powers that the transient nature of strategic advantage must never be discounted.

The concept of strategic superiority in the nuclear age is by necessity imprecise,[1] but it relates to the dynamic interaction between the changing military programs of contesting powers. In the nuclear age, if "superiority" is to be of political value, however, it must be credible to both the nation possessing the advantage and the presumably weaker opponent. Ultimately, strategic advantage or inferiority lies in the perceptions with which the opposing leaderships evaluate their own, as well as their adversary's, strategic capabilities.

The measure of comparative strategic advantage, if ever put to the test, would be the relative survivability of each side following a nuclear exchange. Until recently, the military component of strategic advantage was calculated in terms of the relative size and effectiveness of opposing strike forces. A concise evaluation of strategic advantage is found in biblical history and was stated in Luke 14: "What king, going to make war against another king, sitteth not down first, and consulteth whether he be able with ten thousand to meet him that cometh against him with twenty thousand? Or else, while the other is yet a great way off, he sendeth an ambassage, and desireth conditions of peace." Now, the calculus of strategic advantage must be adjusted for the interaction of both offensive and defensive systems.

Although the nuclear factor makes calculations far more esoteric,

---

[1] "The term strategic superiority is difficult to define in precise terms. Obviously, *it implies both offensive and defensive capabilities that will allow us to come out of any war in better shape than our adversary*. One measure might be the ability to strike second and still come out better—or less badly—than the adversary did striking first. The unspoken leverage of such deterrent strength is likely to be very important in deciding the outcome of confrontations short of nuclear war, even though losses in a nuclear war would be so great on both sides that escalation to that level is very unlikely to take place [italics added]."— Harold Brown, Secretary of the Air Force, Supplement to the "Air Force Policy Letter for Commanders," Number 4-1966, April, 1966, pp. 2–3.

governments have so far been able to measure strategic advantage and act accordingly. This ability was dramatically illustrated in the Cuban missile crisis. The clandestine Soviet effort to place intermediate-range missiles in Cuba was calculated to upset the world balance of nuclear power, and it came perilously close to succeeding. When the Soviet missiles were detected (shortly before their emplacements were completed), the United States brandished its full power to induce the Soviet Government to remove its weapons. President Kennedy's speech to the American people and the Soviet leaders on October 23, 1962, affirmed that a nuclear attack from Cuba against any nation in the Western Hemisphere would be regarded as an attack by the Soviet Union on the United States and would require "a full retaliatory response."

McGeorge Bundy, reflecting on the value of strategic superiority in the Cuban missile crisis, later stated that "this power should exist, and . . . there should be confidence in its future as well as its present effectiveness."[2] During that major nuclear crisis, the United States, as the superior power, had military resources capable of destroying Soviet weapons, which, had they been used first, would seriously have damaged the United States. Since the Cuban missile crisis, however, the realities and perceptions of international power have changed.

The Record of U.S. Advantage

In all the major crises that have punctuated the Cold War, U.S. nuclear superiority has exerted an influence on the policy of the Soviet Union. Generally, the Soviet Union instigated these crises by exploiting situations potentially disadvantageous to the United States or its allies. In meeting a crisis, the United States had to demonstrate its capacity and determination to honor a commitment, whereas the Soviet Union and Communist China were able to withdraw a probe with little or no damage to the dynamic thrust of their foreign policy.

A study of the major crises of the Cold War shows that the possession of clearly superior strategic forces, the capacity to apply those forces in a crisis, the resolve to do so, and the ability to communicate power and intentions to Soviet or Communist Chinese leaders have

[2] "The Presidency and the Peace," *Foreign Affairs*, April, 1964, pp. 353–65.

been crucial to their successful resolution.[3] Strategic forces, though, are designed for direct nuclear attack against military targets and other vital installations in the adversary's homeland, and thus they have played only an indirect role in crisis management. The United States has been best able to control a crisis when its conventional superiority in the area operated under the umbrella of over-all strategic superiority. This combination has held the greatest potential for political bargaining at lower crisis levels.

In times of crisis, when strategic capabilities influence the opponents in one way or another, it is difficult to determine who is influenced, in what direction, by which military factor, and under what circumstances. It is even more difficult to determine what psychological processes are at work in the individual who is perhaps being influenced. Nor is it easy to determine how strategic superiority communicates itself, or is imparted, to policy-makers on opposing sides. Yet, an examination of eight Cold War crises yielded evidence that U.S. strategic forces played a part in conducing fear of unwanted consequences in the minds of Soviet leaders.[4] The analysis generally confirmed the positive assumptions underlying theories of deterrence and escalation—namely, that there are salutary effects in inducing or reinforcing an adversary's fear of undesired consequences. In these specific crises, in fact, interaction took a discernible pattern. Leaders of the Soviet Union often initiated or supported crisis policies despite their awareness of clear U.S. strategic superiority. But as the United States increased its resolve and readied itself strategically and tactically to deal with a crisis, the Soviet Union significantly modified its assessments of the relative merits, consequences, and costs of its policies and generally backed down from crisis-stirring actions. These findings suggest an important relation between U.S. strategic capability and national resolve, on the one hand, and the adversary's perceptions of U.S. policies, on the other.

The ebb and flow of Soviet pressures against the Free World have corresponded with Moscow's idea of its own power position in rela-

[3] *A Study on Crisis Management*, a report to the U.S. Air Force, William R. Kintner, principal investigator, David C. Schwartz, project director (Philadelphia: Foreign Policy Research Institute, 1965).

[4] *Ibid.* The eight crises were: Korea, 1950; Suez, 1956; Lebanon, 1958; Quemoy-Matsu, 1958; Berlin, 1961; Cuba, 1962; Tonkin Gulf, 1964; Cyprus, 1964.

tion to the United States and its allies. During the late 1940's and early 1950's Soviet offensives took advantage of both the postwar demobilization of the United States and the weakness of its Western allies. The Cuban missile crisis followed a period of Soviet expansionist pressure against the West. From 1958 until the confrontation in October, 1962, Moscow apparently believed that it had a psychological, if not strategic, edge over Washington. Acting on this belief, the Soviet Union almost succeeded in upsetting the world balance with missiles in Cuba. The United States managed to convince the Communist leaders that U.S. military power was superior and would be utilized to protect Western interests. The world may owe the relatively peaceful period following the Cuban missile crisis to that accomplishment. U.S. strategic advantages that have been curbing Russia have been summarized as follows:

> The basic constraints on Soviet policy are created by the superiority of U.S. strategic deterrents. Since the Soviet Union is not able to destroy this deterrent without bringing about its own destruction, it must operate with circumspection and avoid: a) provoking the superior adversary into a major war, b) situations and events which could escalate into a full-scale war, and c) "either-or" situations where the alternatives may be war or severe concessions.[5]

Erosion of U.S. Strategic Superiority

During the past ten years, U.S. strategic superiority over the Soviet Union has been declining. Some of the decline in our relative advantage was inevitable, and there was little we could do—short of an outright attack on Soviet manufacturing facilities—to prevent the Soviet build-up of strategic capabilities. Nevertheless, much of the decline is a result of conscious decision-making on our own part. In international equations, U.S. strategic power is the one independent variable that we can strengthen or weaken at our own volition.

Contrary to some opinions, however, the United States has never engaged in an arms race with the Soviet Union. In fact, the proportion of the U.S. defense budget devoted to strategic forces—always a small fraction of the whole—is shrinking progressively. Because of the sizable conventional build-up in Vietnam, more funds may be diverted from allocations for future U.S. strategic forces. The Great

[5] Roman Kolkowicz, "The Role of Disarmament in Soviet Policy: A Means or an End," in *The Prospects for Arms Control,* ed. James E. Dougherty, with John F. Lehman, Jr. (New York: Macfadden-Bartell, 1965), p. 101.

Society and national defense compete for funds. In a few years we shall have to face a painful question: Should we pull in our international horns to pay for a domestic welfare society? Issues such as these make it difficult for a pluralistic democratic system to conduct a purposeful, consistent, and effective foreign policy. Alexis de Tocqueville, defender of democracy, observed:

> Foreign politics demand scarcely any of those qualities which are peculiar to a democracy; they require, on the contrary, the perfect use of almost all those in which it is deficient. Democracy is favorable to the increase of the internal resources of a state; it diffuses wealth and comfort, promotes public spirit, and fortifies the respect for law in all classes of society: all these are advantages which have only an indirect influence over the relations which one people bears to another. But a democracy can only with great difficulty regulate the details of an important undertaking, to preserve in a fixed design, and to work out its execution in spite of serious obstacles.[6]

One source of the erosion in U.S. strategic superiority has been the adoption of a number of arms control measures. For instance, the United States agreed to the Nuclear Test Ban Treaty although both the U.S. Senate Preparedness Subcommittee and the Joint Chiefs of Staff asserted that the treaty was militarily disadvantageous. The United States and the Soviet Union also agreed to a mutual cutback in the production of fissionable material. The United States has honored its pledge, but the Soviet Union has reneged. The United States has delayed the production and deployment of an antiballistic defense system partially on the grounds that such a system would be provocative, but there is mounting evidence that the U.S.S.R. has begun to deploy such a system.

The United States advocates a nonproliferation treaty, which may ultimately weaken the West's over-all strength, for if the treaty is designed on Soviet specifications, it would rule out an integrated Western European nuclear force. Such a treaty could split the West and deny Western Europe the capability of defending itself.

Strategic Alternatives

Almost all serious students of contemporary conflicts acknowledge the need for a U.S. nuclear strategy, but they disagree about what

---

[6] Alexis de Tocqueville, *Democracy in America* (New York: Vintage Books, 1955), I, 243.

kind of strategy it should be.[7] Opponents of strategic superiority have become more sophisticated in recent years, and their arguments are rooted in a realistic understanding of the present and potential threats that the nuclear power of both the Soviet Union and Communist China pose to the United States.

Many of the intellectuals opposing U.S. strategic superiority admit to some of its blessings; nevertheless, they see harm rather than utility in any U.S. effort to retain this advantage. J. David Singer, a member of this school of thought, after an intensive survey of Soviet and American operational codes, claimed that:

> Both major powers have been appallingly slow in discovering the strategies that may enable them to survive the present while shaping the future. . . . Such a strategic preponderance may, for example, have been crucial in inducing the withdrawal of Soviet missiles from Cuba, but we cannot blink the possibility that it may well have provoked such adventurism in the first place. Though the "full first-strike" superiority is no longer official doctrine, our move toward a more conservative and stabilizing posture has been only partial at best.[8]

In Singer's opinion, faulty organization of the international community is primarily responsible for unnecessary conflicts and is an obstacle to the effective handling of conflict. "Thus the nations are left to rely primarily upon the intelligent calculation of their own and others' utilitarian interests if they are to minimize recurrent threats to their security and remain free from war as the most frequent consequence of such threats."[9] "Since nations are compelled to rely heavily on their own power as a means of protecting their interests, this power, which takes the form of military strength, must be mobilized. To effect a high degree of mobilization, the national political elites find it necessary to paint an increasingly treacherous, if not omnipotent, picture of the opposing nation(s) in the conflict."[10]

[7] A description and analysis of the arguments in this emerging debate can be found in Robert A. Levine, *The Arms Debate* (Cambridge, Mass.: Harvard University Press, 1963).

[8] J. David Singer, "Soviet and American Foreign Policy Attitudes: Content Analysis of Elite Articulations," *Journal of Conflict Resolution,* December, 1964, p. 474.

[9] J. David Singer, "The Political Science of Human Conflict," in *The Nature of Human Conflict,* ed. Elton B. McNeil (Englewood Cliffs, N.J.: Prentice-Hall, 1965), pp. 144–45.

[10] *Ibid.,* p. 146.

Once the preparedness program is under way, it grows by a process of positive feedback. "The tragedy is, of course, that about the time the political elites discover what they have set in motion, it is extremely costly to seek to slow or reverse it."[11]

Since a similar pattern takes hold in the opposite nation, the problem, as Singer sees it, is how to reverse this self-winding process. According to Singer, any method for reversing the normal processes of conflict must meet four conditions:

> First, it must be either initially acceptable to the policy-making subgroups (i.e., those who act on behalf of the national state) or . . . in the direction of diminishing their resistance to it. . . . Second, in order that the policy-makers' pay-off matrix can be modified, one of two domestic phenomena must occur. Either those subgroups which reinforce the hard-line tendencies must be weakened vis-à-vis the "moderates," or the former must experience a shift in attitudes such as to move them away from the implacable hostility end of the foreign-policy continuum.
>
> This requires, in turn, the fulfilling of a third set of conditions, that is, the hard-line subgroups must be persuaded that continued resistance to a co-existence strategy will be costly to them in the middle as well as the long run. And that conclusion is unlikely to be reached unless one or both of their two major sources of support and power seem to be turning away from them and thus depriving them of the legitimacy which is the major pillar of that power. . . .
>
> For the latter condition to obtain, of course, we come full circle, and must then look, *inter alia*, at the international environment again. The adversary nation must be expected (despite all of the experimental evidence to the contrary) to respond to co-existence moves in a manner such as to reward the policy-makers diplomatically in order to minimize their losses (and hopefully, maximize their gains) domestically. The fourth condition, therefore, is diplomatic reciprocity, and this requires, in turn, that essentially the same processes be set in motion within the adversary nation, at approximately the same pace.[12]

With admirable candor, Singer concedes that his model of international conflict is a pessimistic one and that the interaction between the United States and Russia—as they defend their national interests at the risk of war—"now looks very much as if it is, in fact, not reversible."[13] Singer has suggested, however, that the United States should make certain unilateral moves to reduce its strategic advantage over the Soviet Union. He argues that in order to accelerate the

[11] *Ibid.*
[12] *Ibid.*, pp. 149–50.
[13] *Ibid.*, p. 153.

process, the U.S. Government should take the lead and persuade the American people to abandon old-fashioned beliefs about military power and warfare. Or, as Singer puts it, "Surely, there must be a way in which they can disarm their bellicose domestic factions and prepare their publics for some modest *détente*."[14]

No one can predict with certainty what the world would be like if the United States scaled down to strategic parity with its chief adversary. On the other hand, how the Soviets would act if the United States were perceived by Soviet leaders to be strategically inferior is perhaps less speculative. Singer, after chiding the United States for military intervention well within the adversary's sphere of interest, conceded that: "The Soviet Union has likewise found it most difficult to move away from the traditional doctrines of 'self-help.' Perhaps as serious as the Cuban adventure and the constant appeal to violence in the nonaligned areas has been their obsessive obstructionism in the disarmament negotiations."[15]

Perhaps the major objection to this path toward peace is its underlying assumption. Singer seems to take for granted a one-to-one equation between the Soviet Union and the United States. His arguments appear to be addressed to our psyche, and, via ours, to that of the Soviets, which eventually will change because of the change in ourselves—a kind of reverse psychological warfare. Moreover, it assumes a cultural, psychological, and sociological symmetry that now does not exist: The controlled *Pravda* does not equal *The New York Times*, the scope of *International Affairs* does not equal that of *Foreign Affairs*, and an apple does not equal a cucumber.

In reality, Soviet perceptions and Soviet modes of thought are far different from our own:

> Given our necessarily limited perspective, we cannot arrive at an appreciation of the springs of Soviet action solely through the power of logical analysis, no matter how rigorous, or of creative imagination, no matter how ingenious. As the essential starting point of our estimates, we need first to obtain and analyze data which can instruct us about the nature of Soviet perceptions, motives, and fears.[16]

[14] Singer, "Soviet and American Foreign Policy Attitudes: Content Analysis of Elite Articulations," p. 475.

[15] *Ibid.*, p. 474.

[16] Urie Bronfenbrenner, "Allowing for Soviet Perceptions," in *International Conflict and Behavioral Science*, ed. Roger Fisher (New York: Basic Books, 1964), p. 168.

The challenge of the nuclear age is to find methods for resolving international conflicts without triggering a general nuclear war. For the United States, the search is complicated by the equally pressing need to defend its basic values against a persistent and many-pronged attack. Communists have frequently contended that *"the beginning of all wars will be finally eliminated only when the division of the society into hostile antagonistic classes is abolished. The victory of the working class throughout the world and the victory of socialism will bring about the removal of all social and national causes of the outbreak of wars, and mankind will be able to rid itself forever of that dreadful plight [italics added]."*[17]

Most arguments about international security focus on ends rather than means. The underlying debate really concerns the role of nuclear forces and is less concerned with strategy than with some basic, but unstated, premises about the nature of the evolving world order. In other words, if one accepts as valid a particular premise about the real world, then it is not too difficult to choose a strategy to fit.

Premises that concern the international environment and that can influence strategic choice tend to center around two poles. One appraisal is that the Soviet Union voices its revolutionary goals, but in reality it has tacitly abandoned them. Thus, we are told that the "North-South" struggle between the industrialized nations and the developing nations has become more important than the outmoded Cold War, East-West conflict. It is oppositely held that the Soviet drive for world hegemony, although occasionally muted for tactical reasons, is still the central thrust of Soviet policy. And numerous other premises relate to these divergent views.

There are those who assert that a technological plateau has been reached, and they decry the futility of U.S. efforts to maintain strategic superiority. Strategists of this persuasion also tend to favor the search for a nuclear *détente* with the Soviet Union above the preservation of NATO. They consider NATO to be obsolete and in the way of peace. Other strategists credit NATO with whatever mellow-

[17] Nikita Khrushchev, "Report on the Moscow Conference," speech delivered January 6, 1961, in Moscow, cited by U.S. Congress, Senate Subcommittee of the Committee on the Judiciary, *Hearings, Analysis of the Khrushchev Speech of January 6, 1961,* testimony of Dr. Stefan T. Possony before the 87th Cong., 1st Sess., June 16, 1961, p. 63. This theme has been pronounced by Soviet leaders before and after Khrushchev.

ing may have occurred within the Soviet system and particularly the nations of Eastern Europe.

Some strategists regard the Sino-Soviet split as the guarantee of a more benign Soviet Union. The dissenters believe that the split may possibly exacerbate conflict in many parts of the globe and that, for the West, any positive gains from the split will be harvested only in the distant future. Many advocates of U.S. strategic superiority believe that mankind's leaders are motivated by the same drives and greeds that have always brewed conflict. Some of them conclude that the tide of history still runs strongly against the West. Or, as one student of world affairs asserts:

> After nearly 20 years of Cold War, the West is still mostly fighting it by Communist rules. No wonder that the West, trapped in the defensive, has not been winning the Cold War. The expense has been enormous; the returns have been meagre. Hence the mounting sense of frustration that pervades the West's decision-making quarters and, increasingly, the West's intellectual community. Hence the escapist illusions—the new myths—that supersede rational calculation. The West wants surcease from the protracted conflict. What more comforting haven beckons the weary Western warrior than the notion of a Communist change-of-heart? How reassuring is the thought that the Cold War will end because the Communists want to halt it and not because the West needs to prevail, because the Communists, too, dread the spectre of nuclear war; because the Communists are "mellowing"; and because indigenous developments are changing the Communist orbit in ways beneficial to the rest of the world.[18]

It is also argued that many Americans do not want the protracted conflict to cease. The government officials and their advisers who have won their reputations in the numerous engagements marking the East-West conflict may be reluctant to admit that the foundation of their *raison d'être* is crumbling. As our cold warriors, they seek to convince the political leaders of the United States that the Communist challenge, though altered, still remains the overarching problem.

Adherents of the opposite view believe that a new world synthesis, which fuses the best of East and West, will soon emerge. Many of the plans for an amelioration of the U.S.-Soviet conflict would be desirable if they could be effected within a reasonable amount of

[18] Robert Strausz-Hupé, "The Real Communist Threat," *International Affairs*, October, 1965, p. 617.

time. But such sanguine plans can be realized only when Communist countries are controlled by politically influential groups willing to deal with the West on a basis of genuine cooperation. For why should Communist leaders cooperate if they are satisfied with the results of their competitive approach?

An in-depth analysis of these views of world politics would require volumes. Some views are touched upon in subsequent chapters. The important point, however, is that U.S. strategy is determined less and less by an adversary's actual or even estimated military capability. The most important influence is political judgment, which is affected by subjective and normative views of the present and future world.

Power Decisions and Political Aims

Except for the United States, every nation in the nuclear club appears to have joined primarily for political reasons and only secondarily for purposes of security. The Soviet Union has long exploited nuclear weapons for their political value;[19] both the British and the French were motivated to acquire nuclear weapons to improve their diplomatic bargaining power within the Western alliance. The Chinese Communists' atomic bomb symbolizes their claim to future great-power status.

For the United States, too, political choice will settle the key security issue of maintaining or not maintaining strategic superiority. Under both the Truman and Eisenhower administrations, the composition of U.S. strategic forces was influenced by economic and technological restraints and also varied with political perceptions of the world. Break-throughs in technology did not solely describe size and characteristics of U.S. armed forces.

During the Kennedy Administration, however, technological obstacles were often given as the principal reason for the United States not acquiring a particular advanced offensive or defensive weapons system. President Kennedy's scientific adviser, Jerome B. Wiesner, subsequently stated:

> Weapons technology and strategic thinking have reached a plateau. New weapons developments of the past several years have been primarily refinements leading to greater reliability, greater fire power, higher effi-

[19] See Arnold L. Horolick and Myron Rush, *Strategic Power and Soviet Foreign Policy* (Chicago: University of Chicago Press, 1966).

ciency, and greater economy; they have hardly been of a sort to make either side fear that any one development would disrupt, even partially, the established nuclear stalemate.[20]

Many scientists take issue with Wiesner. In point of fact, in the mid-1960's renewed technological acceleration was evident in both the Soviet Union and the United States. The fact of this technological surge casts doubt on U.S. strategic doctrines of only a few years ago. Furthermore, technology has moved forward so rapidly in the past several years that, for the United States, it is rarely a restraining factor in the design of its strategic forces. As things now stand, U.S. strategic forces can be designed for a wide range of political preferences. The Soviet choice, on the other hand, is more limited by economic considerations and, to a lesser extent, by technological restraints. The arguments for or against the United States endeavoring to maintain strategic military superiority (at least until a secure arms control agreement can be reached between the major nuclear powers) may still be couched in terms of economic and technological considerations. Yet the crucial component of these arguments, whether explicit or not, is the political perceptions with which key U.S. officials regard the future world and the role of the United States.

Undeniably, many of the advocates of both a "unilateral initiative" for reversing the arms race and a strategy for interdependence between the United States and the Soviet Union have, more clearly than others, seen the practicality—if not the necessity—of meshing strategic decisions with political aims. Conversely, advocates of strategic superiority have too often viewed a U.S. military advantage over the Soviet Union as an end in itself—a sterile view that has led to much of the current questioning of the value of strategic superiority. Because strategic superiority should not be visualized as an absolute concept but as a relative one, the extent of superiority should always be related to the discernible present and future threat. Far more importantly, strategic superiority has value for the United States only if it serves a policy calculated to bring about in the Soviet system many of the same kinds of changes that the advocates of "unilateral initiative" and "interdependence" seek. In other words, the political implication of our decisions regarding the design of fu-

[20] Jerome B. Wiesner, from Forward to Jeremy Stone, *Containing the Arms Race* (Cambridge, Mass.: M.I.T. Press, 1966), p. viii.

ture U.S. strategic forces must be spelled out to Communist leaders. For, the year-by-year plan of future strategic offensive and defensive forces may not only change the objective situation, affecting Soviet allocation of resources,[21] but also raise either the hopes or doubts of Soviet leaders about their prospects for ever overcoming the U.S. military-technological lead. But the task of communicating to Soviet leaders through the walls of their fears and misconceptions is a formidable one.[22]

> In urging adoption of a psychological perspective in considerations of American policy, I am not arguing for the elimination of other more traditional considerations. Were American decisions to be guided substantially by psychological, economic, and other factors, the outcome would be tragic indeed. But it is the major thesis of this paper that the converse of the foregoing proposition is equally valid. To base our arms control and disarmament policy primarily on considerations of strategy and national analysis is to court disaster just as surely.[23]

The Promise of Strategic Superiority

Replying to the question of whether present and future generations will live in peace, President Johnson predicted:

> Conflict among nations will trouble this planet and will test our patience for a long time to come. And as long as weapons are necessary, wisdom in their control is going to be needed. The man who guides them holds in his hands the hopes of survival for the entire world.[24]

It will be a long time before mankind reaches the peaceful millennium in which conflict will have ceased. But even in this era of disputes and conflict, some observers of international politics suggest that the Soviet Union is gradually awakening to those interests that, presumably, it has in common with the United States. Furthermore, they deem it likely that the Soviets will sooner or later align them-

[21] Ithiel de Sola Pool, with Barton Whaley, *Deterrence as an Influence Process* (Cambridge: Center for International Studies, Massachusetts Institute of Technology, 1963). Among the various ways of influencing the adversary's attitude and decision, Ithiel de Sola Pool includes changing the objective environment and changing the influence's resources.
[22] Bronfenbrenner, "The Place of a Psychological Approach," *op. cit.*, p. 178.
[23] Bronfenbrenner, "Allowing for Soviet Perceptions," *op. cit.*, p. 168.
[24] Address delivered at a dinner honoring United States and Canadian Partnership in Progress, Seattle, Washington, September 16, 1964. See "The Direction and Control of Nuclear Power," *Department of State Bulletin*, October 5, 1964, p. 460.

selves with the United States against the "have-not" nations.[25] In arguing for an antinuclear-proliferation treaty with the Soviet Union, William C. Foster, Director of the U.S. Arms Control and Disarmament Agency, commented that the Soviet Union, following the Cuban missile crisis, "appears to have appreciated to a degree not apparent before that its long-term interests might best be served by increased emphasis on internal development and a relaxation of the Cold War."[26]

Given the proper time and circumstances, even the most optimistic prophecies may eventually prove accurate. In light of today's realities, however, there is little evidence supporting contentions that the rivalries of our time are easing. Although many believe that the October, 1962, events in Cuba represented a watershed in the Cold War, that checkmate may, on the contrary, be a warning that the Soviet Union would move again to gain strategic advantage over the United States.

The United States has frequently proclaimed its intention to create, insofar as it is able, a peaceful world order. Ironically, and even though certain other forms of violent conflict may continue, the U.S. capability to render nuclear war improbable is the overriding contribution that the United States has made, and can continue to make, to the cause of peace. We may succeed in preventing a nuclear war, but transforming this conflict-oriented world into a relatively more peaceful one will take generations. In a paradoxical way, the mere existence of nuclear weapons is contributing to the transformation and, at the very least, counteracts the possibilities of a conventional conflict on the scale of World War II. However, these weapons cannot by themselves induce changes in Communist systems.

In the long view, the best way to promote peace is to help transform the centers of aggressive Communism. But in dealing with the present danger, U.S. foreign policy has to rely on our political, economic, and moral power—employing military strength only when necessary to thwart an enemy's physical aggression. The United

[25] See, for example, Amitai Etzioni, *Winning Without War* (Garden City, N.Y.: Doubleday, 1964), p. 69; and Vincent P. Rock, *A Strategy of Interdependence* (New York: Scribners, 1964).

[26] "New Directions in Arms Control and Disarmament," *Foreign Affairs*, July, 1965, p. 587.

States must be both powerful and skillful to contest the profoundly reactionary concept underlying Communist dogma—namely, that change flows mainly from strife and, more explicitly, from violence. If able to prevent the Soviet Union or Communist China from resorting to nuclear weapons in conflicts, the United States may, in time, induce both powers to abandon the doctrine of violent conflict itself.

But is it possible for a foreign policy designed to secure world peace and a nuclear force designed to be superior to live together? In the world scheme, can the strategic offensive and defensive forces of nuclear powers be tailored to satisfy each nation's conception of a political goal as well as its perception of obstacles to that goal?

Assumptions for U.S. Strategic Progress

Men act on what they believe the future will be, and their assumptions about the future—explicit or unstated—influence, if not dictate, almost every major foreign-policy or national-security decision. By the very nature of things, these assumptions can be tested only by events. On the other hand, actions flowing from a given set of assumptions may themselves produce events invalidating the assumptions. Analogously, since it takes time to conceive and develop complex and costly weapons, responsible decision-makers must anticipate the need of countering a future threat. The threat may never materialize if the counter is procured in good time. But if the seriousness of an incipient threat is discounted and no actions are taken to counter it, the threat may grow and be unmanageable in the future.

There is a feedback relation between assumptions, actions taken because of them, and the effect of these actions on the future. From his conceptions about the future, the military policy-maker deduces certain assumptions which figure in his operational decisions. He then decides on an action—for instance, to build certain weapons, phase out others, or even defer some decisions to a later time. The net effect of these actions, in conjunction with those taken by friendly and adversary powers, will be to alter the very future about which his assumptions were made. At this juncture, the policy-maker may choose to retain his original assumptions or alter them. If he retains them, the future, having already been sidetracked by the

actions and reactions that were set in motion, will skew even more sharply from its assumed character after the next feedback.

Secretary of Defense McNamara has stated that strategic superiority is the "absolute foundation" upon which our military effectiveness rests. And there is no doubt that he has sought to maintain U.S. strategic superiority in a manner that is consistent with his own assumptions about the kinds of threats the United States will face in the future. Since the Soviet Union is the one and only adversary capable of challenging U.S. strategic nuclear superiority during the next ten years, U.S. strategic power will be inversely related to the strategic strength of the Soviet Union, and vice versa. Consequently, Defense Secretary McNamara's stated assumptions regarding the Soviet Union are most relevant to the issue, and particularly pertinent is his assumption that "Communism has eroded—it has changed —in the Soviet Union. It has become less violently aggressive. . . . [This development] is a product of two things. First, the rising standard of living, and, second, the increase of personal freedom."[27]

McNamara is not alone in holding these views. In 1966, Konrad Adenauer asserted that things had changed so much that the Soviet Union is now genuinely seeking peace. Almost simultaneously, Walter Lippmann urged the United States to seek new relations with the greater Europe "from the Atlantic to the Urals," which, he claimed, was struggling to be born.

With respect to Soviet aspirations in the realm of strategic power, McNamara assumes that the Soviet Union is content to remain second best.[28] As he puts it: "There is no indication that they are catching up or planning to catch up. . . . There is no indication they are in a race at this time."[29] McNamara also suggests that:

The focus of the U.S. defense problem has shifted perceptibly toward the Far East. Overt aggression by the Warsaw Pact countries in Europe, particularly against NATO and other nations allied with the United

[27] Interview by Henry F. Graft, "Teach-in on Vietnam," *The New York Times*, March 28, 1966, p. 126.

[28] In the spring of 1965, Secretary McNamara asserted that the Soviet leaders "have decided that they have lost the quantitative race, and that they are not seeking to engage us in that contest."—*U.S. News & World Report*, April 12, 1965, p. 52.

[29] Cited by J. S. Butz, Jr., "The New Soviet Missiles—Technological Storm Warning or False Alarm," *Air Force and Space Digest*, July, 1965, p. 34.

States, seems increasingly unlikely as long as we maintain our military strength and unity. The threat of nuclear war, and even of large-scale conventional wars, has become more latent, while the threat of local insurgency and "wars of liberation" has become more active [italics added].[30]

His assertion assumes that the NATO allies will maintain their military strength and unity and that the Soviet Union has already basically changed. He also assumes "that it's impossible to win an all-out nuclear exchange. Once you realize this, you arrive at certain rational conclusions."[31] The Soviets appear to make the opposite assumption:

A new world war would be a decisive armed conflict of two world systems—capitalistic and socialistic—excluding any sort of compromise. . . . And the result of such a war would unavoidably be the death of imperialism. From the side of socialistic countries subject to imperialistic aggression, it would be a just war, in so far as it would be directed at the liquidation of imperialism—the sole cause of war—and at securing the gains of socialism.[32]

Finally, McNamara assumes that in the nuclear age the offense will always dominate the defense—so much so that "if we had to spend the entire budget of the Defense Department, $50 billion, on the strategic offensive system, we would propose to do so to insure that the Soviets do not develop an effective counter."[33] He conceded the Soviets believe in defense but assumed they erred to do so.

It is an intellectual's task to construct models of the future based on a likely range of realistic assumptions, but the most clairvoyant mind cannot now perceive whether the future will prove any set of assumptions right or wrong. All of McNamara's assumptions about the future may be correct. For instance, if the Soviet Union pursues

[30] *Statement of Secretary of Defense Robert S. McNamara Before the House Subcommittee on Department of Defense Appropriations on the Fiscal Year 1967–71 Defense Program and 1967 Defense Budget* (mimeo.), February 23, 1966, p. 41.

[31] Quoted in an article by Stewart Alsop, "His Business Is War," *The Saturday Evening Post*, May 21, 1966, p. 30.

[32] Marshal of the Soviet Union V. D. Sokolovskii and General Major M. Cherednichenko, "On Contemporary Military Strategy," *Kommunist vooruzhennykh sil* (*Communist of the Armed Forces*), April, 1966, p. 62; unpublished English translation by Harriet Fast Scott.

[33] Michael Getler, "McNamara Says Soviets Err on ABM," *Missiles and Rockets*, May 2, 1966, p. 2.

more conciliatory policies, the United States should be able to maintain its strategic superiority with a decreasing effort. Yet, if the United States acts on these assumptions, it may present tempting opportunities to the Soviet leaders and thereby disturb the vision of a stable future.

My assumptions are that the Soviet Union remains committed to the attainment of its professed revolutionary goals and that the Soviets are planning to catch up with, if not surpass, the United States in strategic nuclear power. If the United States were to act on these twin assumptions, chances are that the Soviet Union would be unable to catch up with the United States in strategic power and might, therefore, be induced to pursue more moderate policies.

Admittedly, there is risk associated with these assumptions. A vigorous U.S. program to retain strategic superiority might goad the Soviet Union into making an intensified effort to surpass the United States. But there appear to be greater risks associated with the "unilateral initiatives" approach.

Likewise, if McNamara's assumptions about the future are incorrect, the U.S. defense programs in the area of strategic nuclear power may prove inadequate to check expansionist Soviet policies. The possibility that the United States might loose strategic superiority must be assessed alongside the proposition that strategic superiority is no longer of value to the United States.

2

The Nuclear Thrust:
From Alamogordo to Cuba

The nuclear age began on a Manhattan Project test stand at Alamogordo, New Mexico, in July, 1945, and the first two-sided contest was waged and won by the United States in the 1962 Cuban missile crisis. The thinking and the preparations leading to this bloodless[1] and novel but crucial confrontation comprise one of the shortest and most turbulent chapters of military history.

The advent of nuclear bombs threw an entirely new element into the military equation. Patterns of strategic thought were rendered obsolete almost overnight. Comprehending the significance of the nuclear weapon, the United States, and subsequently the Soviet Union, slowly began to formulate strategic concepts in keeping with the new era; but the task of the United States was made even more difficult by the Soviet Union's postwar challenge to U.S. power. The strategic revolution had been spurred by the arrival of nuclear weapons, and strategic decisions had to be made for (and in spite of) a politically uncertain future.

The Truman Years

At the end of World War II, the United States demobilized its armed forces and acted as though the world was indeed at peace. But in late 1946 and early 1947, the United States began responding to the challenge of Soviet thrusts in Iran, Greece, Czechoslovakia, and Berlin.

At that time, the relatively small and poorly equipped Strategic

[1] Major R. Anderson, Jr., who was shot down by Soviet missiles while flying a U-2 reconnaissance plane over Cuba, was the only casualty of this conflict.

Air Command (SAC) was the United States' prime instrument for containing Communist aggression. As long as the Soviet Union had neither strategic air power nor nuclear explosives, SAC's mission was clear and simple: to deter the Soviet Union from a land invasion of Europe by threatening a retaliatory nuclear strike against the Soviet Union itself.

The Soviet atomic explosion in the fall of 1949 ended U.S. atomic monopoly and foreshadowed a revision of U.S. strategic concepts.

In response to Communist aggression in South Korea, the United States increased its military outlay and helped to organize the defense efforts of its non-Communist allies. The defense budget rose from $15 billion in 1950 to $51 billion in 1952. In addition to increasing conventional forces, these funds allowed the Strategic Air Command to grow into a full-fledged fighting force.

In 1951, to convince the Soviets that the United States would fight if Western Europe were attacked, President Truman committed U.S. ground forces to the North Atlantic Treaty Organization, which had been formed by the allies in 1949 as a mutual defense alliance. Despite its atomic advantage, the United States began to plan for a conventional defense of Western Europe; and in Korea, combined units of the U.S. Army, Navy, and Air Force, armed with conventional weapons, were fighting a World War II type of war. Although superior U.S. strategic air power was never directly employed, its effect was to limit the Korean War and to keep the Soviets out of Western Europe.

The U.S.S.R. Enters the Nuclear Age

Although by 1945, Soviet prestige as a world power had attained hitherto unknown heights, the Soviets were still militarily and economically weak in comparison with the United States. The Soviet Union ended World War II with essentially one basic force, the Red Army. During the war, the role of the Soviet Air Force remained subordinate to that of the Army, and the Soviet Navy was negligible. Soviet industry had been severely damaged, and probably 20 million Russian people had perished in World War II. The Soviet leaders knew that among the great powers, the United States alone not only survived unscathed but also possessed the weapons of the future—atomic bombs. Until the Soviets achieved equal capabilities,[2] they publicly disparaged the military value of atomic weapons.

In the history of the Soviet armed forces, an institutional bias for defense has been a persistent element. A prime task of Soviet forces since the Allied intervention in Russia in 1918 has been the preservation of Communism within the U.S.S.R. Thus, before the Soviet Union obtained a nuclear capability, it developed an air defense system designed to cope with nuclear attack by U.S. long-range bombers. Hundreds of captured German experts on early-warning radar were pressed into service by Stalin; and by 1950, the Soviets deployed a warning net from the Baltic to the Pacific. The development of jet interceptors kept pace with the Soviet warning system; by 1950, the Soviets had a 2,000-aircraft interceptor force. Billions of rubles were spent on surface-to-air missiles (SAM's), which replaced antiaircraft artillery and supplemented the interceptors.

Despite a traditional defense orientation (seen today in the emphasis on both active and passive defense), neither Russian military tradition nor Soviet military doctrine ever ignored the value of taking the offensive to achieve victory. Parallel with Soviet efforts for active and passive defense and before the Soviets possessed nuclear weapons, great strides were taken to obtain long-range delivery systems. Apparently, the Soviets were embarking on a broad and varied program of their own in the field of rockets and missiles. In April, 1944, a leading specialist in nuclear weapons and long-range missiles, Major General G. I. Pokrovskii, published the first Soviet article on long-range missiles.[3] In 1946, A. A. Blagonravov, who was both a military officer and an academician, was named President of the Academy of Artillery Sciences, an institute that was to play an important role in developing ICBM's and space rockets.[4] As in the case of defensive weapons, the Soviets made use of captured German technicians for

[2] See Marshall Shulman, *Stalin's Foreign Policy Reappraised* (Cambridge: Harvard University Press, 1963), Chapter 2, "Moscow in the Spring of 1949."

[3] *Science and Technology in Contemporary War,* trans. by Raymond L. Garthoff (New York: Praeger, 1959), pp. vi–vii.

[4] U.S. Congress, Senate Committee on Aeronautical and Space Sciences, *Soviet Space Programs: Organization, Plans, Goals, and International Implications,* 87th Cong., 2nd Sess., 1962, p. 64.

developing offensive weaponry. Meanwhile, Soviet interest in nuclear weapon and missile warfare amounted to almost an obsession.[5]

> In 1947, our whole budget for research and development in the intercontinental field was eliminated for reasons of economy. In 1946 the Soviet budget for research and development in these categories was trebled. It reconstituted its research bodies for jet engines, for swept-wing aircraft design, for nuclear explosives, for rocket propulsion. The whole basis for a shift in the balance of power, as the Soviet leaders saw it, was laid in the period at the end of the war; and beginning immediately thereafter, the Soviets turned on an intense concentration of resources in these categories in order to shorten their period of vulnerability as much as possible. The Soviets' expectation was that when these things began to bear fruit, a shift in the balance of power would result.[6]

Under Stalin, early Soviet moves toward obtaining the best that modern postwar technology had to offer were not, however, hand in hand with a basic reformulation of Soviet military doctrine. A number of retrospective Soviet accounts of the postwar development of Soviet military theory make clear that in the period before meaningful numbers of modern weapons were acquired, Soviet thinking was directed toward using new weaponry within the framework of past methods of warfare.[7] Critical nuclear-age problems such as surprise attack and the decisive initial period of a modern war bred new views that were confronting the old outlook. The lag was not unnatural; for from the first Soviet atomic test in the fall of 1949 until the Soviet acquisition of the hydrogen bomb in 1953, quantities of nuclear weapons and numbers of long-range bombers were very small.

Stalin's insistence that Soviet military thinking focus on elaborating the significance for warfare of his "permanently operating factors" was another reason for discrepancy between technology and military doctrine in his time. These "factors" dealt with stability of the rear,

[5] S. N. Koslov, M. V. Smirnov, I. S. Boz, and P. A. Sidorov, *O sovietskoi voennoi nauke* (*On Soviet Military Science*) (Moscow: Voenizdat, 1954), p. 249.

[6] Philip E. Mosely and Marshall Shulman, *The Changing Soviet Challenge* (Racine, Wisc.: The Johnson Foundation, 1964).

[7] Colonel I. Korotkov, "The Development of Soviet Military Theory in the Postwar Years," *Voenno-istoricheskii zhurnal* (*Military-Historical Journal*), April, 1964, p. 43. This account is one of the most candid and critical treatments of the subject to appear in Soviet literature to date.

morale of the army, quantity and quality of divisions, armament of the army, and organizational ability of army commanders. Originally formulated in 1942, these factors of warfare were, in part, an outgrowth of Soviet experience in World War II. The subsequent emphasis given these principles represented an *ex post facto* rationalization for the kind of war conducted by the U.S.S.R. under Stalin's guidance.

With the development of significant strategic capabilities and the death of Stalin in 1953, a dialogue was initiated within the Soviet military establishment by Major General N. Talenskii. In an article in the journal *Military Thought,* Talenskii noted that there were objective rules of war that apply to all armies, both capitalist and Communist. He argued that the "permanently operating factors," which stressed the general superiority of Communist troops mainly because they were Communists, had no significance, especially in the face of a capitalist monopoly of nuclear weapons.[8] In addition, the Talenskii article implied that surprise nuclear attack against the U.S.S.R. was feasible and apt to succeed. A doctrinal debate between the supporters and detractors of Talenskii continued for four years, until, in good Marxist form, a synthesis was eventually reached. It was agreed that there were, indeed, objective laws of war that pertained to capitalists and Communists alike but that those laws applied only to actual combat conditions and not to society as a whole.

When the Soviet Union acquired its first nuclear capability in 1953, the chore of long-range bombardment fell to the Soviet Air Force and its manned bomber forces. Toward the close of World War II, an American B-29 had landed in Siberia and had been interned, giving Soviet aircraft designers a prototype—the TU-4—for a strategic bomber force. The turbo Bear appeared in 1955 and was the first Soviet aircraft of sufficient endurance to bomb the United States and return without refueling. (The Soviet Air Force has continued to modernize and improve its manned bombers even though the Soviets have achieved notable successes in rocketry.)

[8] Major General N. Talenskii, "On the Question of the Laws of Military Science," in *War and the Soviet Union,* ed. Herbert S. Dinerstein (New York: Praeger, 1959), pp. 36–49.

The Eisenhower "New Look"

While the Kremlin was awaiting the construction of a Soviet strategic air force with an intercontinental range, the United States was simultaneously coming to rely more upon its strategic nuclear forces, and their protective cover was extended to areas of the globe other than Europe. A "New Look" stressing U.S. air atomic power was the result of Washington's 1953 strategic reappraisal. By then, the increase in the size and striking power of the Strategic Air Command was truly formidable. Inspired by the Korean War, it was based upon mounting inventories of B-36 and B-47 bombers and rising stock piles of nuclear weapons. The Eisenhower Administration subsequently decided to predicate U.S. security on nuclear weapons as opposed to conventional forces. The Strategic Air Command, operating from overseas bases, gave the United States the capacity to destroy the Soviet Union, as well as Communist China, with little risk of effective reprisal. A considerable portion of the defense budget was allocated to the construction of early-warning systems that would alert the Strategic Air Command to an incoming enemy attack in sufficient time for SAC to launch a massive retaliatory force from domestic bases.

In a speech before the Council on Foreign Relations on January 12, 1954, Secretary of State John Dulles outlined the policy that was to match the "New Look"—the doctrine of *massive retaliation*. He stated that, should deterrence fail, a selective range of actions would be taken "at places and times of our own choosing." The new policy called for a strategy based on America's special assets, particularly "air and naval power and atomic weapons . . . suitable not only for strategic bombing but also for extensive tactical use." This was widely interpreted to mean that instead of using conventional means to meet Communist incursions, the United States would direct strategic nuclear firepower against urban and industrial complexes of the Soviet Union and Communist China. In part, the doctrine represented an effort to capitalize on advanced U.S. technology with the aim of gaining diplomatic flexibility for deterring Communist aggression while avoiding another Korean-type war. A related purpose of the "New Look" and the doctrine of massive retaliation was to reduce defense spending.[9]

Massive retaliation seemed a logical concept at this time, for the unprecedented destructive power of nuclear weapons made it possible for the first time to destroy enemy cities at will. Because the Soviets had few nuclear weapons in the mid-1950's and the chief military threat to U.S. security was the Red Army that was deployed against Western Europe, the U.S. could strike at the heart of the Soviet Union with little fear of retaliation. The Soviet population and industry were designated the objects of attack, since a U.S. attack on the Soviet ground forces deployed in Europe would have injured not only the Red Army but also America's European allies.

In the vocabulary of nuclear war, the strategy of massive retaliation came to be identified as a *spasm* strategy—a cataclysmic attack that would use virtually all available force for one onslaught against any and all enemy targets. Yet, in those days of U.S. nuclear superiority, the United States need not have planned so horrendous a punishment. Since the Soviet Union lacked offensive strategic forces, the U.S. might have retaliated in measured doses offering its enemy the opportunity of accepting U.S. terms to end the conflict.

Massive retaliation was designed as a *first-strike* strategy, which does not necessarily denote an act of aggression. That is, the United States might have waged the first strategic nuclear strike in response to a Soviet invasion of Western Europe. A first strike should not be confused with *pre-emptive war*—for instance, a U.S. attack launched because of an impending Soviet attack that is clearly indicated by intelligence reports or the actual deployment of Soviet forces. During the heyday of the massive-retaliation strategy, such a pre-emptive attack would have been both wanton and unnecessary, for the Soviets did not possess sufficient forces even to contemplate attacking the United States.

Under the doctrine of massive retaliation, nuclear forces became the principal military support for U.S. foreign policy; army and navy

[9] President Eisenhower cut President Truman's proposed defense budget for the fiscal year 1953–54 from $51.2 billion to $46.6 billion and also reduced his Mutual Defense Assistance proposals by nearly 25 per cent (from $7.9 billion to a little over $6 billion). On April 3, 1953, President Eisenhower announced a further reduction of $8.5 billion in the defense budget. He later made other reductions, and Congress eventually voted $34.4 billion for defense.

forces were relegated secondary roles. The critics of massive retaliation, who grew more vociferous as the Soviets became capable of launching a nuclear strike against the United States, lumped together massive-retaliation strategy, first-strike attack, and U.S. reliance on nuclear forces as if the concepts were synonymous. Unfortunately, the arguments against massive retaliation became arguments against both a first-strike capability and the use of nuclear forces in support of U.S. foreign policy.

Early in 1954, only a few months after Secretary Dulles unveiled the policy, the United States practically abandoned the strategy of massive retaliation. President Eisenhower rejected the use of U.S. strategic and tactical air power to save the French forces besieged at Dien Bien Phu.[10] The French were subsequently defeated in Indochina, and another Communist state, North Vietnam, was created.

In December, 1954, the NATO Council agreed to base the defense of Europe upon atomic weapons, so that a major conventional attack on the Continent would be countered by nuclear weapons. The Eisenhower Administration, whose "New Look" was extended to include the defense of Europe, envisioned NATO strategy as the "sword" and the "shield"—the "sword" of U.S. strategic air power operating behind the "shield" of NATO's conventional power.

On March 8, 1955, Secretary of State Dulles announced that the Southeast Asia Treaty Organization (SEATO) would "rely upon mobile allied power which can strike an aggressor wherever the occasion may demand." Two months later, the flight of fifteen Soviet Bison long-range jet bombers over Moscow's Red Square revealed Soviet capability to strike at targets within the continental United States. For the first time in its history, the United States was vulnerable to direct and destructive attack from abroad. Although it was believed that the United States would mount a nuclear attack in defense of so vital an area as Europe, the strength of U.S. protection for other parts of the world became less credible.

The acceptance of the "New Look" by the officialdom of NATO did not silence the critics of the Eisenhower defense policy. The dissenters argued that it was irrational to extend the SAC umbrella

[10] The compelling political reasons for leaving the French to their fate are discussed by Chalmers M. Roberts in "The Day We Didn't Go to War," *The Reporter,* September 14, 1954, pp. 31–35.

over the entire Free World at the very time when growing Soviet strategic capabilities rendered that guarantee less credible. In sum, they charged that the doctrine of massive retaliation was not broad enough to take into account changing Communist capabilities, but it was too broad to cope with anything but the most unlikely, apocalyptic contingency. Soviet technological break-throughs and shifting Communist tactics seemed to favor increased conventional capabilities to meet Communist challenges, which, they projected, would more likely come on the local level. In retrospect, Mr. Dulles' critics seemed to have overlooked the fact that as long as the main component of strategic forces was the manned bomber, the American strategic lead probably was insurmountable. (At this time, the rapid development of the intercontinental ballistic missile had not been foreseen.) Because the Soviet manned bomber force was quite small compared with the SAC force and, even more importantly, because the Soviets could not match the rich experience of the United States in building bombers and planning and executing strategic bombing operations, the small Soviet long-range air force did not basically change the strategic equation.

In the 1950's, during the course of debates about massive retaliation, Secretary Dulles and his supporters were arguing that a capacity for massive retaliation would deter the potential Communist aggressor. But the critics of the Dulles doctrine stressed the dire consequences should the threat of massive retaliation fail to deter Soviet aggression.

While the nuclear capability of the United States grew, the Sino-Soviet bloc attempted to extend its sphere into many "soft" areas of the Free World. By avoiding a direct clash with regular forces and pressing for advantages in less "sensitive" regions, the Communists sought to undermine the credibility of the massive-retaliation strategy. The Communists moved on many fronts, confronting the West with a series of "ambiguous challenges" without presenting any single challenge that might trigger nuclear retaliation. Whether fortuitous or not, the Communists gained very little for their efforts during this period.

In an address to the Dallas Council on World Affairs on October 27, 1957, Secretary Dulles somewhat modified his doctrine. Conceding the possibility of localized Communist aggressions, he stated that "we and our allies should, between us, have the capacity to deal with these without our actions provoking a general nuclear war." The Secretary's revision had been immediately preceded by the Soviets' successful firing of an intercontinental ballistic missile and launching of the first sputnik. These events gave substance to the fear, unjustified in retrospect, that U.S. strategic nuclear forces might soon be inferior to those of the Soviets.

Khrushchev's Course

The political victory of Nikita Khrushchev had brought to the ranks a man who foresaw the possibility of an atomic war that a properly armed Soviet Union could win. Also, the successful 1957 launching of a space satellite by the Soviet Union infused Soviet leadership with a new measure of confidence.

Khrushchev enunciated his nuclear doctrine in a speech to the Supreme Soviets on January 14, 1960. He proclaimed that although an armed struggle of some magnitude might occur between the present and the Communist millennium, it would be a thermonuclear war only by imperialist design. The implication was that the Soviets would have to be prepared to fight both limited and general wars in order to achieve their goal.[11] Khrushchev asserted that in any future war, missiles would play a dominant role to the virtual exclusion of conventional ground forces, manned aircraft, and navies. Stressing the superiority of Soviet long-range delivery systems, he declared that "barring the actions of a madman," the West was now decisively deterred from launching a surprise attack.

On January 6, 1961, Khrushchev amplified the strategic position that he had presented in January, 1960. His underlying thesis appeared to be that until such time as the U.S.S.R. surpassed U.S. industrial production and military technology, the struggle between capitalism and Communism would take the form of "peaceful" competition—a competition, however, neither precluding Communist support of "wars of national liberation" nor excluding the U.S.S.R.'s use of nuclear blackmail to protect its own vital interests.

Khrushchev also called for disarmament, peace offensives, and negotiations designed to convey the impression of a sincere Soviet

[11] See J. M. Mackintosh, *Strategy and Tactics of Soviet Foreign Policy* (New York: Oxford University Press, 1963), pp. 299–314.

desire for peace. To Khrushchev, disarmament represented a means of "restricting the military potentialities of the imperialists,"[12] and peace propaganda, aimed primarily at bourgeois elites and intellectuals, could contribute to the general moral paralysis of the West. He was setting the stage for the Cuban missile crisis.

The Missile Revolution

The so-called missile gap in the latter years of the Eisenhower Administration had been sired by questionable information, inadequate analysis, and bad politics; and we now know that the Soviet missile force was not superior in either quantity or accuracy. The Soviets had built a large force of some 700 to 800 intermediate missiles that could strike Western Europe—a missile preponderance over NATO that still exists. They were ahead in some aspects of medium- and long-range-missile development, and in this sense, there was indeed a missile gap; but an intercontinental-missile gap never existed. The Soviets did not exploit their developmental advantage in booster thrust and did not procure large quantities of expensive, vulnerable, and inaccurate ICBM's. In view of the uncertainty of the strategic situation, President Eisenhower had placed part of SAC on airborne alert and energetically (though without fanfare) launched a crash missile-production program.

Regardless of the confusion surrounding the missile gap, Soviet development of the ICBM drastically and irrevocably altered the strategic balance—far more so than Soviet long-range bombers had. Under the pressure of growing Soviet strategic capabilities, the United States began to develop a command and control system that could survive a nuclear attack. If the command facilities of the Strategic Air Command could be destroyed by a few Soviet missiles, the President, as Commander in Chief, might not be able to communicate the "go" code to U.S. forces in case of war. Constitutionally, the decision of going to war or attacking the Soviet Union could not be left to subordinate commanders; and if the President's survival and his ability to communicate with American commanders could not be

[12] "Report on the Moscow Conference," speech delivered January 6, 1961, in Moscow, cited by U.S. Congress, Senate Subcommittee of the Committee on the Judiciary, *Hearings, Analysis of the Khrushchev Speech of January 6, 1961,* testimony of Dr. Stefan T. Possony before the 87th Cong., 1st Sess., June 16, 1961, p. 68.

assured, there was a real possibility that under attack, the United States might never launch its retaliatory force (or what was left of it after the enemy's strike). During the later years of the Eisenhower Administration, measures were taken to provide sufficiently invulnerable command capabilities. Since then, the National Command and Control System has been further improved.

By 1960, U.S. military strategy was in a state of flux. Voices of dissent grew more strident both within and outside the Eisenhower Administration, and from this opposition developed the strategic concepts that initially guided the military program of the Kennedy Administration.[13]

The Vocabulary of Nuclear Strategy

Since the period when massive retaliation was in vogue, nuclear strategy has become subtler and more complex, and the vocabulary used to describe nuclear confrontation has become a language of its own.[14] To understand the issues and nuances of the Kennedy-McNamara strategic doctrine, one must first understand the semantics of nuclear war.

Terms describing various strategies are used to convey a general attitude toward nuclear conflict rather than to depict the complex reality of a given strategic posture or nuclear confrontation. The U.S. strategic posture has never fitted precisely into these or other descriptive molds, nor is it ever likely to for several reasons. Strategies have overlapping boundaries. Furthermore, there are always weapons around from an earlier strategic era that, for political and economic reasons, are difficult to discard abruptly even though they do not fit the prevailing strategy. None of these strategies could be used in warfare with strict adherence to its presumed distinctions. The execution, for example, of a *finite-deterrence* (FD) strategy, which hypothetically includes only cities as targets, would also destroy military forces located in urban areas. Likewise, some damage to cities would

[13] See General Maxwell Taylor's criticism of the massive-retaliation strategy in his *The Uncertain Trumpet* (New York: Harper & Brothers, 1960), which had a profound effect on President Kennedy and, later, on President Johnson.
[14] One of the most articulate contributors to the Western glossary on nuclear warfare has been Herman Kahn. See Herman Kahn, *On Escalation: Scenarios and Metaphors* (New York: Praeger, 1965), Appendix, "Relevant Concepts and Language for the Discussion of Escalation," pp. 275–300.

result from a *counterforce* (CF) exchange, which, in theory, would be directed only toward enemy strategic forces. Shorthand terms, however, permit orderly distinctions between alternative force levels, targeting concepts, and even strategic intent.

Long before nuclear weapons, heavy bombers, and ballistic missiles were introduced, the Italian General Giulio Douhet foresaw, almost prophetically, how total war could one day be waged by means of strategic bombing, with ground and naval forces playing a defensive, holding role. For many years, technology lagged behind Douhet's vision. With the development of the atomic bomb and then, and more importantly, the thermonuclear bomb, the defeat of an enemy without the need for ground combat became possible.

In the early days of the Cold War—the period of U.S. monopoly of not only the atomic bomb but also strategic air power—most U.S. political leaders assumed that the complete solution to problems of national security had been found. As long as the United States constituted an invulnerable Western base from which an aggressor could be struck a devastating blow, it was unnecessary to build up ground forces for waging long-drawn-out wars like World Wars I and II. The enemy would instead be deterred from aggressive war by the very magnitude of the inevitable retribution.

When the Soviets developed atomic and nuclear weapons, as well as intercontinental aircraft and missile systems, Western strategists realized that it might become impossible to attack the enemy's forces so effectively as to annul his ability to retaliate. The array of opposing forces might be such that neither side could afford to initiate attack against the other without risking enormous damage to its own social and industrial structures.

As armies came to depend more and more on the full resources of the country, war progressively became more total. Industry became a target because troops depended on vast quantities of munitions and other implements of war. Before the airplane was developed, factories could not be directly attacked, so attempts were made to blockade the flow of raw materials or to seize areas that were producing war material. The airplane made it possible to reach over enemy defenses and attack the heartland of a nation. Thus, with the introduction of the airplane, three classes of targets emerged: enemy forces, industry, and population—the latter two comprising *value targets*. If, however, strategic bombing missions could destroy the enemy force in a matter of hours, why proceed to bomb his industries and his population? With its air force destroyed, a nation would lie helpless before an opponent. Yet, the strategists of the nuclear age only gradually perceived this theoretically simple point. Consequently, for some years, targets for nuclear war remained the same as the World War II targets. For example, the concept of bonus damage persisted for some time in strategic war planning: *bonus damage* or *collateral damage* is a result of bombing a military target so that nearby towns and industries are simultaneously destroyed. To an unprecedented degree, thermonuclear bombs made it possible to strike civilian targets in the proximity of the intended military objective; but the conditions of nuclear war made destruction of such targets both unnecessary and undesirable. For a long period of time, however, U.S. targeting doctrine remained tied to the concept of bonus damage.

Western military strategists now recognize that it is not necessary to maximize damage by extending it to nonmilitary targets. On the contrary, the more desirable objective may be to limit damage to hostile populations by a judicious combination of high-delivery accuracy and low-yield weapons. The logical use of nuclear weapons leads to a military strategy that pits armed force against armed force rather than against civilians. Yet, paradoxically, the civilian populations now play a key role as potential hostages, for in a nuclear war the fate of a civilian population is the final bargaining issue. Even though strategic military forces rather than people are the operational targets of nuclear war, the very life of a nation is still threatened. In "escalating" a limited conflict, not only military forces and supplies but also industrial and population centers could become targets.

Alternatives to Total War. As the strategic nuclear capability of the Soviet Union grew, the potential disaster of a general war came to be appreciated. Belatedly, the West, seeking alternatives to total war, sought a doctrine of war that would relate nuclear arms to the values they were supposed to defend.

When the Kennedy Administration assumed power, the two most commonly advocated strategies for U.S. strategic nuclear forces were finite deterrence and counterforce.

By 1960, spasm war was no longer regarded as the only possible nuclear confrontation with an adversary. Moreover, an all-out disarming attack on the enemy's strategic forces was no longer considered feasible, since, as a practical matter, it was impossible to prevent some retaliatory attack. For this reason, an attempted *disarming strike* —a strike directed at all strategic weapons to compel *unconditional surrender*—was no longer a suitable strategy for the thermonuclear era.

Both finite deterrence and counterforce provide alternatives for dealing with the basic attribute of nuclear weapons—the ability to inflict almost unlimited damage. The counterforce concept is intended to lessen nuclear damage by inducing the enemy not to strike our cities because we would not strike his. The enemy would be assured that we would hit his cities if he attacked ours; that we could reduce his offensive striking power (and hence the damage he could do) by attacking his offensive forces that had not yet been launched; that we could defeat the attack that had been launched by means of active defense measures; and that we could minimize the destructiveness of his weapons that reached target by using our fallout shelters and blast shelters. In essence, this strategy focused on the destruction of enemy offensive forces rather than cities, so that ultimately the surviving populations would be the final bargaining issue.

Finite deterrence rejects the counterforce concept that nuclear wars can be fought in a controlled fashion, that a country's industry and population might be spared, and that damage can be held to acceptable limits. The goal of finite deterrence is to make nuclear war so catastrophic as to be unthinkable, and its purpose is to deter any nuclear attack on the United States by fact of a U.S. capability to destroy the enemy's cities in retaliation. In effect, this strategy would force each opposing state to offer the other its respective population and economy as hostage. The posture makes only limited provision for active air defense; it does not seek an antimissile system; it provides for only minimal civil defense. This strategy is also called *basic deterrence,* a felicitously descriptive name that conveys the key idea; it is a strategic posture that can deter attack on only this country and cannot offer protection to U.S. allies. In other words, by making the possibility of a first strike totally incredible, it repudiates the extension of U.S. deterrent capability, or "nuclear umbrella," to the NATO countries or other allies.

Second-strike Forces. As the Soviet Union gained the capability of launching a nuclear attack against the U.S. mainland, it became necessary for the United States to develop a *second-strike force*—a force capable of absorbing the enemy's blow and then striking back. Confusion then arose between first-strike *strategy* and first-strike *weapons*. First-strike weapons are delivery systems that could not survive an enemy attack and hence could be used only for a first strike, that is, for attacking the enemy before he is able to land his blow. When the Soviets acquired ICBM's, the United States faced a radically altered strategic situation, one in which the possibilities of a pre-emptive attack by either side became too great for comfort. At this point, the Soviet strategic force was as vulnerable as the U.S. force, both of which were comprised of bombers located on unprotected fields and vulnerable first-generation ICBM's. The danger of accidental war was considerably heightened by the instability of a tense international situation in which either side, anxiously aware of the vulnerability of its entire force, could launch a pre-emptive attack. The need for a second-strike force was clear.

Fundamentally, second-strike forces are to some degree invulnerable. *Invulnerability* can be acquired through a variety of means: (1) *dispersal of forces* from a few sites to many sites—for example, SAC bombers were dispersed from seventeen bases to sixty-one bases; (2) acquisition of *warning systems*—for example, the Ballistic Missile Early Warning System (BMEWS) was added to the already existing Distant Early Warning (DEW) line, which served to deter bomber attacks; (3) *mobility* and *concealment*—for example, the development of Polaris missile-firing submarines; and (4) *hardening*—for example, the placing of missiles in concrete silos for protection against the effects of nuclear warheads. Bombers, like missiles, were protected by a combination of warning and dispersal (permitting the bombers to take off before the enemy warheads exploded) and mobility.

Invulnerability, though, is never absolute. It depends not only on the measures taken to protect one's own forces but also on the kind and number of offensive weapons the enemy builds. A weapons system that is highly invulnerable today, such as Polaris, may become vulnerable if a break-through—for example, in antisubmarine warfare (ASW)—should occur.

No single hardened missile site is invulnerable, but the combination of the number of missiles and the hardening of the missile sites safeguards the whole force against destruction in an initial attack. Also, the degree of protection given to each missile site may compel the enemy to employ more than one missile in attacking it; on the other hand, improved accuracy and higher-yield warheads will reduce the number of missiles required to destroy a given target. For hardened missile sites, invulnerability may be lost by 1975.

An invulnerable, hardened, fixed-site command and control system may be difficult, if not impossible, to build, man, and operate because of practical limitations. Since they are complex and costly, command sites cannot be dispersed by the hundreds as can missile sites. Thus the *exchange ratio*—the cost to the enemy of destroying a military command center in relation to the cost to the defender of adding an alternative command center—would be highly favorable to the enemy. For missile sites, the exchange ratio favors the defender as long as it is more than 1:1—that is, if it takes more than one attacking missile to destroy a single defending missile. If, for example, the missile exchange ratio is 5:1, an aggressor must build five missiles for every one that the defender adds to his force. In the case of command and control sites, however, a 5:1 ratio would be highly favorable to the attacker, since the cost of building five missiles is far less than the cost of adding another command site.

A second-strike force need not be inconsistent with a first-strike strategy. Invulnerable weapons systems, which constitute a second-strike force, could be launched in a first strike; however, the invulnerability of a second-strike force may inhibit its use in a first strike. The key concept is *credibility*.[15] Any weapon can be used in a first strike, but the question is: How credible is a threat to do so? In the days when the Soviets did not have the capability to retaliate against the United States, the U.S. threat was entirely credible. Now a nuclear strike in response to Soviet aggression in Europe could lead to terrible damage to the United States. Hence the U.S. nuclear guarantee to Europe seems less credible.

Ironically, the U.S. first-strike threat remained credible as long as

[15] This question was reviewed in Herman Kahn's defense of a credible first-strike strategy. By adding the term "credible" to "first strike," Kahn attempted to deal with the problem of a U.S. first-strike strategy in reaction to a Soviet attack on Europe, in a situation in which the United States was vulnerable to a missile attack. See *On Thermonuclear War* (Princeton, N.J.: Princeton University Press, 1961), pp. 27–36.

the United States had only a vulnerable force; for with such a vulnerability, the United States could not afford to sit out a Soviet attack on Europe. We would have had to attack to keep our own force from being destroyed on its home base. Similarly, the Soviets could not attack Europe without first attacking the United States for fear that the United States in turn would have to attack them. Mutually vulnerable systems, despite their advantages for deterrence, posed excessive dangers of war by accident or miscalculation; whereas secure second-strike forces removed the necessity for a virtually automatic U.S. nuclear strike against the Soviet Union in the event of aggression against NATO. The United States, secure in its ability to ride out a Soviet attack, would be able to assess a threatening situation. Paradoxically, as the invulnerability of the U.S. force increased, the credibility of the U.S. nuclear guarantee to NATO declined.

A first-strike threat could, however, be made by a nation possessing a credible first-strike force—a force that possesses one of the merits of a second-strike force, namely, invulnerability. The primary purpose of a credible first-strike force is not to initiate war but to warn the adversary that he cannot attack Western Europe, for example, without running an unacceptable risk of U.S. retaliation. The expectation is that, faced with the necessity of attacking the United States, the Soviets would be deterred from major aggression in Europe.

The invulnerability of a second-strike force does not rule out the threat of an enemy's first strike against it; however, the term "second-strike force" can be, and often is, understood to rule out its credibility as a first-strike strategy. The force need not be—and this is the key to many strategic disputes—merely an invulnerable one, but logically it should be incapable of striking first. This would be the case if an invulnerable missile force had low accuracy and weapon yield—too low to strike first and successfully or even to issue a credible first-strike threat.[16]

Parity, Stability, and Stalemate. A situation in which both sides have armed themselves only with vulnerable weapons, which are therefore suitable only for a first-strike strategy, is inherently unstable and accident-prone—like a Western gun duel in which the faster draw wins. Yet, when both sides possess invulnerable offensive forces and neither can rationally contemplate an attack given the retaliatory

---

[16] The French *force de frappe* fits this description.

power of the other, a *stalemate* exists. According to many experts, the objective of U.S. second-strike forces should be the achievement of stalemate by such a margin of superiority that a potential enemy would realize that by attacking he would worsen his relative position rather than improve it.

In a strict sense, a condition of *parity* exists if two forces are approximately equal, although it is often asserted that parity exists even though the forces of the two great nuclear powers are quite unequal. In the latter sense, parity refers to a situation in which the party with the larger arsenal cannot afford to attack because the other side, though weaker, still is able to retaliate with a countervalue attack. Parity in the sense of equality of strategic forces is sometimes advocated as the U.S. goal in lieu of strategic superiority.

Opposing views on a strategic posture for the United States reflect a basic disagreement on the meaning of *nuclear stalemate*. According to one school of thought, nuclear stalemate renders nuclear weapons useless for any positive political purpose; consequently, their negative role—deterring nuclear attack—could just as well be played by *nuclear disarmament*. Since nuclear forces impose a burden on national economies and since nuclear war might be triggered by accident or miscalculation, nuclear disarmament is a more rational course of action. But since unresolved political issues bar the road to total nuclear disarmament for the near future, it is proposed that *arms control* measures either lead step by step toward disarmament or take the place of disarmament. Arms control can be accomplished by numerous methods, all of which have in common the objective of either reducing the risk of nuclear war or mitigating its effects.

The Kennedy Phase

New strategic concepts for nuclear weapons began to be articulated during the late 1950's, and in the spring of 1961 President Kennedy called for new U.S. strategy and tactics to meet the continuing Soviet challenge. Early in his administration, President Kennedy announced the broad outlines of his military strategy:

> The primary purpose of our arms is peace, not war—to make certain that they will never have to be used—to deter all wars, general or limited, nuclear or conventional, large or small—to convince all aggressors that any attack would be futile—to provide backing for diplomatic

settlement of disputes—to insure the adequacy of our bargaining power for an end to the arms race. . . . Our military policy must be sufficiently flexible and under control to be consistent with our efforts to explore all possibilities and to take every step to lessen tensions, to obtain peaceful solutions and to secure arms limitations.[17]

President Kennedy intended to achieve a wider range of strategic options primarily by increasing U.S. general-purpose forces and by increasing the invulnerability of our bombers and missiles. Doctrinally, Kennedy pioneered the concept of a deliberate, selective, flexible, controlled response to be prepared for any type of warfare at whatever level and to force on the adversary the onus of striking the first nuclear blow. A flexible response necessitated not only conventional forces capable of meeting limited aggression but also, and most crucially, second-strike nuclear forces capable of fighting a controlled nuclear war. The Eisenhower nuclear control system had tied virtually all the U.S. strategic forces together under "one button," leaving the President with the single option of pushing or not pushing. The Kennedy-McNamara combination was designed to give the President a series of options on his "nuclear console" as well as a range of nonnuclear options, thus avoiding an "all or nothing" dilemma.

An inherent part of the selective-response doctrine was a rapid build-up of conventional "below-the-threshold" forces, for without additional means to cope with limited conflicts, the new flexible strategy would be useless. A substantial increase in funds was consequently allotted for conventional armaments and forces. Concurrently, emphasis was placed on special forces for aiding nations subjected to Communist "wars of national liberation," and the number of personnel authorized for these activities was increased. Although conventional forces that are sufficient for meeting a range of contingencies are essential for Free World defense, these forces were never intended to be a substitute for a credible nuclear deterrent.

The policy developed by the Kennedy and Johnson administrations for strategic nuclear weaponry differed essentially from that of their

[17] U.S. President, *Recommendations Relating to Our Defense Budget*, U.S. House Document No. 123 (Washington: Government Printing Office, 1961), p. 2. The concepts in this document were developed in the Pentagon under McNamara's aegis and were accepted *in toto* by President Kennedy.

predecessors. Rather than a missile gap, as had been touted during the 1960 Presidential campaign, the United States possessed nuclear superiority and a considerable lead in strategic delivery vehicles (primarily the manned bomber) on the day Secretary McNamara arrived in the Pentagon. Revised intelligence estimates, based on some new data, led to a changed assessment of the United States–Soviet strategic balance. Secretary McNamara nevertheless decided to increase the U.S. missile capability and to convert strategic retaliatory forces to second-strike forces, which entailed hardening the delivery systems and otherwise making the force invulnerable to an enemy first strike. To carry out these decisions, Secretary McNamara stepped up the production of first-generation Minuteman missiles and increased the number of nuclear bombers on fifteen-minute alert.

The Kennedy Administration took steps to assure civilian control over the military commanders of U.S. strategic forces. Constitutional provisions for civilian control of military forces have never been questioned; but in 1961, civilian control halted at the same point as did military control, namely, before the giving of the "go" orders. By his own authority, the SAC commander could put his force on alert and, if he concluded that an enemy attack was under way, could order his aircraft to fly to the positive control point. But without a direct order from the President (or a lawfully designated successor), he could not command his force to attack the enemy. When a Soviet surprise missile attack on the United States became a possibility, appropriate civilian authorities had to be endowed with means for surviving the initial attack and for commanding a controlled nuclear war; thus, a *national control system* became the capstone of the U.S. military posture.

By 1965, the Kennedy and Johnson administrations had demonstrably raised the levels of readiness, modernity, versatility, and combat power of U.S. armed strength. Although history may count the 1961 Berlin crisis, the 1962 Cuban crisis, and the 1965 Vietnam build-up as limited political successes, these events are excellent examples of how conventional forces determinedly deployed under the umbrella of nuclear striking power can support U.S. policy without leading to all-out nuclear conflict.

Secretary of Defense McNamara has been responsible for momentous changes in the U.S. military posture; and regardless of differing opinions about his methods and judgments on certain programs, his reign over the military establishment has introduced some beneficial changes. Some critics have cast McNamara as a technocrat with little regard for the human element of the vast organization he manages. He has been criticized for ignoring the available wealth of professional military advice, for affronting the will of Congress with his centralization of direction and operational control, and for making arbitrary operational, technical, and procurement decisions.

Secretary McNamara took as his charter these instructions of President Kennedy: "To develop the force structure necessary to our military requirements without regard to arbitrary budget ceilings; and procure and operate this force at the lowest possible cost."[18] From the outset, McNamara concluded that he could not comply with these instructions and conduct business as usual at the Pentagon. Faced with archaic organizational and jurisdictional practices, he apparently felt that only shock treatment could effect an appreciable improvement. National-security problems seemed more unmanageable each day, and most of the people living with these problems considered some form of "drastic" action imperative. McNamara proceeded to carry out his mandate under the aegis of "budgetary management." In the process, he established a composite approach to national-security objectives in terms of forces, missions, and tasks —an accomplishment that had come to be regarded as impossible. By 1964, budgets and programs were being related by means of uniform criteria and according to function, such as strategic offense or defense.

Secretary McNamara required justification and convincing logic for each service's recommendations to continue old efforts or to start new ones. Various analytical methods, particularly economic operational trade-off considerations, or "cost effectiveness," became general tools in decision-making. McNamara also set up a series of new functional agencies, which reported directly to him, in the fields of common supply, intelligence, and communications. In the fullest sense, McNamara revolutionized the management of U.S. national-security affairs; and notwithstanding the inevitable errors and shortcomings that have attended the managerial, conceptual, and operational upheavals in the Defense Department, his managerial tools, particularly systems analysis, have greatly assisted national decision-making. Un-

[18] *Ibid.*

fortunately, these tools have sometimes been used to confirm prede-
termined solutions rather than to aid in an open-end search for
answers to the exceptionally complicated and many-sided security
problems confronting the United States.

McNamara's managerial talent has been less successful in the realm
of policy and strategy. The U.S. choice of weapons and strategy has
been coolly calculated, but it has also been improvised. Even if one
supports President Johnson's policy to stand firm in South Vietnam,
the U.S. piecemeal engagement in that country cannot be deemed a
masterpiece of strategic foresight. And the decision to reach the moon
by 1970, whether desirable in itself or not, was made unsystematically
and with scant regard for its impact on critical national-security programs:

> The moon program was worked out over a hectic weekend in May of
> 1961 at the Pentagon following Alan Shepard's successful suborbital
> flight. It was a political response to the Gagarin venture and to the
> Cuban disaster, among other things. Reportedly, Secretary McNamara,
> James Webb of NASA, and a few others met round the clock starting
> Friday evening and worked out the crash program that was presented
> to the President for a decision the following Monday.[19]

The NATO Alliance was rocked by the abrupt cancellation of the
Skybolt project during a two-day meeting between President Kennedy and Prime Minister Macmillan in Nassau. McNamara's advice
dominated the decision.

> The Pentagon had precipitated the ill-advised Skybolt controversy with
> a computor decision to cancel development of the missile; the difficult
> project was held to be proceeding too slowly, too expensively and too
> uncertainly. . . . The President nevertheless accepted and later re-
> confirmed Secretary McNamara's timetable: a budget ruling abandon-
> ing Skybolt for U.S. forces before the end of the year. It was a decision
> that should have been postponed until new arrangements could have
> been made with the British that would not have endangered vital U.S.
> objectives abroad; the bill for a six- or twelve-month postponement
> would have been cheap compared with the political issues that later
> ensued.[20]

[19] Meg Greenfield, "Science Goes to Washington," *The Reporter,* September 26, 1963, p. 26. It should be noted, however, that U.S. space achievements
to date have resulted from massive efforts to reach goals that were beyond the
state of the art when the decision to go to the moon was made.
[20] See Robert Kleiman, *Atlantic Crisis* (New York: W. W. Norton, 1964),
pp. 52–53.

The legitimate controversy that has surrounded the development of the TFX aircraft[21] is additional evidence that Secretary McNamara's judgment has not always been as sound as many of his managerial innovations.

The Search for Options

In 1961, Secretary of Defense McNamara, a major force in reorienting U.S. nuclear strategy in the years just before and after the Cuban missile crisis, began to seek new doctrine with which to govern U.S. strategic nuclear forces. Massive retaliation with its specter of spasm war was categorically rejected, but some consideration was given to the concept of finite deterrence, which was developed in the late 1950's. According to that strategy, anything beyond a capability to destroy a certain portion of enemy society would be considered "overkill" and would therefore be undesirable and unnecessary. Finite deterrence, which could not be used as a credible threat against the U.S.S.R., would provide minimal military support for U.S. allies and would have little usefulness in meeting crises. In the event of a Soviet attack, the United States, incapable of waging a controlled attack on the enemy's forces, would have no alternative except countervalue retaliation and thus would undoubtedly assure a similar retaliatory response from the enemy.

The United States sought an incentive for the Soviets to avoid targeting our cities in the event of nuclear war. A two-pronged concept of nuclear strategic war gradually emerged that would provide for: (1) retaliation against a large-scale Soviet attack, if American cities were avoided, using systems and command and control that would permit a deliberate, selective, and controlled option; and (2) a carefully controlled, discriminating response against a small-scale, ambiguous, or accidental attack. Furthermore, the use of conventional forces for NATO's initial defense was stressed repeatedly by U.S. authorities.

These innovations of the Kennedy and Johnson administrations signified a major reappraisal of the role of strategic weapons in supporting U.S. foreign policy—a role subsequently centering around two major alternative strategies. Counterforce reached its high point by mid-1962; the other strategy, *damage limiting*, gradually evolved

[21] See J. Richard Elliott, Jr., "Point of No Return," *Barron's*, August 15, 1966, pp. 1–12.

after the Cuban missile crisis. The difference between these and other possible strategies is one of intent, degree, and emphasis. Counterforce hews to the classic military doctrine that the proper objective of military action is the destruction of the enemy's armed forces. It may be defined as the neutralization of hostile military actions against the United States through: (1) direct attack against enemy strategic bases and missiles sites; (2) in-flight destruction of launched hostile aircraft, missiles, and space vehicles; and (3) the blocking, interdiction, or destruction of hostile surface or undersea forces.

Secretary McNamara expressed the reasons for his initial attraction to the counterforce concept in a speech at Ann Arbor, Michigan, in June, 1962:[22]

> By building into our forces a flexible capability, we at least eliminate the prospect that we could strike back in only one way, namely, against the entire Soviet target system including their cities. Such a prospect would give the Soviet Union no incentive to withhold attack against our cities in a first strike.

He explicitly espoused the counterforce option:

> If, despite all our efforts, nuclear war should occur, our best hope lies in conducting a centrally controlled campaign against all of the enemy's vital nuclear capabilities, while retaining reserve forces, all centrally controlled.

Yet, McNamara gave two substantially different reasons for seeking a counterforce targeting strategy. On the one hand, he stated:

> The United States has come to the conclusion that to the extent feasible, basic military strategy in a possible nuclear war should be approached in much the same way that the more conventional military operations have been regarded in the past. That is to say, principal military objectives in the event of a nuclear war stemming from major attack on the Alliance should be the destruction of the enemy's military forces, not of his civilian population.

On the other hand, he declared:

> [It is] possible for us to retain . . . reserve striking power to destroy an enemy society if driven to it. In other words, we are giving a possible opponent the strongest imaginable incentive to refrain from striking our own cities.

[22] Robert S. McNamara, commencement speech, University of Michigan, Ann Arbor, Michigan, June 16, 1962, cited in Department of Defense news release No. 980-62.

By introducing this thought, the Secretary suggested that the threat of a massive retaliatory attack could be used to deter an enemy's nuclear attack on U.S. cities—an objective quite different from the goal of a pure counterforce strategy: to disarm.

A U.S. counterforce posture also offered a powerful argument against proliferating national nuclear forces, particularly the French force. In returning to the more traditional view of warfare, in which battle is waged against enemy armed forces rather than population, McNamara cited the fact that small national nuclear forces could not wage such a war against a major power like the Soviet Union. Moreover, the existence of small national nuclear forces within the Western Alliance would make it impossible for the United States to wage a controlled counterforce campaign in the event of Soviet aggression against Europe.

It subsequently became clear that strategy could take various forms either of counterforce or of the strategy known as damage limiting. Objections were quickly raised against the nascent counterforce doctrine. For one thing, a counterforce attack could not be easily distinguished from a countervalue attack if very high-yield warheads were used. This problem would be aggravated if some counterforce targets were located in urban complexes, as many Soviet targets were believed to be. At the time of the Cuban missile crisis, the United States fortuitously possessed superior nuclear delivery systems capable of both countervalue and counterforce targeting. Most of these forces were available because of the weapons decisions previously made by the Eisenhower Administration, and President Kennedy exploited these inherited capabilities to bring about the Soviet missile withdrawal.[23]

A Soviet Bid to Upset the Balance of Power

With the emplacement of missiles in Cuba, the Soviets climaxed a bid to break the delicate nuclear balance of power.[24] By the mid-

[23] The subsequent evolution of U.S. strategy will be discussed in Chapter 8, "U.S. Strategy in Crisis."

[24] For an account of this period, written in the Soviet Union, see Oleg Penkovskiy, *The Penkovskiy Papers,* trans. by Peter Deriabin (Garden City, N.Y.: Doubleday, 1965). Colonel Penkovskiy was shot as a spy by the Soviet Union on May 16, 1963. See also, Frank Gibney, "When the West Had a Man in the Kremlin," *Washington Post,* October 31, 1965. According to Gibney, Penkovskiy conducted the most amazing single-handed campaign of

1950's, the Soviets were developing, testing, and producing nuclear and thermonuclear warheads and long-range strategic missiles. (The Soviets consider both ICBM's and IRBM's as long-range strategic missiles, and in view of the Soviet geographical position, they are.) Initial test firings of the intercontinental missiles revealed problems with the guidance systems that would limit their military employment. However, the combined testing of missiles and their warheads by the Soviets was never duplicated in the West.[25]

The allocation of Soviet research and development funds for advanced weapons was greatly increased in 1956–57. Surface-to-air missiles were deployed on an unprecedented scale, and by 1962 some 1,000 SAM sites had been constructed. To support this massive air-defense program, radar systems blanketed the entire Soviet Union and the manned-interceptor force was increased on almost the same scale as the surface-to-air missiles. The air-defense system, probably manned by at least 1 million men, was set out to blunt any possible retaliation from SAC manned aircraft. The Soviets decided to deploy approximately 750 of their very efficient medium-range ballistic missiles—more than enough to destroy the military installations of the U.S. and its allies in Western Europe.

The Soviets did not build a large intercontinental-ballistic-missile force. They believed that planting their more efficient, accurate, and

---

espionage in modern history. He rocked Nikita Khrushchev's policy to its foundations. The two years 1961–62, during which Penkovskiy worked for British and American intelligence, marked the freezing point of the Cold War.

In June, 1961, Khrushchev risked war by his decision to force an Allied retreat in Berlin. In August, he put up the Berlin Wall. In September, 1961, he resumed nuclear testing, breaking agreements with the United States. His missile build-up of 1962 was climaxed in the Cuban confrontation with the United States, when he almost threw the world into total war. How badly Penkovskiy hurt Moscow's plans for an aggressive break-through against the West in these two critical years can be gathered from the public aftermath of his arrest: one chief marshal of the Soviet Union demoted and disgraced; the chief of Soviet military intelligence, General Ivan Serov (the "Hangman of Hungary" in 1956) demoted; some 300 Soviet intelligence officers recalled to Moscow from their foreign posts.

[25] "All nuclear tests have had and some still have two phases. The first phase deals with the explosive force in TNT equivalents. In these tests the bombs were dropped from aircraft or from special masts. The second-phase tests are of the latter type, in which missiles are fired for distance and accuracy without a nuclear charge. Next, the same type of missiles are launched at the same targets with nuclear warheads."—Penkovskiy, *op. cit.*, pp. 335–36.

reliable intermediate-range missiles in Cuba could, however, compensate for deficiencies in their intercontinental-missile force.

By June, 1961, Khrushchev was ready to test the U.S. position in Berlin and, in essence, issued an ultimatum to President Kennedy to pull out. President Kennedy responded with a partial mobilization and an increase in the U.S. defense budget. Undeterred, the Soviets pressed forward with plans to resume testing missiles and warheads. On July 8, 1961, the Soviet troop reduction that was programmed was canceled, and the defense budget was increased from 9.3 billion rubles to 12.3 billion. Significantly, Khrushchev returned to the view that nuclear war would lead not to mutual annihilation but to the total destruction of imperialism.[26]

Later that same year, the Soviets announced a series of troop maneuvers in conjunction with the Warsaw Pact[27] and also made preparations for "general strategic military exercises. . . . There have never been exercises like these in the history of the Sovet Army. All the staff of military districts and groups will participate. . . . That is, absolutely every Soviet military installation will take part in these games."[28]

For a Soviet "win" strategy—and 1962–63 was a period of opportunity—the development of high-yield weapons was another requirement. The Soviets had broken the tacit test-ban moratorium in 1961 and tested again in 1962. This was the greatest single period of open high-yield nuclear testing by either the United States or the Soviet Union. The Soviet Union was testing both offensive and defensive operational weapons with regular combat troops and made its first tests of the large-megaton bomb. "On September 8, 1961, there was a regular experimental explosion of a bomb of such force in the Soviet Union. . . . When a fifty-megaton bomb was tested . . . the explosion's actual force equalled that of eighty megatons."[29]

Soviet intentions may be gleaned from the Penkovskiy papers, written during this same period:

> From what I have learned and what I have heard, I know that the leaders of our Soviet state are the willing provocateurs of an atomic war. At one time or another they may lose their heads entirely and

[26] Mackintosh, *op. cit.*, pp. 264–65.
[27] *Ibid.*, p. 267.
[28] Penkovskiy, *op. cit.*, p. 243.
[29] *Ibid.*, pp. 334–35.

start an atomic war. See what Khrushchev has done over Berlin.

In Moscow I have lived in a nuclear nightmare. I know the poison of the new military doctrine, as outlined in the top-secret "Special Collection"—the plan to strike first, at any costs.[30]

In retrospect, it appears that Premier Khrushchev "was undoubtedly looking for a way of offsetting the superiority of the American long-range strike forces."[31] The Soviets had hoped that by installing their efficient intermediate-range missiles geographically near the United States, they would be able to nullify the American ballistic-missile early-warning system. If the Soviet missiles in Cuba had become operational before they were discovered, they could have altered the global balance of power, but this calculated bid fortunately failed.

Soviet Perspective on Nuclear War

In the aftermath of the Cuban missile crisis, Soviet leadership undoubtedly reassessed its nuclear strategy, but we can only speculate on what transpired and reinforce our speculations with whatever evidence is available. Two articles in Moscow's *Red Star* hinted at some resolution of the strategic controversy that followed the crisis.[32] Written by two Soviet military leaders, the articles referred to strategic forces twice as frequently as to nonstrategic forces. Discussing the broad outlines of Soviet military forces and capabilities, the authors asserted that "the operational art of the strategic rocket troops as well as that of the troops of the country's defense against air attacks have now become the main feature." They went on to say that "the strategic rocket troops have become the main, most reliable force; they will accomplish the main tasks of the war." An apparent capitulation by the "traditionalists" to the "modernists" is contained in the admission that "combat, battles, and operations in the conventional sense will lose their importance as the only means of destroying the enemy and gaining victory."

Another statement, representing a reversal in long-standing Soviet doctrine, concluded that "in our opinion thermonuclear war cannot

[30] *Ibid.*, p. 57.

[31] Mackintosh, *op. cit.*, p. 274.

[32] Marshal of the Soviet Union V. D. Sokolovskii and Major General M. Cherednichenko, "The Revolution in Military Affairs, Its Significance and Consequences: Military Art at a New State," *Krasnaya zvezda* (*Red Star*), August 25 and 28, 1964.

last long. Hence it is necessary . . . above all to make preparations for a short war."[33] What appears to be a retreat of the "traditionalists" does not, however, contradict the Soviet belief that the poststrike stage of a thermonuclear war could be protracted. For although published Soviet documents spell out the nuclear thrust that is central to Soviet military doctrine, many questions are left unanswered—in particular, how a specific military concept would be executed.

The problem of understanding Soviet strategic writings is compounded by fundamental differences in our approaches. In the Soviet Union, the strategy recommended to the Politburo is made by military professionals and not by a comparable cortege of economists, physicists, sociologists, psychiatrists, and comptrollers, the groups that have sought to monopolize strategic thinking in the United States. According to one Soviet military professional:

> In foreign bourgeois military literature there are statements which in essence come to this: that supposedly nuclear rocket weapons lead to the liquidation of military art, that waging armed combat in nuclear war does not require any military theory preparation of an officer cadre.
> Soviet military science categorically rejects such groundless and oversimplified assertions about the nature and the ability to wage armed combat with the use of nuclear rocket weapons.[34]

By the rules of the game in the United States, military professionals do not engage in public discussions of strategy. The field has been pre-empted by a growing body of articulate and increasingly vocal social scientists and academicians. Herbert Spiro accurately reported that in the West:

> Neither professional military nor professional diplomats retain their monopoly over the warlike or peaceful relations between states. Each is involved in the affairs that used to be the preserve of the other and, more important and on a larger scale, both are being pushed out of their realms by members of quite different professions.[35]

[33] For a fuller discussion of these and other current Soviet military views, see Thomas W. Wolfe, *Soviet Strategy at the Crossroads* (Cambridge, Mass.: Harvard University Press, 1964).

[34] General Colonel Nikolai A. Lomov, "The Influence of Soviet Military Doctrine on the Development of Military Art," *Kommunist vooruzhennykh sil* (*Communist of the Armed Forces*), March, 1965, p. 16; unpublished English translation by Harriet Fast Scott.

[35] Herbert J. Spiro, *World Politics: The Global System* (Homewood, Ill.: The Dorsey Press, 1966), p. 230.

U.S. strategy is a publicly drawn and beautifully structured model. The Soviets have learned the value of secrecy, and the Soviet debate concerning the nature of future war is made public only in part, permitting only the most general conclusions about Soviet directions in the decade ahead. Important details are either omitted or obscured by a haze of ideology and semantics. According to General Colonel Lomov: "The most important feature of Soviet military doctrine is that it is oriented not to past but to future war, taking into account its features, which pose specific demands on the art of the use of armed forces in it."[36]

Many Western scholars view the simplicity and directness of the Soviet military as a reflection of the primitive nature of Soviet thought, and in Soviet strategic literature they find a gross lack of sophistication and expression. American analysts, tending to search for features that are comparable to those in U.S. strategy, often overlook critical differences; the power of the dialectical approach to strategic analysis is almost completely ignored in the West.[37]

Soviet strategic thinking, particularly in understanding the organic relation between force and nonviolent forms of conflict, is extremely sophisticated. A significant unstated premise in Soviet military writing is that until the Soviets are able to attain their announced force objectives, they must necessarily practice restraint. The Soviets rarely enunciate, other than in ideologcal terms, their blueprint for waging restrained conflict—sabotage, subversion, infiltration, revolution. What Western analysts view as a Soviet doctrinal gap may merely be an understandable reluctance to reveal their operational thinking to the public.

Disappointment has been expressed that the Soviets do not give out highlights of their society's vulnerability to nuclear attack. Soviet authors illustrate their technical writing with characteristics of Western weapons, and their strategic and arms control discussions make use of some of the terms common to American strategic analysis. Certain terms such as "deliberate" and "selective" are never used to describe a nuclear attack. Presumably, the Soviets have a targeting doctrine from which they develop their target lists, but in public dis-

[36] Lomov, *loc. cit.*
[37] See Chapter 4, "The Balance Sheet: Strategic Assets and Liabilities," for amplification.

cussions their strategic doctrine calls for "the simultaneous action on populated centers and the armed forces of the enemy with nuclear weapons"[38]—an indiscriminate targeting that suggests little Soviet interest in restraint.

What Soviet writers do stress is of considerably greater importance. It points out what might be expected from the oldest and most combat-experienced group of military professionals now on active duty in any country: Initiatives short of war can best be risked from a position of massive superiority. If war is to be waged, it must be done so totally and from a position of clear initiative. This is the single most pervasive theme in the more than 90 per cent of contemporary Soviet writings on strategy that deal with the value of nuclear superiority.

The Soviets believe that a future war will begin with a surprise attack without a formal declaration of war. America will be the main Soviet adversary.[39] Further:

> The next world war will be a nuclear conflict involving the use of ballistic missiles. Such a war, however, cannot be waged with nuclear weapons alone. It may be of a long duration and call for the utmost effort by all the armed forces involved. It will bear the character of a coalition war and, from a spatial angle, be of tremendous dimensions. The military operations will be intercontinental in their scope and the role of space will undergo a fundamental change. The struggle for mastery of the seas will mainly take place below water, since even surface vessels equipped with the most up-to-date technical devices are too vulnerable. As the initial phase of a nuclear war is of decisive importance for the outcome, armies will no longer occupy the leading position but will be superseded by strategic missile forces, though this does not imply that their development can be neglected.[40]

In view of the acknowledged destructiveness of nuclear war, the Soviets have come to recognize one essential precondition for such warfare—namely, the first strike, which they call a "pre-emptive" strike:

[38] Marshal of the Soviet Union V. D. Sokolovskii and Major General M. Cherednichenko, "On Contemporary Military Strategy, *Kommunist vooruzhennykh sil* (*Communist of the Armed Forces*), April, 1966, p. 64; unpublished English translation by Harriet Fast Scott.

[39] Sokolovskii and Cherednichenko, "The Revolution in Military Affairs," p. 393.

[40] T. F. M. van den Buch, "Strategic Concepts of the Russian High Command," *NATO's Fifteen Nations*, December, 1965–January, 1966, p. 60.

As a result of the mass use of strategic nuclear means, the possibility becomes real of the quick removal from the war of a series of countries of one or another coalition even without the simultaneous seizing of the territory of these countries by land forces and airborne troops.

This new feature of modern military strategy decisively influences the nature of waging war. *Using intercontinental means of combat can at once, from the very beginning of the war, achieve results of great strategic meaning* [italics added].[41]

Since the concept of the pre-emptive strike dominates the Soviets' strategic doctrine, their major weapons emphasis is on strategic rocket forces rather than on conventional forces. The targeting doctrine to be employed would be a combination of counterforce and urban-industrial and population targets.[42] Each side will have to employ its nuclear arsenal in a surprise attack. "It is for this reason that the nuclear weapons, and more especially the strategic nuclear weapons, still occupy a predominant place in the strategic thinking of the Soviet army commanders. . . . [Strategic rockets] determine the basic principles and procedures for military operations. . . . Rocket troops form the chief component of the whole military machine."[43]

By attacking targets in the enemy's rear as well as groupings of his armed force and other important targets on the various battlefields, rocket forces in combination with the strategic air arm will dominate the initial phase of nuclear hostilities.

Since the Soviets believe that the initial plan of a nuclear war will be decisive, "to repel the nuclear blows of the enemy, especially in the beginning of the war, when the enemy evidently will try to use the maximum of his nuclear power, is a problem of great national significance."[44] For this reason, the Air Defense Command (PVO) is "one of the most important branches of the Armed Forces."[45] And, by Soviet military doctrine, it was a logical decision for the Soviets to proceed with the development and deployment of an antiballistic-missile system.

---

[41] Lomov, *op. cit.*, p. 19.

[42] *Soviet Military Strategy*, ed. V. D. Sokolovskii, trans. by Thomas Wolfe, Herbert S. Dinerstein, and Leon Gouré (Englewood Cliffs, N.J.: Prentice-Hall, 1963), pp. 59–60.

[43] Van den Buch, *op. cit.*, p. 59.

[44] *Ibid.*

[45] *Ibid.*, p. 22.

Soviet Organizational Adaptation

Just as a revolution has taken place in the Pentagon, so, too, have the armed forces of the Soviet Union experienced major changes in organization, management, and the development and production of weapons systems. By the mid-1960's, various reorganizations had divided the Soviet armed forces into six coequal services—Army, Navy, Air, Strategic Rocket, Air Defense (PVO), and the Forces of the Rear. The Strategic Rocket Force is regarded as the elite group of the military organization. The six services are headed by coequal marshals under the supervision of the Minister of Defense, who is also a marshal.

The military-industrial complex of the Soviet Union has, in the last few years, been managed with growing efficiency. In the summer of 1964, the former chief of Soviet armaments production, D. F. Ustinov, was promoted to First Deputy Premier as a result of his superior performance. Authority has been decentralized among managers who each function, in effect, as scientist, industrialist, and general. Production and efficiency have been encouraged and increased through a system of incentives that matches Western capitalistic societies. By 1966, Soviet production of highly accurate ICBM's capable of carrying payloads five to six times as large as U.S. Minuteman and Polaris missiles was accelerating at an impressive rate. This is but one example of the performance of the Soviet military-industrial complex.

Conclusions

The Cuban missile crisis has been widely hailed as perhaps the major watershed of the nuclear age. Presumably both the United States and the Soviet Union have digested its lessons and have oriented the design of their respective strategic forces according to what they have learned.

The United States subsequently adopted the damage-limiting strategy, which is described in Chapter 8, "U.S. Strategy in Crisis." It has, however, been reluctant to invest in the deployment of an ABM system or to initiate a large-scale civil-defense program—both implicit in the damage-limiting strategic design. The United States is placing its primary emphasis on offensive missiles, while the Soviet Union is investing proportionately more in defensive systems. In April, 1966, Secretary McNamara asserted at a press conference:

> "If we had to spend the entire budget of the Defense Department, $50 billion, on the strategic offensive system, we would propose to do so to insure that the Soviets do not develop an effective counter." The Secretary, in response to a query regarding the logic behind a Soviet decision to build an ABM system, viewed such a decision, "if they have decided that," as "simply a carry over of the same philosophy into ABM defense that they made in connection with air defense. And, I think, with the same error. . . . The Soviets for years have placed a different emphasis on strategic defense than we have. They have felt that they could obtain a higher level of protection than we believed was technically feasible."[46]

The many uncertainties regarding the future orientation of Soviet strategy are discussed in Chapter 5, "The Soviet Dilemma." Although Soviet strategy is defense oriented, the Soviet Union has also invested heavily in offensive weapons and space activities. There is little or no basis for believing that the Soviets will be forever content with second-best strategic capabilities. Geographical and industrial asymmetries between the United States and its Communist adversaries and even some of its allies will affect the future choice of both U.S. and Soviet strategy. Significant improvements by the United States, the Soviet Union, or Communist China in offensive and defensive systems, in research, development, and testing, should exert a considerable influence upon the still uncertain outcome of the strategic revolution. Political trends among the aligned and nonaligned nations of the world and the perceived prospects and desires for arms control will also help shape the development of future U.S. and Soviet strategic postures. But in the last analysis, the choices the United States will make concerning the design of its strategic forces will depend largely on how its leaders perceive the value of power in the future.

[46] Michael Getler, "McNamara Says Soviets Err on ABM," *Missiles and Rockets*, May 2, 1966, p. 12.

3

The Technological Arena

A nation that is first to envision a strategy for exploiting technological superiority holds within its grasp decisive political as well as military advantage. During World War II, the miracle of U.S. production was the key that opened the door to victory. Since World War II, the United States has successfully used science and technology to enhance its security and has become the acknowledged leader in basic research and many areas of applied technology. In their bid to achieve military superiority by deliberately exploiting science and technology, the Soviets have made their share of mistakes. They have also demonstrated their capacity to correct deficiencies in the planning and management of their research and development (R&D) effort. Few people in the Western world, however, can accurately assess the state of Soviet science and technology today. But we car extrapolate from past Soviet achievements,[1] from the magnitude of the resources allocated to Soviet R&D, and from the future-oriented character of Soviet planning, and we can conclude that the Soviet challenge to scientific and technological leadership will become increasingly serious. It is against this threat that the adequacy of U.S. technological management and level of R&D should be assessed.

The Soviet Drive to Master Technology

Marxist-Leninist dogma contends that the sphere of production is the decisive sphere of human relations. Hence, the Soviet system is institutionally committed to gaining technological superiority as one means of furthering its political ambitions. Lenin, in 1920, believed

---

[1] The Soviets were first in space, first to hit the moon, photograph its dark side, place a man in orbit, test nuclear weapons in operational missiles, and detonate the largest-yield weapons.

that electrification was the key to victory;[2] now the Soviets seek mastery in almost every realm of technology.

The manner in which the Soviets have conducted basic scientific research and have organized their research and development programs suggests that they have evolved a coherent plan for making the most of their scientific and technological gains. From the day it came to power in Russia, the Communist regime has strived to educate its people as a way toward mastering science and technology. Lenin declared that "education must be a weapon for moving people forward on the road to communism." Stalin emphasized that "to build socialism . . . we must master science. . . . To master science, we must learn from our friends and particularly from our enemies." In Communist thought, applied technology can transform not only the class structure of society but also the order of international power. For this reason, the Communists seek to break the West's advantage and to outdistance the West in those strategic military capabilities that will form the future core of international power.

By 1965, the Soviet scientific effort had equaled the U.S. effort.[3] Between 1 million and 1.5 million Russians are engaged in R&D; approximately 440,000 of these are scientists and engineers.[4] In 1966, the Soviets spent about $7 billion on R&D—an increase of 9.9 per cent over the previous year.[5] This represents about half of the U.S. expenditures ($15 billion), but U.S. research costs are several times those of the Soviets.

Soviet R&D is centrally organized in conceptual planning and the

[2] "Communism is the Soviet power plus electrification of the whole country. Otherwise the country will remain a small peasant country, and that we must clearly realize. We are weaker than capitalism, not only on the world scale but within the country. Everyone knows that. We have realized it and we shall see to it that the economic basis is transformed from a small, peasant basis into a large-scale industrial basis. Only when the country has been electrified, when industry, agriculture and transport have been placed on a technical basis of modern large-scale industry, only then shall we be finally victorious."—Lénin, "Work of Council of People's Commissars," Report to 8th Congress of Soviets, December 22, 1920, in *Selected Works* (New York: International Publishers, 1937), VIII, 267–77.

[3] *The New York Times*, December 19, 1965, p. 20.

[4] In the Soviet Union, many technicians are referred to as "engineers."

[5] Harry Schwartz, "Soviet Budget Implying Peace," *The New York Times*, December 12, 1965, Sec. 3, p. 12.

assignment of priority, but it is highly decentralized in execution. A 1961 decree, based on many years of experimenting with forms of administration, established a system for coordinating scientific and technological programs under the State Committee for the Coordination of Scientific Research.[6] The committee not only is attached directly to the Council of Ministers, but also is a formally constituted body with the duty and power of mobilizing the scientific community to serve the ends of the Soviet state. The committee's task is to establish research priorities on key problems for some 170 agencies responsible for conducting R&D in the Soviet Union and to focus on those weapons applications that appear to have the greatest military potential. This arrangement allows for rapid, authoritative decisions on the planning, priorities, and execution of Soviet research and development. The task of exploiting knowledge and executing projects is conferred on separate government bureaucracies. As noted earlier, each manager functions on a number of levels, and the system has been reinforced with the dynamic incentive of competition, which is deliberately spurred among leading research teams.

Although the quality and volume of Soviet basic and applied research are salient, two other immensely important factors aid Soviet achievements. The U.S.S.R. has a vigorous program for acquiring, translating, and exploiting Western scientific literature and (when possible) applied technology. Designs of weapons systems or components that can be obtained from other countries are promptly copied or adapted. Soviet collection of Western technical information increased during and after World War II, and at the present time, more than 25,000 technically competent translators comb, abstract, or relate in full the mass of published Western scientific data.

In the mid-1940's, farsighted and discriminate investments in education, the expertise of captured German scientists, and the rich hauls of espionage enabled Soviet scientists to make several far-reaching decisions in the field of military technology. Having recognized at an early stage the importance of technology for both industrial devel-

---

[6] "The Committee has many different sections and directorates which work strictly in the field of the national economy. The direction of our so-called coordination of scientific research work, however, is undoubtedly of a military nature."—Oleg Penkovskiy, *The Penkovskiy Papers*, trans. by Peter Deriabin (Garden City, N.Y.: Doubleday, 1965).

opment and military supremacy, the Soviets created the base from which they would methodically launch the drive for technological superiority.

In the early 1950's, Soviet leaders apparently decided to rely more on missiles than on long-range bombers. The first Soviet ICBM was a great achievement—possibly representing the U.S.S.R.'s first major weapons development not borrowed in whole or in part from foreign technology. The Soviets had to break new ground and, at the same time, master "sausagelike" production of shorter-range systems that would secure their flanks. They took an early lead in developing ICBM's, but they did not mass-produce them. That turn is difficult to interpret since, whatever the answers, it is apparent that the Soviets did not succeed in capitalizing fully on their initial ICBM advantage. Perhaps Soviet military commanders and technical directors did not order large-scale production because they were not confident that the missiles, if deployed, could achieve anticipated results.[7]

The first-generation Soviet ICBM's would not provide a dependable striking force—particularly in comparison with the proven effectiveness of the U.S. Strategic Air Command. The Soviets deployed medium- and intermediate-range missiles vastly in excess of what the United States had anticipated; and it can be reasoned that the Soviets produced these missiles for the purpose of securing the periphery and the land approaches to the U.S.S.R., their most immediate strategic concern. It is not clear why they did not produce more ICBM's. Their initial ICBM's were bulky, difficult to handle, and possibly costly to produce; they were also limited in range, requiring forward deployment into the inhospitable Soviet north until lighter and improved re-entry vehicles and warheads were deployed. Nevertheless, they were surprisingly reliable work horses and continued to serve as primary boosters for Soviet space programs.

The mystery of how many of these ICBM's were produced with refire capabilities has never been satisfactorily resolved. The extraordinary effort in 1962 to redress the strategic balance by deploying medium- and intermediate-range missiles to Cuba implied the availability of a considerable reserve of ICBM force. Probably the Soviets'

[7] For a discussion of the pertinent factors, see Donovan P. Yeuell, Jr., *Missile Dependability* (Washington, D.C.: American Security Council, February, 1964), pp. 1–2.

military purpose was to achieve successful surprise in the face of the U.S. BMEW's and alert-force capabilities. By attacking U.S. command and control centers from Cuba, they might have been able to vitiate U.S. warning capabilities. The Soviets have not, unfortunately, volunteered their analysis of the Cuban venture, and so the mystery remains.

Early Soviet ICBM's were considerably more powerful than, and about as accurate and reliable as, the first-generation U.S. Atlas missiles. The Soviets readily capitalized on the high-thrust of their early ICBM as the basic building block of their space-research program. They were also quick to perceive the extraordinary political and psychological potential of moving into space; and while the world watched, they reaped psychological gains both at home and abroad from their space spectaculars. Yet, the Soviet boosters, which were capable of putting a satellite three times larger than a Gemini vehicle into orbit, were being used principally for the systematic development of military space capabilities, especially in the fields of orbital bombardment and reconnaissance. Unlike the United States, the Soviets were not compelled to develop subsystem miniaturized components for space. Because they diverted the development of their ICBM boosters for space, they were able to put up larger payloads and carry sensory and other equipment—a capability that the United States could match only after a lapse of several years.

The difficulties alluded to in the Penkovskiy papers[8] concerning Soviet missiles were not unlike those experienced by the United States with the Atlas missile. Not mentioned in the Penkovskiy papers was the unusual success and magnitude of the Soviet development, production, and deployment of medium- and intermediate-range ballistic missiles. The correctness or soundness of Soviet deci-

---

[8] "While Khrushchev rattles his missiles the fact is that as far as launching a planned missile attack to destroy definite targets is concerned, we are not yet capable of doing it. We simply do not have missiles that are accurate enough. . . . Many of our big missiles are still on the drawing boards, in the prototype stage, or are still undergoing tests. . . . The launching of the first *sputnik* required the combined efforts of all Soviet scientists and technical personnel with the entire technological capacity of the country at their disposal." Of the 1962–63 period, Penkovskiy wrote that it was difficult "to speak of strategic missiles as perfected. Accidents and all sorts of troubles are daily occurrences. In this connection, there is much talk about shortcomings in the field of electronics."—Penkovskiy, *op. cit.*, pp. 339–40.

sions concerning missiles and space boosters cannot yet be assessed. Had not crash programs been ordered to place U.S. strategic bombers on alert and to develop the Minuteman and Polaris missile systems, the strategic balance might have been upset in 1962 by the Soviet Union.

The failure to wrest strategic superiority from the United States between 1957 and 1962 has not discouraged the Soviet leaders from trying again. Perhaps they are on the threshold of succeeding; an information gap exists in the West on this subject. We do know that the Soviets are building and rapidly deploying highly accurate, hardened ICBM's with a payload far greater than that of either the Polaris or the Minuteman; they are also deploying an antiballistic-missile (ABM) system and are continuing to develop a military space capability.

U.S. Status in the Technological Race

Some scientists in the United States are taking the position that a technological plateau has been reached. In an article in *Scientific American,* Jerome B. Wiesner, who was scientific adviser to President Kennedy, and Herbert F. York, who was chief scientist at the Pentagon during the Eisenhower and Kennedy administrations, asserted that the United States is confronted "by the dilemma of steadily increasing power and steadily decreasing national security,"[9] and they advocate virtual unilateral disarmament. They maintained that "nothing on the horizon suggests that there is a solution to the anti-missile problem."[10]

Equally competent scientists, however, including those responsible for the design and engineering of antiballistic-missile systems, contend that the solution to this particular problem is well in hand. Eugene P. Wigner of Princeton University, replying to Wiesner and York, contended:

A justified "extrapolation" made from the article is that no further methods of offense or defense need be explored, that is, that military science is a complete and closed book. . . . Statements of this sort mean partly that those who make them have, at the time of making the

[9] Jerome B. Wiesner and Herbert F. York, "The Test Ban," *Scientific American,* October, 1964, pp. 27–35.
[10] *Ibid.*

statements, no promising ideas in the field about which they speak. Others have such ideas, and those making the statements may themselves conceive such ideas at a later time.[11]

Dr. James R. Killian, Jr., chairman of the Massachusetts Institute of Technology and former scientific adviser to President Eisenhower, joined Wigner in taking issue with the plateau thesis:

> I am troubled when I hear statements about our having reached some kind of plateau in our invention and development of new weapons. I don't think we have, but I think it is of the utmost importance that we continue a high level of creative activity in this area. . . . Our science and technology must be so good and so far out on the frontier that it is we who have the capability to anticipate advances and do things unimagined by others.[12]

The 1965 resignation of Dr. Eugene Fubini as deputy director of Defense Research and Engineering in the Department of Defense provoked further discussion of the idea of technological stalemate. Fubini did concede that the development of weapons was limited only by man's imagination, but he contended that a plateau may have been reached in the development of strategic weapons. In the field of nonstrategic weapons, however, Dr. Fubini believed that a technological revolution was still possible.

The United States is, of course, seeking to improve the weapons and equipment needed to deter or win future Vietnam-type conflicts. This book focuses, however, on the technological confrontation in the strategic zone of the conflict spectrum, for the other military and nonmilitary elements essential to a viable U.S. policy can be taken for granted.

Leaders of the Soviet Union do not subscribe to the idea of a "technological plateau" for any kind of weapon. Good Marxists that they are, the Soviet leaders clearly believe that mastery of technology will inevitably lead to mastery of the political order. Their intentions to be in the lead in all branches of science have been proclaimed with impressive candor and regularity. Soviet Major General Talen-

[11] Eugene P. Wigner, letter to the editors, *Scientific American,* December, 1964, p. 22.
[12] "Dr. Killian's Warning," editorial, *Aviation Week and Space Technology,* April 27, 1964, p. 21.

skii, for example, emphatically rejects the thesis of stalemate—material or intellectual:

> There are no limits to creative human thinking, and the possibilities offered by modern sciences and technology are tremendous. And I think that it is theoretically and technically quite possible to counterbalance the absolute weapons of attack with equally absolute weapons of defense, thereby objectively eliminating war regardless of the desires of resisting governments. In our day, the human genius can do anything.[13]

Because of the scope of Soviet research and development and a philosophical commitment to attain superior military technology, we can anticipate the Soviet Union's challenge to the United States and its industrial allies for world technological leadership.

Of central issue in a technological race is whether a decisive military advantage can be maintained through the exploitation of technology, whether both sides will recognize the existence of such an advantage, and whether the advantage can be sustained over a sufficient period of time to be politically useful. Within the valid restriction of a second-strike policy, the United States needs military-technological superiority as the essential foundation for its world position. But is the United States doing all that needs to be done to maintain its military-technological superiority?

Management of U.S. Technology

U.S. pioneering efforts of the 1940's and 1950's in nuclear and thermonuclear projects and in the production of supersonic fighters are well known. The technological and managerial achievements that spawned Polaris and Minuteman are a credit to the Department of Defense. Now, while military technology stands on the verge of unprecedented technical possibilities and opportunities, the government's approach to technological innovation appears to be halfhearted at best. Many weapons or delivery vehicles under development or in production (such as the C5A—a large transport plane) do not fully push the state of the art. Time delays and possible failures may be the result of stretching technology too far, but this is a lesser risk than consciously choosing product improvement rather than innova-

[13] Major General N. Talenskii, "Antimissile Systems and Disarmament," *Bulletin of the Atomic Scientists*, February, 1965, p. 26.

tion as a technological goal. Admittedly, resources have to be allocated, funds controlled, and costly mistakes avoided.[14] Yet many constraints are imposed on U.S. technological progress by managerial decisions and policies. It is noteworthy that the word "superiority," as it is used to describe weapons goals, has been replaced by such terms as "balance," "adequate," "parity," and "not inferior." Obviously if requirement goals do not demand that the state of the art be pushed to assure superiority, the end results will be a good deal less.

Despite many improvements in the Department of Defense and its management of research and development, there are some discernible flaws. Hanson Baldwin, military analyst for *The New York Times,* has described some of the imperfections of the system and contends that the Department of Defense has increasingly emphasized cost rather than effectiveness criteria. Baldwin commented on this statement by Secretary McNamara:

> Before full-scale development is initiated, the specific operational requirements and the cost effectiveness of the system must be confirmed, and goals, milestones, and time schedules must be established. . . .
> All the aspects of a development are tied together into a single plan which defines, for Government and industry alike, what is wanted, how it is to be designed and built, how it will be used, what it will cost, and what systems and techniques will be used to manage the program.[15]

Baldwin pointed out that five to seven years ago, "it required four to five months to execute a contract from the time an acceptable price quotation was received in the Pentagon to the time the contractor received the final document. Today . . . an average of nine to twelve is needed for the same process." The development of weap-

[14] We have avoided the costly mistakes and wasted time that characterized development of the SAGE (Simulated Air Ground Environment) air-defense control system because the decision to develop it was preceded by thorough analysis. Current procedures call for a program-definition phase, which allows full-scale study and detailed definition of a particular system before development is authorized. The energy required to explore various approaches and make detailed estimates of the time, effort, and money that will be involved if a given weapons proposal is approved for operational development has been worthwhile in many cases.

[15] *Statement of Secretary of Defense Robert S. McNamara Before the House Armed Service Committee on the Fiscal Year 1965–69 Defense Program and 1965 Defense Budget* (mimeo.), January 27, 1964, p. 100.

ons systems is also retarded by a "prevalent negativistic Pentagon philosophy about new weapons systems and of the difficulties of developing new systems under hydra-headed controls."[16]

Baldwin also alleged that the source of the delay originates in the Pentagon "from the overcentralized organization established by Mc-Namara and the attempts to achieve 'perfection on paper' before any steel is bent." Although there was little support for Baldwin's thesis in the upper echelon of the Pentagon, the former director of Defense Research and Engineering, Dr. Harold Brown, conceded:

> There are too many echelons, I believe. I believe my own way of looking at it is to say there should be the project officer, then there should be one echelon of technical review in the service—in the Air Force, probably Systems Command, say, or in the Navy, the Chief of Naval Material—and then it should be reviewed by me jointly with the service Assistant Secretary of the military department concerned. That would be three technical people looking at it. Then any separate administrative review should be done at the top at the same time as I do it. That would be the three layers. At the moment, I think it is true that there are at least two or three times as many layers as that. Some of them are administrative, some of them are technical."[17]

Perhaps even more crucial is the fact that the Pentagon has employed cost effectiveness as the basic value criteria of R&D management, with prime stress being placed on cost. Not all aspects of R&D can be pinned to a cost-effectiveness criterion, for the very nature of forward-oriented R&D makes it a high-risk operation in which some failures are inescapable.

Promising strategic weapons have been vetoed with some frequency in the United States since 1962. An air-breathing, nuclear-powered vehicle with a high potential speed, designated "Pluto," was abandoned in May, 1964. It could attack targets below radar-detection altitudes almost half the earth away—an excellent attack mode—yet was eliminated because it had "no apparent military utility."[18] Some de-

[16] Hanson W. Baldwin, "Slow-Down in the Pentagon," *Foreign Affairs*, January, 1965, pp. 262 and 266.

[17] Dr. Harold Brown, testimony, U.S. Congress, House Subcommittee of the Committee on Appropriations, *Hearings, Research, Development, Test, and Evaluation*, 89th Cong., 1st Sess., 1965, Part 5, p. 38.

[18] "The cause of the project's death is a combination of indecision, indifference and lack of support by the Defense Department. . . . The closing out of the once promising project is being carried out in embarrassed privacy, without so much as an official announcement from the Commission of the death

sirable weapons have been kept in the development stage for long periods of time, while promising ideas for future weapons have been neglected. The United States quite sensibly seeks to improve what weapons it has, but it seems more concerned with marginal improvements than with exploration of future technological vistas.[19]

The problem of making future weapons choices is immensely difficult. Cost-effectiveness methods have not completely solved this problem but at least have made it more manageable. The idea behind cost-effectiveness is that comparative dollar costs can help measure military effectiveness, for there is an element of uncertainty in all alternative weapons choices. For instance, would putting one's money into penetration aids be the best initial answer to ABM's, or vice versa? Under certain circumstances, it might be both prudent and cunning to keep certain systems under lengthy consideration.

Doubts have nevertheless arisen on the specific decisions made on the actual mix and levels of offensive and defensive strategic forces and on the Defense Department's wisdom in dealing with space and ballistic-missile defense. The U.S. has thus far postponed the decision to deploy an ABM because, as of 1966, it was believed to be far cheaper to overcome a defense than to build one. Yet, technology is rapidly changing this picture. Richard Foster, Stanford Research Institute, suggested:

> One must consider the rate at which the cost-exchange ratios may change in the future between offensive and defensive weaponry. If they continue at the present rate, the defense planners may become indifferent to whether they buy offensive weaponry or defensive weaponry since the cost-exchange ratios will be virtually the same.[20]

Although repeated delays in producing operational systems can be traced to some technical difficulties and the high costs of such sys-

---

of the program. It was only in response to newspaper inquiries that the A.E.C. acknowledged the project had died earlier this month."—*The New York Times,* July 13, 1964, p. 11.

[19] "Because of the growing number of weapons systems which have passed the full-scale development stage, greater stress is now being placed on improving these systems and on developing advanced components which can be used in the future in a number of different weapons systems such as strategic and tactical aircraft and ballistic missiles."—*The New York Times,* January 26, 1965, p. 28.

[20] Richard Foster, "The Impact of Ballistic Missile Defense on Arms Control Prospects," an address given at the Third International Arms Control Symposium, Philadelphia, April 1, 1966.

tems, they are also partly related to U.S. confidence in its own estimates of future Soviet intentions—to the neglect of Soviet capabilities.[21]

There has been, however, a steady increase in funds allocated to
R&D.[22] We have sought to develop some new systems and to find
answers to some crucial problems. For example, Project Defender is
a study of other forms of ABM defense, and the Manned Orbital
Laboratory (MOL) is a test vehicle designed to measure man's military potential in space. Yet the Defense Department has tended to
concentrate on developments that are predictable within proven technologies and can therefore be more easily programmed and controlled.

We have not allowed sufficiently for the exponential growth of
technology. We have not always sought open-ended answers to
problems and situations that, by their very nature, escape precise
definition and solution. More funds could be allocated to research not
directly related to a specific weapons concept. Currently, less than 20
per cent of the defense R&D budget is allocated to such exploratory
or speculative ventures in weaponry. Likewise, prototypes of promising weapons should be bought far more frequently than is now the
case. General Bernard Schriever, who prematurely retired in the
summer of 1966 from the pivotal leadership of Air Force Systems
Command, believed: "If the U.S. is to maintain its military superiority, it must sometimes gamble large sums on chancy projects. Mc-
Namara's philosophy is that the need for expensive new weapons and
other equipment must first be objectively proved to his satisfaction. 'I
have tried and tried,' Schriever said recently, 'but he won't listen to
me.' "[23]

Because these issues, posed by Schriever and others, are crucial to
the future of U.S. security, they are objects of legitimate inquiry and
debate. The Secretary of Defense, because of his responsibility, should
welcome debate to guard against the possibility that either he may be

[21] Arms control considerations, discussed in Chapter 6, also influence U.S.
decisions.

[22] The impact of the Vietnam war may have reversed this trend. "Harsh re-
appraisals of Defense Dept. research and development programs plus at least
some cancellations and cutbacks as well as major Fiscal 1967 supplemental
budget requests appear inevitable as the Administration searches for additional
funding to finance the war in Vietnam."—*Aviation Week,* September 12, 1966.

[23] *Time,* September 9, 1966, p. 24.

wrong or his view of the situation or the situation itself might change. In a rapidly changing world, security is a continuous problem.

The Crucial Time Element

Any serious lag in countering a hostile military threat based on superior technology cannot be quickly redressed. There are several courses open for obtaining timely strategic advantage through the exploitation of technology. Demand can be placed on the state of the art to develop a product several years before it would normally emerge. When the Minuteman and Polaris programs called for missiles with solid-fuel boosters by 1961, an accelerated effort was made to exploit solid-fuel propulsion techniques. Thus, this kind of booster, which the Soviets were beginning to acquire in 1965, was available in the United States by 1960–61 rather than some years later. The initial requirements for developing the Polaris and Minuteman missiles were so advanced that the feasibility of producing them in eight or nine years—let alone four—appeared dubious. Yet the development period of four years was met for both systems as well as for the nuclear-powered submarine. These achievements were possible because of an early decision to invest adequate resources and because project managers were given the necessary authority to produce results.

Rarely is a break-through the key to military superiority. Incremental improvement involves refining and improving existing designs by such a method as to lead ultimately to the development of almost new weapons; it is typified by the jump from Minuteman I to Minuteman II. Even if the incremental method does not yield entirely new weapons, it does provide an improved weapons system. Another option is to integrate existing technology in new weapons configurations.

Since the U.S.S.R. possesses approximately the same level of scientific resources and technological ability as the United States, the future power positions of the two countries will be critically affected by the comparative speed and managerial skill[24] with which both

24 "There is a thin line of good administrators. It does not go very deep."— Brown, *op. cit.*, p. 33.

apply technology to developing an advanced weapons system. The Soviet technological advance has often proceeded at a faster rate than the West's for two reasons: For the Soviets, reduced lead time for complex weapons-systems development stems from their capacity to make crucial decisions early in the R&D cycle and from a will to stick with their decisions. Since the crucial factor is the target date for making the device operational, the Soviets allocate funds according to strategic priorities; they rarely settle strategic priorities according to available funds.

The United States often decides to study a weapons concept for an excessively long time or to finish a project at a later date because of an unwillingness to assign priority funding to the undertaking. The United States has become increasingly reluctant to launch new programs. "We have exercised a certain degree of control over the beginning of big new programs, with the result that, although we are doing a number of new programs, it is only, say, half or so of what the services would like to do. I think we have picked the right half to carry on."[25]

The U.S. Department of Defense divides the research and development cycle into five significant steps:

1. Research—the effort directed toward the expansion of knowledge of natural phenomena and our environment. . . .
2. Exploratory Developments—the effort directed toward the expansion of technological knowledge and the development of materials, components, devices and sub-systems which *it is hoped* will have some useful application to new military weapons and equipment [italics added]. . . .
3. Advanced Developments—the effort directed toward the development of experimental hardware for technical or operational testing of its suitability for military use, prior to the determination of whether the item should be designed or engineered for actual Service use. . . .
4. Engineering Developments—the effort directed toward the development of a particular system engineered for service use and for operational employment, but which has not yet been approved for production and deployment. It is at this point that large commitments of resources must be made to single projects.
5. Operational Systems Development—the effort directed toward the

[25] *Ibid.*, p. 36.

continued development, test, evaluation and design improvement of projects which have already entered (or have been approved for) the production-deployment stage.[26]

In the United States, these steps, as a rule, are taken sequentially; but years may transpire before step 5 is reached. Even after a weapon does reach step 5, more time will elapse before its production is ordered and the weapon is in the hands of operational units.[27] The Soviets, in contrast, often try to accomplish comparable steps concurrently for the sake of gaining a time advantage. Whereas it is not necessary to match the adversary system for system, it is necessary to speed the development and deployment of critical systems such as the ABM.[28] One possible way of telescoping the R&D production cycle would be to order prototype production of critical weapons when they enter operational systems development, step 5. This would permit initial tooling for subsequent production. Prototype weapons could also be used for preliminary crew training so that the effective operational date for a critical weapons system could be advanced.

Zones of Technological Confrontation

The primary area of technological conflict encompasses those weapons and communications systems, existing and potential, that are or may be deployed for strategic warfare. These are land-, sea-, or air-based offensive and defensive systems that operate through either the atmosphere or space and whose development has critical implications for future U.S. military security.

[26] *Statement of Secretary of Defense Robert S. McNamara Before the House Armed Services Committee on the Fiscal Year 1966–70 Defense Program and 1966 Defense Budget* (mimeo.), February 18, 1965, pp. 129–30.

[27] By strict definition, step 5 may continue for the active life of the system.

[28] "There have been a very few weapons system developments which have been critical in the sense that without them the security of the United States would have been perhaps fatally impaired. These include in the nuclear weapons field the fission bomb and the thermonuclear weapon. Had we been forced to face an opponent which had either of these while we had not, our national survival might very well have been threatened. In the same category of importance were the development of the first radars, the ICBM's and the entire POLARIS system. I believe I would put the nuclear submarine, even in the absence of the POLARIS missile, in this same category. *The critical category also includes an anti-ballistic missile capability.*"—Dr. Harold Brown, speech at the Armed Forces Communications and Electronics Association Convention, June 12, 1962. (Dr. Brown became Secretary of the Air Force in 1965.)

The Delivery System. Advanced versions of familiar weapons systems will comprise a large part of the weapons used by the United States and other nuclear powers in the next decade. The West will be threatened by formidable ballistic and supersonic cruise missiles capable of sea, air, ground, or space launch. The capability to launch these weapons from submarines and preanchored containers places a great burden on the crucial area of antisubmarine warfare. For, if it proves difficult to make significant gains in detecting nuclear submarines with either current or new methods, a greater burden will be placed on antiballistic-missile defense.

Developments in offensive weapons systems inspire counterefforts. The missile, which has become a prime component of strategic offensive forces, has been no exception. The U.S. ABM—the Nike-X—which is presently envisioned for deployment, is a combination of a long-range (Zeus) rocket and a high-acceleration short-range (Sprint) rocket. One is designed to destroy incoming missiles high above the earth; the other, as they reach deep into the atmosphere; together, they are known as the Nike-X antiballistic-missile system. This system's ability to destroy incoming ICBM's is a product of several technological developments—including at least the fast-reacting Sprint missile and the multifunction array radar, with its quick-scanning, detection, and high-discrimination capabilities. Also, the development of special heat-resistant materials for the interceptor missiles and a special computer helped to make the Nike-X system feasible.

The development of the ABM is forcing the offense to work out new tactics of penetration. For example, today's ABM system can effectively discriminate among a large number of incoming objects. If the ICBM is to stay effective, it will have to incorporate sufficient decoys or penetration aids to frustrate discriminators in the ABM defense system. This may be accomplished by improving missile technology in the direction of allowing for more penetration aids without sacrificing payload, range, or accuracy. Attempts are being made to reduce a vehicle's cross section in order to make it "invisible" to the enemy's sensors—whether radar, infrared, or optical. Decoys shot from the nose cone of an incoming missile are also a means of aiding penetration; their purpose is to confuse the defender's radar as to the identity of the vehicle containing the bomb. Electronic warfare is the highly complex conflict between defense radar's effort to identify and "lock in" on incoming targets in the face of the target's effort to confuse, deceive, and "throw off" the defender's radar.

The amount of money allocated since 1962 to advanced ballistic re-entry systems indicates a growing concern that missile defenses are beginning to overtake present means of penetration and that new means must be sought. According to Secretary McNamara:

> Our deterrent strategy depends upon our ability, under all foreseeable conditions, to destroy the attacker as a viable society, and this means that our strategic missiles must be capable of penetrating any kind of defense the Soviets may be able to devise. In this connection, it is interesting to note that we have applied almost $1 billion to our development efforts on penetration aids during the period FY 1962 through 1965.[29]

This large increase over three years in funding U.S. penetration aids tends to refute the views of Drs. Wiesner and York—namely, that problems posed by saturation and discrimination negate the development of an ABM system. The search for new delivery systems to supersede present ones must begin when the possibility of countering an existing system appears feasible.

Another consideration affecting U.S. and U.S.S.R. missile forces is the interaction of a missile's warhead yield and accuracy on nuclear strategy; for the greater the yield, the greater the area of destruction. Reducing circular error probability (CEP) by half is equivalent to an eightfold increase in yield against a single, concentrated target such as an ICBM site. It is normally easier and cheaper to increase the yield (provided the rocket is capable of lifting the larger warhead) than it is to increase the accuracy (that is, decrease the CEP). Since Soviet rocket warheads are much more powerful than U.S. warheads, any improvement in accuracy in Soviet ICBM's will yield an even greater increase in their destructive power than a corresponding increase in the accuracy of U.S. ICBM's. The quantitative missile superiority that the United States possessed in 1966 could lose its strategic value if the Soviet Union obtains a more favorable exchange ratio based on high missile payload and increased accuracy. For the Soviet Union, with its penchant for high-yield warheads, the

[29] *Statement of Secretary of Defense Robert S. McNamara Before the House Armed Services Committee on the Fiscal Year 1966–70 Defense Program and 1966 Defense Budget* (mimeo.), February 18, 1965, p. 132.

payload (warhead megatons on target) is the pay-off as long as accuracy continues to increase; for with large warheads and high accuracy, the need for large numbers of missiles decreases. If the programmed U.S. strategic force is not increased by 1970, the Soviets will have a counterforce capability greater than that of the United States.[30]

Unless Soviet planners are confronted with prospects of a U.S. ABM, the Soviet Union does not have to focus efforts on penetration aids or decoys. If, however, the Soviets begin a penetration-aid R&D program, they would be ready to install such devices as soon as the United States begins to deploy an ABM. Then the battle would ensue between penetration aids and the ABM's increasingly discriminating detection and tracking devices.

The United States miniaturized and reduced the weight of electronic components and warheads for its missiles, but did not stress thrust for its initial ICBM boosters. U.S. rocket thrusts are only one-third to one-quarter as powerful as the Soviet ICBM boosters; payloads of existing U.S. missiles are about one-sixth of the weight of Soviet payloads. Because of these intrinsic characteristics, the U.S. capability to deliver megatonnage on specific targets would greatly depreciate if the Soviets were to deploy an ABM. Decoys and penetration aids must be incorporated into the re-entry vehicle to ensure penetrability—at the expense of the weight of the nuclear warhead. The attendant loss of nuclear yield, regardless of the accuracy, will necessitate more U.S. missiles and a corresponding rise in costs. By their projected deployment of accurate missiles with much higher payloads than those possessed by the United States, the Soviets would be taking advantage of the present characteristics of the U.S. missile.

More and more, strategic superiority is becoming a matter of the optimum offensive-defensive mix. In the absence of a U.S. ABM, the cost of maintaining a credible offensive deterrent will increase. Even if the United States builds more of its smaller payload missiles, the Soviets will need to build proportionately fewer of their larger missiles to achieve an exchange ratio in their favor. The quest for higher accuracy in offensive missiles is a primary part of the technological conflict. Higher accuracy—whether it is due to better guidance, im-

[30] See Chapter 5, "The Soviet Dilemma," for a projection of the Soviet–U.S. missile ratio in 1970.

proved separation procedures, or better target location—means greater confidence in the ability to destroy hardened military targets. At the same time, higher accuracy enables the United States to lessen collateral damage by reducing the required yield of warheads. The Soviets, on the other hand, appear less interested in mitigating collateral damage and have repeatedly emphasized the high yields of their rockets.

There are other areas of technological competition. The world is on the threshold of another revolution in aircraft technology, and new systems utilizing new technology can dramatically enhance existing aircraft capabilities. Research on fuels, metallurgy, heat transfer, aerodynamic configurations, and ingenious new compressors is responsible for a renaissance in aircraft technology and design.[31]

The Weapons. The increased effectiveness of thermonuclear weapons over atomic warheads was a quantum jump equivalent to the advance from chemical to atomic explosives. Even though the weight of nuclear and thermonuclear warheads has been radically reduced without losses in yield or effectiveness, further miniaturization and efficiency is still possible. The development of new weapons such as focused-energy beams and enhanced-radiation weapons appears likely. The laser is an example of a focused-energy device, which conceivably may be used for a variety of reconnaissance and communication purposes; also, the absence of any energy-dissipating atmosphere in space may make lasers an extremely lethal method of attack in space.

On another front, biological and chemical weapons could become extremely significant during the next decade. With the Soviet capability and emphasis on B-C weapons, it will be necessary for the United States to recognize, in both the military and public spheres, the threat these weapons impose. New varieties of agents will allow degrees of lethality and incapacitation that could increase the flexibility of attacking and defending forces at the strategic as well as the tactical level. Certain agents can achieve almost complete incapacitation with little or limited injury to populations, cities, and industrial plants. As has been done in Vietnam, anticrop agents can be used in limited areas as defoliants in counterguerrilla operations. Antimaterial items can be used to attack metals, plastics, fuels, and lubri-

[31] No decision has been made, however, to procure an advanced manned strategic aircraft as a follow-on bomber to the B-52.

cants in the enemy's industrial or military establishments without seriously affecting personnel. It is possible that, in certain specific situations, biological or chemical warfare will become an alternative to nuclear weapons.

Reconnaissance, Command, Control, and Communications. A superior military posture requires excellent warning systems, trans- and postattack reconnaissance, and efficient command and control. More and more attention is being given to reconnaissance and command and control during the actual exchange, or transattack, phase of the conflict, the aim being to have at hand an up-to-the-moment (real-time) picture of all crucial elements in the global strategic situation. An instant transattack assessment and command and control capability could greatly reduce the number of offensive weapons needed in the strategic inventory by permitting efficient retargeting while the exchange is in progress. Search and detection systems will gain increasing importance in future years as new operational delivery systems complicate the identification, tracking, and neutralizing of space-, air-, and sea-borne systems.

Limitations inherent in radar have led to the development of other sensors for the detection of targets—infrared, optical, electronic, radiation emission, and laser. Over-the-horizon radar recently became operational; but presently the reliability, accuracy, rapidity, dissemination, and display of information from the newer sensors leave a great deal to be desired. The inability of present analysis and display equipment to handle numerous targets at high speed puts U.S. defense at a disadvantage, for a wide range of data must quickly be processed, evaluated, and transmitted before any subsequent attack mission can be conducted. Obviously, if the U.S. command and control system is to function, our intelligence structure, which gathers, analyzes, and stores strategic information, needs protection, and sensory technology should be advanced.

New Frontiers

The "technological revolution" has already pushed U.S. security programs across new strategic frontiers—under the sea and in space —and these environments have become crucial to national strategy. Although seas have historically been the theater of military conflict, in recent years they have become a base for projecting strategic power into the heart of many countries. To the attacker, the seas offer concealment and mobility as well as access to most of the earth's land surface. The submarine has relative security from attack yet freedom of action against an enemy's sea power. Nuclear propulsion enabled submarines to remain underwater for long periods of time and gave them an expanded role (although, like the airplane, submarines will always require a base).

The U.S. geopolitical position and its military and political obligations make it paramount for the United States to maintain superior subsurface, air, and amphibious capabilities that can be projected to and over every ocean.

The Soviet Union's appreciation of sea power is readily discernible, for its efforts in oceanography are more than double those of the United States.[32] A large part of the total Soviet oceanographic research work is devoted not only to matters of significance for general naval operations but to submarine operations particularly. The Soviet Union now has the second-largest navy in the world, the largest submarine fleet in the world, an effective fleet air arm, and an excellent mining capability. Also, the Chinese Communist submarine capability cannot be ignored.

The undersea threat compels both sides to try to destroy each other's missile-carrying submarines before the missiles can be fired. If and when hunter-killer systems can counteract the effectiveness of submarines, the search for even more secure systems will begin. Although the U.S. program for antisubmarine warfare (ASW) currently faces certain unsolved problems, ASW's prospects against future nuclear-powered submarines may be even more adverse. Consequently, successful ABM defense against submarine-launched missiles remains the essential complement to ASW.

Over the last several years, the rapid progress made on space systems and vehicles has altered the strategic confrontation. To both the United States and its adversaries, applications of space technology are presenting a new military frontier, which will add novel dimen-

[32] See Bernard M. Kassell, "Soviet Oceanography," *U.S. Naval Institute Proceedings*, July, 1963; and Desmond Wattern, "The Coming Cold War of the Sea Lanes," *U.S. Naval Institute Proceedings*, August, 1962, p. 71.

sions to strategy during the next ten years and may become the primary confrontation in the period beyond.[33] One of the emerging debates of the mid-1960's concerns whether a future decisive advantage could be gained by utilizing space for both manned and unmanned military missions. Could either side realize a significant position or technological advantage in space for the purpose of winning major concessions without provoking all-out war?

A number of unmanned military space systems are already in operation or will be in the near future. These include reconnaissance, early-warning, communication, nuclear-test-detection, and navigation satellites. Satellite-interceptor missiles, designed for launching from the ground, are now operational; but more sophisticated techniques are under development in the United States and, undoubtedly, in the Soviet Union. These systems are the prelude to the manned systems that will be the successors of the MOL and are likely to fulfill military missions in space within a decade. However, the growing reliance on unmanned space systems for early warning, reconnaissance, communications, and navigation tends to obscure the fact that these systems are vulnerable. At present unmanned satellites do not have any on-board maneuvering capability and must "fly" a predictable path. They are thus susceptible to interception, countermeasures, and surveillance. Their relatively short operating life requires constant effort to recover their information quickly or else to keep it from being exposed to public scrutiny (exemplified by the British and U.S. interception of the Soviet's moon pictures).

Reconnaissance and early-warning satellites are already vital to strategic planning and operations and could be even more important to a future strategic system. An effective strategic system requires high delivery accuracy in order to eliminate the opponent's striking forces with a reasonable expenditure of warheads. High accuracy and small yields allow a choice between "force" and "value" targets, which may be geographically close together. Satellites have already been used to lessen geodetic error, and it is expected that future satellites will reduce that error to less than 50 feet. It may also be possible to use satellites to trigger terminal guidance systems that

---

[33] The scope, rate of development, and emphasis of the Soviet space programs were portrayed by Robert A. Kilmarx in "The Soviet Space Program," *Current History*, October, 1963.

could strike within a few hundred feet of targets, permitting the destruction of hard targets with very low-yield warheads.

President Johnson's decision on August 25, 1965, to proceed with the development of the MOL signified an administration commitment to explore man's military usefulness in space. No longer would NASA be the sole supporter for manned military space systems. The launching of this system, planned for late 1968 or early 1969, will be the first U.S. attempt to explore near-orbital space with manned systems for national-security purposes.[34] MOL has certain potential advantages over unmanned space systems. A manned system should allow for immediate comprehension of intelligence data—for example, the instantaneous recognition of a missile launch. Rapid transmission of such information to a command center should be of inestimable value in strategic warfare. Gemini missions have established the feasibility of rendezvous, endurance, and extravehicular activity; MOL will provide additional opportunity to test man's endurance in space and the contribution that man can make to surveillance, inspection, interception, identification, and reconnaissace of other space and ground systems. Even though weapons will not be aboard, tests can be made of the feasibility of armoring or defending both manned and unmanned systems. Other experiments might include maneuvering, flying in formation, visual earth observation, the study of infrared phenomena, and radio- and radar-signal propagation. Further tests will determine the feasibility of using space platforms for command and control and arms control.

The reliability of present satellites is impeded by their susceptibility to power shortages and failures as well as to a host of other space-environment phenomena. The importance of the MOL experiment becomes evident in light of what can happen to a system in space. Experiments have been attempted to study man's ability to assemble, maintain, and repair structures and equipment in space.

Whether or not bombs are placed in orbit,[35] the threat of the new antisatellites will undoubtedly stimulate improvements in the satellite

[34] There is a good chance that these dates will have to be delayed because of the funding required for the Vietnam conflict.

[35] The Soviets claimed they had developed an orbital-bomb–missile combination and publicly displayed this weapon in the 1965 parade commemorating the Bolshevik Revolution. See Michael Getter, "Soviet Claim Could Spur Space Track," *Missiles and Rockets,* November 15, 1965, p. 14.

systems themselves. Because the United States has an imperative need for intelligence, this country is particularly concerned with threats to reconnaissance satellites. Improvements that would make the difference between a vulnerable "passive" satellite and an effective spacecraft include maneuver, defense, and higher-altitude capabilities, larger cameras or other equipment, and particularly the addition of crews. Studies have been initiated on many such systems, and successive MOL flights should supply sufficient test information for the selection of operational vehicle designs.

Manned operations in space will open up new vistas, and according to Dr. Edward C. Welsh, executive secretary of the National Aeronautics and Space Council:

> So rapid is the pace of change that we must look ahead just to keep abreast of the current that leads us. Given the atom's almost limitless energy and the computer's almost limitless ability to remember and to organize, the future beckons to us as an era of almost limitless attainment. Within the next several decades one can confidently predict such developments as space ships ferrying tourists as well as scientists and explorers to space stations and to nearby planets; and aerospace planes spanning oceans and continents in tens of minutes.[36]

This statement suggests that manned space vehicles will be able to take off from land bases, operate in the atmosphere and beyond, and return to earth without the complicated recovery procedure now necessary. When this development occurs, military operations in space will assume an identity of their own. Still tied to complicated launching and recovery techniques and susceptible to countermeasures launched from earth, present space systems are generally incapable of evasive action or self-protection. Hence, space, like the land, sea, and atmosphere, has become a complementary theater of military operations. But once this military role of space is visualized as distinct and uniquely useful, space forces and space warfare may come into being.

The United States has tended to judge Soviet efforts in space largely in terms of psychological gain or of cost comparisons with ICBM's for firepower delivery; whereas, it may be that the Soviets envisage military uses for space vehicles. Because they have long been able to lift big payloads into space and consequently did not have to devote efforts (as did the United States) to superminiaturization of component equipment, the Soviets were able to search sooner for pos-

[36] Address to the Churchman's Club, Baltimore, Md., May 5, 1966.

sible military applications of space. (As U.S. rocket thrusts catch up, however, the U.S. lead in miniaturization should be of advantage.)

It would be imprudent to attribute Soviet successes entirely to "accident." The orderly and systematic building-block approach taken by the United States is matched by the Soviets, and the near-space orientation of many of the efforts of the Soviets indicates their sensitivity to the military implications of space operations.

The Importance of Innovation

If the Soviets believed that mutual deterrence would not fail, they would hardly waste time and money to seek a first-strike counterforce capability. If they believe that the effort will pay off and if we allow them to achieve a sufficient margin of advantage to justify this belief, they may try their luck. The United States cannot maintain deterrence by merely wishing for it but must continually pioneer weapons innovations that keep the opposition off-balance. If the United States makes no technological innovations except in response to Soviet efforts, the Soviets may defeat or neutralize U.S. capabilities.

The underlying issue is the "will" to innovate. Under the present system, the armed services are apparently held responsible for proposing innovations, and the Department of Defense subsequently judges whether service recommendations are sufficiently justified to be funded. Justification is generally evaluated against an adversary's innovation or threat, for the United States innovates, for the most part, in a defensive context. If we continue down this road, we may one day lose our technological initiative and superiority.

The fundamental issue is whether or not it is desirable to maintain U.S. technological leadership. The technological realms that modern science will open by the year 2000 promise to match those that have reshaped so much of human life since the dawn of this century. However, new technologies are less likely to be the product of individual or spontaneous innovation. Instead, they will result from the conscious decisions of governments to allocate resources to competent research teams in order to attain a given technological objective. Because exploration of new technological frontiers will increasingly require a scale of resources that only governments can provide, technological leadership will depend upon political decisions influenced by scientific and engineering judgment. Thus, the political insights that inform our strategic choices will, in the long run, channel the direction of technological development on which future strategy will depend.

To maintain strategic superiority in the 1970's requires a willingness to invest adequately in the scientific future, despite the many other competing demands. The country can perhaps afford to pay for the war in Vietnam, the war against poverty, and other segments of the Great Society program, as well as the Apollo project to reach the moon. Yet, to do all these things simultaneously and to sustain our scientific and technological dynamism, we must meet our present and future problems according to a set of realistic priorities.

Unfortunately, the absence of a positive policy for technological innovation impedes U.S. efforts to make the most of science and technology for assured U.S. strategic superiority in the decade ahead. One reason for the absence of such a policy is a prevalent belief that the presumed nuclear stalemate is regarded as a constant factor in the international framework rather than as a variable that is subject to change. As one writer stated:

> Distinctions between strategic superiority, strategic parity, and strategic inferiority . . . are now generally recognized to have little meaning, which is why the "missile race" has petered out. The meaningful factor in the situation is the ability to inflict unacceptable nuclear damage on the opponent, something which might be done from a level of gross "nuclear inferiority."[37]

This conclusion assumes that the Soviets have accepted "strategic inferiority" and have abandoned the offensive and defensive missile race. Evidence to the contrary is presented in Chapter 5, "The Soviet Dilemma."

Admittedly, no amount of hardware will give us security if we do not harness technology to farsighted political, economic, and military programs geared to a purposive view of the world and our place in it. We can stagnate at a self-induced technological plateau, or we can safeguard our future security with a vigorous program of scientific exploration and technological innovation. The path we choose will depend not on what we are capable of doing but on what U.S. leaders decide to do.

[37] Carrol Quigley, "Some Inadequate Nuclear War Assumptions," a review of *Strategic Power and Soviet Foreign Policy* by Arnold L. Horelick and Myron Rush (University of Chicago Press), *Washington Star*, September 18, 1966, p. 19.

4

The Balance Sheet:
Strategic Assets and Liabilities*

For the next decade, the relative strengths of the United States and the Soviet Union will be the determining factor in the equation of international politics. The two superpowers will seek to maintain, gain, or regain the preponderance of power. Their power positions, in turn, will be fortified by their global membership in military alliances or in less formal bilateral and multilateral arrangements. The other nations of the world will, by their actions, weight the balance with the strengths or liabilities they each choose to add. Among U.S. allies, for instance, it is possible that France, at least, will pursue an independent course. But unless other nations approach the two powers in absolute strength, only the United States and the U.S.S.R. will be capable of restraining each other from pursuing a given objective.

The existence of thermonuclear weapons has inspired the concept that neither superpower can exploit its predominant strength. Yet, on the other hand, if either the United States or the Soviet Union were removed from the international scene, the remaining superpower could, if it chose to do so, dominate the world.

The United States is the leading world power and has every possibility of keeping its status for the indefinite future. But in designing its strategy for the next decade, the United States will have to assess the policies and security programs of both the Soviet Union and Communist China, even though the Soviet Union will possess vastly greater capabilities for strategic warfare than will Communist China.

* This chapter is based largely on an article entitled "Strategic Asymmetries," by William R. Kintner and Stefan T. Possony, which appeared in *Orbis* (Spring, 1965).

National power is a composite of many factors, including tangibles such as geography, population, and raw materials and intangibles such as leadership, national character, and ideology. In a contest between two power centers, some of these factors may redound to the benefit of both sides; others might carry advantage for one side alone because the opposing side either does not possess them at all or is inhibited from effectively exploiting them. Elements of power that are available to one side in greater quantity or quality will also affect the power symmetry; one advantage may cancel out another, whereas other inequalities may be very difficult or costly to offset. Since imbalances affect the design of strategy that a major power should or could logically pursue, each power's strategy may differ markedly.

The United States benefits from a situation in which the efforts required of the Soviet Union for engaging in a direct military confrontation far exceed its own. The United States retains its leadership across the broad spectrum of science and technology, although in several important technological areas—defensive weapons systems and space—U.S. supremacy is in doubt. In addition, a vast and diversified economic base enables the United States to exploit new technologies with greater freedom than can the Soviet Union.

Intelligence, conflict doctrine, and psychological warfare, on the other hand, favor the Soviet Union and Communist China. The "open societies" of the West offer opportunities for gathering information that are not available in the closed Communist world. Moreover, the techniques of conflict management developed by the Communists give Moscow and Peking an advantage over Western statesmen, with their predilection for seeking lasting solutions to such complex problems as disarmament. The Communists have shown themselves adept at the manipulation of such desires. In fact, the capabilities of the Communists to play upon yearnings in the West for a surcease of conflict provides Moscow and Peking with a means of influencing the evolution of U.S. strategy.

This suggests a paradox. The over-all power advantage of the United States should foreclose a Soviet option of completing the world revolution by nuclear war, but we have been less successful in preventing the Soviets from adversely influencing U.S. policy during the long haul of the Cold War. Consequently, we have not yet persuaded the men in the Kremlin that their hope of global victory through the harnessing of forces of history and the political exploitation of advanced technology is an irrational dream.

The Setting

The globe is the theater in which the struggle is waged, and the strategies that are appropriate to either side are shaped by their geographic setting.

The United States has lost the military invulnerability that it once possessed by virtue of its remoteness from Europe and Asia. Direct and free access to the Atlantic and Pacific oceans and to three-quarters of the earth's surface remains an advantage to American sea power; but the advent of Soviet ICBM's and, potentially, Chinese missile-carrying submarines have increased U.S. vulnerability to attack. To support overseas allies, the United States must, even with its large airlift capability, make use of shipping, which is vulnerable to submarine attack.

The Soviet Union is well situated for pursuing a policy aimed at ultimate world domination. Astride the world's largest land mass, it enjoys proximity not only to Western Europe but also to the Middle East and Asia. Although its virtually landlocked location may hinder its submarine capability, its position provides a measure of security to interior areas—an advantage unshared by the United States or Western Europe, where most major cities are located on or near the coasts. Population is far more concentrated in urban centers in the United States than is the case in the Soviet Union; and that distribution, within a total land area one-third as large as the Soviet Union, would favor the Soviets in a nuclear exchange. The Soviet Union's vast land area must therefore be reckoned as an advantage.

Command of the air and of the seas gives the United States access to Africa, Latin America, Europe, and Asia. Nevertheless, the United States must maintain its forward positions in Europe and Asia, and in most instances, it is more costly to defend these positions than it is for the Soviet Union and Communist China to threaten them. Inadequate surface transportation, however, hinders the Soviets and the Chinese Communists from exploiting this potential advantage. For the geography of the United States dictates a strategy emphasizing air and maritime capabilities; whereas, the Soviet Union and Communist China must develop continental land power. Each side has adapted itself to the nuclear missile age in accord with these fundamental considerations.

For reasons of geography and ideology, genuine allies are less important to the Soviet Union than they are to the United States. The Soviets have developed a forced alliance system rather than cooperative relationships with those nations now within the Communist orbit. Although this type of alliance is to some extent vulnerable to disaffection, the countries in Eastern Europe serve as a buffer to hostile action against the Soviet heartland.

Economic Profiles

Communist Party leaders are responsible for all Soviet economic decisions, and historically their decisions have been based first and foremost on increasing the power of the Soviet state. In 1957, the Polish economist Oskar Lange, a prominent partisan of the political order of the U.S.S.R., publicly expressed his own carefully weighed judgment of the Soviet economic system: "I think that, essentially, it can be described as a *sui generis* war economy."[1] The essential characteristics of a war economy are a high degree of centralization in all economic activities, a centralized disposal of resources, and the replacement of economic incentives with political incentives.

The Soviet economic system is characterized by total governmental ownership of the means of production, and consequently the Soviet citizen is deprived of any influence over major economic decisions. The Communist Party determines how economic resources will be distributed and issues directives to see that its decisions are carried out. Because key Party leaders occupy key administrative positions, the control of allocations is easily reinforced.

In the national planning for the Soviet Union, the Soviet system is treated as a total economic unit that is operated for the maximizing of state power rather than for the satisfying of individual needs—a crucial distinction that should be kept in mind in comparing U.S. and Soviet strategic asymmetries.

The disparity between the economic systems of the United States and the Soviet Union is such that the ordinary terms of economic

[1] *Dimensions of Soviet Economic Power,* studies prepared for the Joint Economic Committee, Congress of the United States, 87th Cong., 2nd Sess., 1962, p. x.

reference used in the West do not accurately apply to the U.S.S.R. Even such measures as the official ruble-dollar exchange rate do not allow precise comparisons. If, according to this exchange rate, Soviet production is expressed in U.S. dollars, the Soviet economy appears larger than it actually is, for the real-value exchange rate varies from item to item.[2] The information that is available on the Soviet economy is fragmentary, although in recent years the Soviet Government has released more accurate statistical data. These data have deflated Western notions of over-all Soviet economic achievements but have raised respect for Soviet technological and military performance.

As Bernstein computed in his accounts for 1955, the U.S.S.R. was relatively efficient in the production of defense goods and services and of capital goods, while inefficient in consumer goods output. Thus, the purchasing power of the ruble in terms of dollars averaged 8.6 to the dollar, but for consumer goods and services it was worth only about 11 to the dollar, while its value was 5 for investment goods and services, and 4.5 for defense goods and services. When these varying ruble-dollar conversion ratios are applied to Soviet end-use magnitudes and their dollar values compared with U.S. equivalents, the results show that while Soviet GNP was well under half that of the United States, defense expenditures were on a parity with the United States, investment outlays were somewhat larger, and consumption less than a third as great. The seeming paradox of the U.S.S.R. economy, half as large as the U.S. economy with about the same proportion of its resources devoted to defense spending—the dollar equivalent of the U.S. defense effort—is explained by the disparate internal purchasing power of the ruble relative to the dollar.[3]

The Soviet economy is now the second largest in the world. Its size and level of development enable the Soviets to procure weapons systems in the quantity necessary for modern warfare. Although plagued by a shortage of skilled labor and an inadequate internal transportation network, the Soviet economy is responsive to military needs. Basically, the Soviet Union has a war-oriented economy comparable to the U.S. economy of World War II. Such an economy may contain the seeds of long-term economic weakness—namely, the disproportionate allocation of resources to the military effort and an under-

[2] See Stanley H. Cohn, "The Gross National Product in the Soviet Union: Comparative Growth Rates," *Dimensions of Soviet Economic Power*, pp. 67–89.
[3] *Ibid.*, p. 76.

investment in other key sectors. The "delay" in investment in certain sectors of the Soviet economy is most easily illustrated by such blunders as, in agriculture, the neglect of the fertilizer industry and the losing gamble on the cultivation of virgin land. The December, 1966, Soviet budget called for an 8.2 per cent increase in defense expenditures, made possible by further delay in essential investment in agriculture.

The Soviet Union has made considerable propaganda mileage by claiming that the percentage of the state budget allocated for military expenditures is relatively small compared to that of the United States. But the Soviet budget incorporates everything from investments in industry to expenditures for cultural activities and includes the budgets of union republics and even smaller local units.

Concerning the Soviet military budget, Francis Hoeber has written:

> At times, real expenditure increases may be hidden in the covert budget, as was done extensively in the 1958–61 period in order not to disturb the sleeping giant. At other times, increases may be publicly exaggerated, by transferring previously hidden expenditures to open account. This appears to have explained part of the large increase in armed forces expenditures announced in 1961. In the present instance, a 5 per cent increase for 1966 does not appear to be major and is certainly not out of line with recent trends. The real increase may be a little lower than 5 per cent. The allocation to science is up 9 per cent and may conceal some increased military RDT&E expenditures. Over-all investment is up more than military expenditure, which is certainly in line with announced policy, but may always conceal military increases.[4]

The total budget represents more than half of the national income of the Soviet Union. The military budget represents only those funds allotted for direct military purposes. Other expenditures, such as those for the defense industry, research and development, and strategic defense-reserve materials, are hidden in other sections of the state budget. Furthermore, some defense expenditures are reflected not in the state budget at all but in other sources.

Analysis of the *entire* Soviet military budget for 1964 revealed that

---

[4] Letter dated December 14, 1965, to the author. (Francis Hoeber is staff economist at the Stanford Research Institute.)

provisions for direct military expenditures (R&D, defense industry, and state defense reserves), which were distributed in the budget under nonmilitary headings, totaled 14.1 billion rubles. Expenditures *not included* in the state budget at all, such as funds for espionage, Communist parties in other countries, and the defense industry, were estimated to total 4.5 billion rubles. The sum total of expenditures for national defense amounted to 31.9 billion rubles—more than two and one-half times the 13.3 billion publicized for direct military expenditures. In terms of percentage of national income, the *total* military expenditures (31.9 billion rubles) amounted to 17.8 per cent of Soviet national income (estimated at 179.5 billion rubles in 1964).[5] In 1964, the U.S. budget allocated $54.2 billion for national defense, or 8.7 per cent of the GNP ($623 billion). Yet within these respective defense budgets, the Soviet Union over the past five years has allocated to strategic offensive and defensive weapons systems approximately twice as much as has the United States.

Although it has been widely assumed in the Free World that the system of central economic management constitutes a Soviet strength, the assumption that the U.S.S.R. will soon out produce the West is based on little supporting evidence. Lenin anticipated that a system of centralized economic planning, which was introduced by Stalin, would be a "bureaucratic utopia." The Soviet system does have some advantages in the heavy and defense industries and perhaps in those sectors of the economy where output is dependent upon a small number of large plants. But productivity in the Soviet Union lags far behind that of the United States and other industrial nations.

Although Soviet economic planning has improved markedly since the fall of Khrushchev, Soviet planners cannot push to increase productivity by means of industrialization and modernization on all fronts simultaneously, so their efforts are concentrated in the areas of relatively high productivity—electronics and machinery industries. They also plan to computerize operations in heavy industry. To increase productivity while sustaining a modern military machine, the Soviet Union must maintain a high rate of investment. Since the foreign investment that has often triggered and sustained economic

[5] These figures are taken from Timothy Sosnovy, "The Soviet Military Budget," *Foreign Affairs*, April, 1964, pp. 487–94.

growth elsewhere in the world is not available to the Soviet Union,[6] its investment must come from internal savings. Because the Soviets were supporting the Korean "incident" in the early 1950's, the rate of investment was restrained. The Seven Year Plan (1958–65) provided for large increases in investment not only in absolute terms but also in proportion to GNP. However, from 1959 to 1963, a second round of increases in military expenditures stepped up R&D, procurement of sophisticated weapons, and space activities, and a considerable amount of capital goods was diverted to military use. Soviet data suggest that by 1960, military procurement was consuming more than 50 per cent of the Soviet machinery output. The rate of growth of Soviet GNP decreased, though perhaps not as sharply as was announced by the CIA in January, 1964.[7] When machinery was diverted to the military, the low-priority areas, notably agricultural and consumer goods, suffered. The growth of state housing construction slowed appreciably after 1959, perhaps as a direct result of the diversion of massive amounts of construction materials to missile sites, supporting roads, and other military constructions. Thus, recent history amply confirms the contention that the Soviet Union can maintain a guns-or-butter economy but not, in marked contrast with the United States, a guns-*and*-butter economy.

In 1962 and 1963, despite continued high levels of activity in ICBM and space technology, the Soviet planners were taking steps to restore the required trend of nonmilitary investment, especially for machinery. A renewed upswing in military spending would have postponed major programs in neglected sectors of Soviet industry (as it had done during the Korean War and again after 1953) and would have led to a still further decline in the rate of Soviet economic growth.

Whatever the respective U.S. and Soviet growth rates may be, there is no chance for the Soviet Union to catch up with and overtake

---

[6] This situation has been modified insofar as the Soviet Union has had some success in obtaining long-term credits from countries outside the Communist bloc. For example, Britain has given the Soviets $84 million over a fifteen-year period and Japan has made $10 million available for an eight-year span. There is speculation that France will also lessen its credit requirements. Additional trade benefits will be gained if Germany enters into trade negotiations with the Soviet Union.

[7] Khrushchev had hinted at such a decline almost one year earlier.

total American productive capacity in the near future. In 1962, the gross national product of the Soviet Union was half that of the United States. The economic strength of all NATO countries, including the United States and Canada—measured as the sum of the several gross national products—is more than twice as large as the total economic strength of the Communist world. The economic capacity of the European NATO countries is almost three times larger than that of the Eastern European Communist states, and since 1962 the relative economic superiority of NATO vis-à-vis the satellites has improved slightly. A more accurate indication of the flexibility of a nation in wartime is provided by the measurement of per capita income. In this context, Western superiority is even more pronounced: U.S. per capita income is almost three times larger than per capita income in the Soviet Union.[8]

The over-all economic strength of the United States far surpasses that of the U.S.S.R. and constitutes this country's most significant element of power. Such factors as dispersed industry, available (mechanical) repair and maintenance facilities in every town and village, a fully developed infrastructure, enormous resources of energy, and a population that is technically resourceful—factors that might play a decisive role in the latter phases of a nuclear war—have not been duplicated anywhere outside the United States.

The actual potential economies of the United States and the Soviet Union differ considerably, but they share one disposition in common: They do not place a major constraint on the military efforts of their respective countries. The Soviets have been able to increase their overt military expenditures whenever they thought it necessary or advantageous. In 1961, for example, the defense budget was increased by 3.1 billion rubles; in 1962, there was a further rise of 4.1 billion rubles; in 1965, after a modest reduction, the Soviet military budget was boosted another 5 per cent. It was increased again by more than 8 per cent in 1966.

[8] These figures are based on the conversion of Communist currencies according to official exchange rates. There is little question that the respective GNP's of the Soviet Union, China, and, to a somewhat lesser extent, all Eastern European satellites are overstated. The purchasing power of the Soviet currency varies among industrial sectors. It is highest in the strategically crucial heavy and defense industries and lowest in mining, agriculture, and consumer goods. If we assume that a dollar is worth a ruble and exclude the agricultural sectors from our computation, then U.S. GNP is 2.9 times larger than the Soviet GNP.

The U.S. capability to support a high-level defense budget was clearly stated by Secretary of Defense McNamara after a meeting with President Johnson in Texas, December, 1964:

> I want to emphasize, we don't build the defense program against a predetermined budget limit and I don't make any effort to add up the proposals of the Services. We have a Gross National Product of something on the order of very close to $650 billions of dollars. Now we can afford $45 billion, $50 billion, $60 billion, $70 billion—whatever we need for defense. So Mr. Vance and I approach our task of preparing a military program, or preparing a defense budget, purely from the point of view of our security and the forces required to maintain that security. And it's for that reason that I haven't added the initial requests of the Chiefs. We didn't consider them against a restricted financial budget; we didn't consider them against a predetermined financial feeling. We considered each element of their requests against the military benefit that would accrue from granting that request and that in relation to the requirement that we have military forces sufficient to service a solid foundation for our foreign policy. . . . That's the only basis and the only standards against which we compare specific proposals.[9]

A Nuclear Count

The test explosion of an atomic bomb by the United States in July, 1945, and the destruction of Hiroshima in August, 1945, jolted us into the age of nuclear weapons. For a few years only the United States held these weapons; but in the autumn of 1949, the Soviet Union exploded an atomic device and ended the monopoly. Since 1949, three other countries have gained membership in the nuclear club: Great Britain in 1953, France in 1960, and Communist China in 1964. More than a dozen countries are now capable of building nuclear weapons, including Canada, Israel, Sweden, Switzerland, West Germany, Japan, Argentina, and India. In 1965, India displayed interest in developing nuclear capabilities, and several other nonnuclear countries appeared reluctant to renounce the option of "going nuclear" at some future date. The urge to join the nuclear club may diminish if the benefits of membership appear more questionable; yet, over the next decade, other nations can be expected to attempt to build nuclear weapons of their own.

In 1966, the British arsenal consisted of approximately 180 me-

[9] *Journal of the Armed Forces*, January 9, 1965, p. 25.

dium-range planes and some short-range air-to-surface missiles. These weapons, armed with nuclear warheads, provided a minimum strategic deterrent for Britain even though the British force was partially integrated into NATO. In addition, Britain possessed one nuclear submarine, and others are to be completed. The presence of the British deterrent, so long as it does not become obsolete, enhances the nuclear capability of the Atlantic Alliance.

The French nuclear power and related delivery systems are being developed far more vigorously than Britain's. Unless blocked by outside political pressures, France will test a hydrogen bomb in due course. The rapid development of the French nuclear deterrent is consistent with President de Gaulle's intention to enlarge French influence in European and world affairs and, correspondingly, with his effort to reduce U.S. influence in Europe. The creation of a *force de dissuasion* is an inherent part of this design and signals France's increasing independence from NATO and U.S. policy. In comparison with the 1966 British deterrent, the French force was small; but it represented the initial French bid for enhanced nuclear influence and, in some respects, may have been more technologically advanced than the British nuclear force.

By 1966, Communist China had exploded five nuclear devices and weapons, presenting the United States with new psychological and political dangers in Asia as well as with a potentially serious future nuclear threat. China's nuclear program needs at least a decade to mature,[10] and until Communist China acquires a sizable atomic stock pile and advanced delivery capabilities, Peking's threat will be primarily psychological. But even a few atomic bombs, together with delivery systems including aircraft, will enable Peking to pursue a "blackmail" strategy against her Asian neighbors. Eventually Communist China's nuclear arsenal will confront both U.S. and Soviet policy with serious problems.

Intelligence: Area of Uncertainty

In the past, the Communists have enjoyed a notable intelligence advantage over the Free World. They have drawn on world-wide clusters of parties, subsidiary organizations, front groups, and clandes-

[10] See Lewis A. Frank, "Nuclear Weapons Development in China," *Bulletin of the Atomic Scientists,* January, 1966, pp. 12–15.

tine intelligence networks that, in sheer numbers and diffusion, have been more extensive than anything the world has ever known. The intelligence services of those Communist states associated with Moscow work closely together, whereas intelligence cooperation within the Free World leaves much to be desired.

Although the Soviet Union undoubtedly is able to collect enormous masses of data and documents about the plans and activities of the Free World governments, it is conceivable that much of this information is not properly interpreted. There is evidence, however, that Communist understanding of Western—and, more particularly, American—psychology, politics, and strategies has improved in recent years.

The Free World not only has suffered from a dearth of various types of intelligence, but has customarily had difficulty in protecting itself against deliberate Communist techniques of deception and misinformation, which are employed to obscure Communist activities and intentions. A frequent Western bias toward overrating Soviet performance in the area of economics has been matched by a persistent bias toward underrating the sophistication of Soviet military technology and strategy. The United States has generally lagged behind the Soviet Union in intelligence-gathering.

Since the advent of technical data collection, such as space-satellite systems, there has been a growing belief in this country that this asymmetry no longer favors the Soviet Union. U.S. officials are confident that they know Soviet weapons deployments. President Johnson has stated that satellite reconnaissance alone has justified spending ten times what the nation has already spent on space. Specifically, he asserted, "because of this reconnaissance, 'I know how many missiles the enemy has' "[11] Beyond doubt, many gaps in Western knowledge have been filled by reconnaissance satellites, and a more accurate assessment of Soviet capabilities is possible.

Photography, the primary tool of satellite reconnaissance, has enabled a major break-through in our knowledge of previously inaccessible areas of the world. It can record a rich amount of surface detail and may reveal many identifying characteristics of underground installations, particularly during their construction. An underground missile site, for example, could probably be identified, but its refire

[11] *The New York Times,* March 17, 1967, p. 13.

capability might not be discernible. Although certain types of film can be used to reveal camouflage attempts, camouflage may conceal from normal overhead photography objects that cannot be placed underground. For example, operational equipment or an identifiable type of installation may be concealed from view by dummy equipment or buildings that have been quickly and inexpensively constructed. Photography, however sophisticated, can do little to reveal the nature of work going on in Communist scientific laboratories or R&D facilities—an area in which we suffer a genuine intelligence gap.

Obviously, reconnaissance satellites cannot discern political and sociological factors or strategic intentions. A great deal of uncertainty remains. There are also possibilities of error. Can full and complete reliance be placed on intelligence data derived mainly from mechanical means of inspection? Faulty assessment, based on the assumption that the visual data are unquestionably correct, could court disaster. The structure of U.S. forces, future weapon systems, proposals for disarmament—all are influenced by our confidence in U.S. intelligence estimates of Soviet capabilities.

In addition to cameras, a satellite may also carry other sensors, such as infrared and electronic devices; but, potentially, a given sensor can be countered by another device. A reconnaissance aircraft, for example, carries countermeasures against enemy radar systems that seek it out; on the ground, discriminating radar devices work against or detect these countermeasures. During World War II, measures and countermeasures were constantly at odds, and the struggle continues. It would be highly unusual for the Soviets not to attempt to jam, counter, and deceive satellite sensors by means of ground devices more sophisticated than units that can possibly be carried in the satellite itself. And it is unrealistic to believe that the Soviets have not sought or will not seek to shield from U.S. reconnaissance satellites their true capability in technology, weaponry, production, and deployment of weapons.

Few Americans can fully appreciate the scope of Soviet security measures. Historically, Russia has used security as an important adjunct to military strategy, and stringent security laws remain in effect today. The Soviets have consistently refused to allow on-site inspection in arms control agreements, but on-site inspection is necessary to make certain that an installation is actually what it appears to be in photographs or from information provided by other sensors. Communist diplomatic personnel, including military attachés from Soviet satellite countries, can travel practically at will throughout the United States and visit almost any area that is open to a U.S. citizen. In the Soviet Union, less than 1 per cent of its total land area can be visited by foreigners.[12]

The Soviet Union has a long history of deception and secrecy:

> Deception is practiced by communist organizations of all types, including the Russian state, cryptocommunist organizations, and transmission belts, as well as by secret communists infiltrated into the armed forces, government, communications channels, educational agencies, and so forth. The main purposes of deception include: hiding of the true strength of communism; distorting the true strength of the anticommunist camp; covering vulnerabilities in both camps; concealing infiltration; hiding communist intentions; preventing proper evaluation of the politico-military situation; and, in general, forestalling and paralyzing effective action.[13]

The Soviets' secrecy and deception have caused the West to misjudge Soviet development rate, military moves, capability, and intentions: The Soviets exploded their atomic and hydrogen bombs ahead of U.S. estimates. Although the West knew about the MIG-15, having deliberately been shown by the Soviets in an air show over Moscow, the numbers of aircraft they deployed to Korea came as a surprise. The Soviets were far along in their ballistic-missile effort before their progress was realized by other nations. The first sputnik burst on the world like a bombshell, and the first Soviet manned space flight again caught the United States off guard. Major and significant Soviet technological advances have been allowed to reach a mature stage of development before being revealed to the Free World. Prior to the Cuban missile crisis of October, 1962, the Soviets had managed to transfer thousands of troops and considerable numbers of ground-

[12] In "Big Brother Is Still Watching," Edward Crankshaw states: "The tourist's image is the image of the display put on for his special benefit in certain selected places: half a dozen great cities, half a dozen collective farms, half a dozen villages, and one or two resorts. And if it is objected, as it so often is, that it is impossible to turn a whole city—Moscow, Leningrad, Tashkent, Alma-Ata, Tiflis—into a shop window, the answer is that you don't know the Russians. Because this is precisely what the Soviet Government can do and does."—*The New York Times Magazine*, December 29, 1963, p. 8.

[13] Stefan T. Possony, *A Century of Conflict* (Chicago: Henry Regnery Co., 1953), p. 386.

to-ground missiles from the Soviet Union to Cuba—some ninety miles from the United States mainland—without being detected. Missiles with nuclear warheads were already installed in Cuba and ready to be fired when, belatedly, the U.S. ordered manned reconnaissance flights using conventional photographic equipment.

It can be assumed that the Soviet Union has the same satellite-reconnaissance capability as the United States. Further, Soviet surveillance reports can often be checked and verified through ground observations by Communist diplomatic personnel or the many Communist sympathizers operating in an "open society." Relevant information on the U.S. armed forces and, even more important, on U.S. scientific and technological efforts (including funding, direction, and successes) can also be gleaned from American publications, which are available to anyone.

The outside world does not know today, and is not likely to know tomorrow, the actual capabilities of the Soviet Union. Uncertainty will continue to plague the assessment of Soviet intentions and capabilities. We can, however, make the following summary comparison of selected U.S. and U.S.S.R. geographic, demographic, economic, and cultural characteristics.

Characteristic	*U.S.*	*U.S.S.R.*
Area (in millions of square miles)	3.55	8.65
Population, 1965 (in millions)	192	229
Number of cities exceeding 500,000 population	45	49
Total population living in cities exceeding 500,000 (in millions)	77	42.5
GNP (1963 dollar value)*	584	265
GNP per capita (1963 dollar value)	3,084	1,178
Energy output–production (in millions of kwh)	1,011,215	412,400
Number of institutions of higher learning	2,037	742†

* The U.S. GNP for 1966 is estimated to exceed $700 billion; that of the U.S.S.R., $300 billion.

† This figure does not include 3,626 technical colleges.

SOURCES: *The Statesman's Year-Book 1965–1966* (New York: St. Martin's Press, 1965): area, population, and energy-output–production figures; *Current Economic Indications for the U.S.S.R.*, Joint Economic Committee, Congress of the United States, 89th Cong., 1st Sess., 1965: GNP and institutions-of-higher-learning figures.

Psychological Inroads

The American view of conflict in general and the Cold War in particular makes the United States fertile soil for psychological warfare. Americans tend to regard conflict merely as an interlude in the normal course of foreign affairs. Because they find the notion that international strife is a continuing phenomenon repugnant, many Americans succumb to concepts and programs that prescribe painless cures for the ills of international life. An ambiguous conflict is particularly irritating to Americans—as the 1965 "teach-in" campaign against U.S. policy toward Vietnam demonstrated. When possible, the Communists attempt to exploit such attitudes both in the United States and abroad.

At the same time, Western communication and the record of life under free governments have had considerable impact on the popular psyche in the Soviet Union. Soviet vulnerability to psychological penetration is far greater than the Western effort to exploit it. In fact, the exposure of many Soviet citizens to Free World ideas and achievements troubles Soviet leaders because it gives rise to pressures for reform that may weaken the Communists' control system.

But Soviet propaganda messages find greater receptivity in the Free World than U.S. messages find within Communist spheres. Propaganda themes suggested by Moscow are often taken up by the Western press; Western leaders sometimes pick up topics suggested by Moscow and discuss them within the framework of the original propaganda theme. The widespread use of the term "peaceful coexistence" is an apt illustration: Many nations in the Free World have adopted peaceful coexistence as a principal political objective. However, the Leninist meaning of this term signifies "mobilizing the masses" and "restricting the war-making capacity of the imperialists" to gain time for completing the preparations for world revolution.[14] A peaceful strategy is explicitly defined in Soviet documents as a strategy suitable for a specific phase of the conflict. Communists ad-

---

[14] According to Lenin, the "duty of communists is to try to avoid war, to wait until the conflicts between the imperialists weaken them still more, and bring the revolution in other countries still nearer."—*Selected Works* (New York: International Publishers, 1934), VII, 353.

mit that peace and peaceful coexistence are not synonymous; and yet, in presenting this term to both Communist and non-Communist audiences, Soviet propagandists have often succeeded in conveying the *correct* meaning of their strategy to fellow Communists and the *opposite and false* meaning to non-Communists.

The psychological dexterity of the Communists is not always matched by an analogous skill in the Free World. Communist psychological warfare is facilitated by the West's freedom of speech and by the unconscious "cooperation" of Western audiences with Communist propagandists. Westerners are easy prey because of their inability to detect and counter hostile propaganda—itself a tribute to the effectiveness of Soviet psychological warfare.

Among the least understood techniques of Soviet conflict operations are those of "neutralization" by "paralyzing ideas." The most effective type of psychological warfare is not to induce large numbers of people to do certain things but *to prevent them from doing those difficult and costly things that they ought to do for their own safety*. An operation designed to achieve the "neutralization" of groups who either do not comprehend the significance of the conflict or are torn between diverse assessments of its nature is an assignment an efficient psychological-warfare staff can handle with ease. Once a sufficient part of the target audience has been mentally neutralized, paralysis of action follows in due course. "Neutralization" is more easily accomplished if the conflict is lengthy and if a majority of the people, wearied by periodic tensions, become accustomed to repeated failure. Defeatism sets in as doubts about the possibility of victory increase and non-resistance becomes attractive.

Even sophisticated Westerners overlook the organized effort mounted by the Soviet Politburo to promote defeatism in the ranks of its opponents. As Cyrus L. Sulzberger pointedly stated: "The interesting thing about Moscow policy is that it is conceived by the Communist Party, not the Soviet Government, and it is largely applied by the K.G.B. or secret police (once called Cheka, O.G.P.U. and N.K.V.D) and known among party members as 'the sword of the revolution.' "[15] After stating that "almost half of Russia's 75 envoys

[15] Cyrus L. Sulzberger, "Behind Mother Russia's Smile," *The New York Times,* June 19, 1966, p. E12.

to non-Communist countries today are affiliated with K.G.B. or G.P.U.,"[16] Sulzberger made this observation:

> The work of K.G.B. and G.P.U. is enhanced by agents in key foreign positions. Kim Philby, once considered a possible future chief of British Intelligence, was a Soviet spy. Heinz Felfe, head of West Germany's counterespionage against Russia, was Moscow's man. A French official in NATO, arrested in 1963, was recruited by Russia nineteen years earlier. So called "agents of influence"—persons working secretly for Moscow to influence the decisions of their own governments—include the President of one West European country, parliamentarians, politicians and ambassadors.[17]

It is not possible to identify precisely the degree to which the Free World and the United States have been "neutralized" and "paralyzed"; but since these campaigns have virtually been ignored by the West's political and intellectual leadership, it is not particularly surprising that the Free World is handicapped by the psychological war.

Conflict Doctrine

The Communists manage conflict in accord with a "doctrine" embracing a peculiar and, in many respects, unique methodology of thought. Probably the most authoritative statement of Communist conflict doctrine was issued during the Sixth World Congress of the Communist International, held July–August, 1928.[18] This document is ignored by many American experts—some are apparently unaware of its existence, and others assume that it is no longer relevant. The Communists have since, of course, assimilated new ideas into their system, but the document did provide a general philosophical basis for the rationale of Soviet operations.

The Soviets have developed a body of strategic thought that is far richer in content and far more responsive to the requirements of modern conflict than any doctrinal thinking in the Free World. At the risk of oversimplification, it can be said that the United States has, at best, only a military doctrine and lacks a counterpart to the Soviet doctrine of conflict as an organic whole. Whereas U.S. doc-

---

[16] *Ibid.*

[17] *Ibid.*

[18] *The Struggle Against Imperialist War and the Tasks of the Communists: Resolution of the Sixth World Congress of the Communist International* (2nd ed.; New York: Workers Library Publishers, 1934).

trinal thinking is linear, Soviet conflict thinking operates along the time axis and is dialectic. Dialectics is the tool for handling dynamic situations, whereas logic deals, on the whole, with comparatively static relationships. Whereas we tend to ignore historical experiences and reason in a narrow time span, the Soviets make a major effort to master and fully relate their past history and future orientation. The Soviets cultivate and build upon the "theory" of political, social, and economic change embodied in dialectical materialism, or "diamat." Under the one informing idea that the entire conflict must be waged as a political struggle, the Soviets pay the greatest attention to the interplay of conflicting social forces, to psychological warfare, and to the integration of violent and nonviolent means of struggle. From this philosophical base, they derive and refurbish their military doctrine as well as their guidelines for technological innovation.

U.S. doctrinal thinking, by contrast, is oriented chiefly toward material and geographic factors. Thus far, we have been unsophisticated in combining violent and nonviolent methods of conflict; and although we appreciate economic factors, we tend to ignore social forces and psychological processes. The United States establishes "civilian" control, and the Soviets insist on "political" control. In the Soviet scheme, technical military decisions are generally made by military professionals (who are often Party members), although the Party collectively decides on some "technical" questions, such as whether to procure a major weapons system. The professional expert—the political-conflict manager—integrates all conflict operations and tailors a particular "mix" of specific techniques and arms to a particular situation.

In conflict, more than in other human activities, phenomena are interdependent. Within the context of war, the phenomena of peace —and within peace, the phenomena of war—are dialectically related. Increases or decreases in the level of one phenomenon produce qualitative changes in another. Actions call for counteractions, and the clash of countervailing actions results in a new synthesis from which a new series of actions will ensue. Friendship, cooperation, and alliances do not rule out hostility, and the benefits of peace are most readily grasped in the midst of conflict.

To the Western mind, there is a contradiction between launching a war in Korea and at the same time launching the Stockholm peace appeal.[19] In 1965, the Soviet Union was fueling the war in Vietnam with surface-to-air missiles while pursuing an apparent *détente* policy toward the United States. Such seemingly contradictory actions spring from the dialectical conflict thinking that is so alien to the Western mind infatuated with legal definitions of "war" and "peace." The West's inability to come to grips with these thought patterns may also be illustrated by its difficulty in comprehending "surprise." Americans think about surprise usually in terms of a sudden unexpected military attack and give little attention to technological, organizational, psychological, or political surprise. Nor do Americans show particular interest in techniques of surprise—concealment, camouflage, secrecy, and deception. We have found it particularly difficult to cope with deception, and most of our decision-makers, although aware of the potentialities of tactical deception, have given little serious thought to the notion of strategic deception and techniques such as misinformation. In fact, the over-all method by which the Soviets wage conflict is still baffling to most Americans.

That strategy is not one of the crucial functions of its government reflects the doctrinal inferiority of the United States. Even members of the National Security Council do not devote themselves exclusively to strategy, for they are full-time administrators of vast departments and programs. Instead, U.S. strategic thinking flows from subordinate echelons, and final decisions are made by top-level administrators who do not always fully understand the conceptual relation among military, political, and economic strategies.

Strategy is an elusive art and cannot be mastered by anyone, however talented, who comes to it without thorough preparation. In the Soviet Union, strategy is the primary, and probably the principal, function of the Politburo of the Central Committee of the Communist Party. (Soviet Foreign Minister Gromyko, for example, is merely a diplomatic technician carrying out the policies of the Cen-

[19] "The peace policy of the proletarian State certainly does not imply that the Soviet State has become reconciled with capitalism. . . . It is merely another—and under present conditions—a more advantageous form of fighting capitalism, a form which the U.S.S.R. has consistently employed since the October revolution. . . . There is no such contradiction, however, between the Soviet Government's preparation for defense and for revolutionary war and a consistent peace policy. Revolutionary war of the proletarian dictatorship is but a continuation of revolutionary peace policy 'by other means.' "—*Ibid.,* pp. 32-33.

tral Committee.) Soviet strategy against an external adversary is intimately related to Party and personal struggle for domestic political survival. This steady preoccupation with strategy produces a singleness of purpose and enormous determination in the Communist leadership as a whole. The history of conflict teaches that, of all factors, the will to victory is the most decisive. The Soviet leaders' dedication to victory, their strategic skill, organizational structure, and mental and psychological energy—all devoted to the struggle— combine to make them superior in conflict techniques.

The Character of Political Decision-making

Although the pragmatic bent of modern Communism resembles that of Western systems, a number of classical Communist tenets exert a strong influence on Soviet strategy, including a continuing belief in the determinism of history and the inevitable demoralization of the Free World, a commitment to pursue goals "actively," an emphasis on "violence" if it is necessary to attain revolutionary objectives, a commitment to attain technological supremacy, and a notion that various forms of struggle are organically related to one another. The "rationality" of the Communist dictatorship also differs from that of a Western government with regard to questions of war and peace, risk and cost, and the use of violence.[20] To Western minds, a nuclear war appears "rational" only if it is a matter of national survival; and many consider nuclear war, for any purpose, to be completely and utterly "irrational." In calculating the risks of fighting for national survival, Western statesmen would consider the long-range consequences of nuclear war on national survival and the preservation of a democratic way of life. A Western leader would hesitate to advocate openly a "rational" decision on war that means the acceptance of certain loss of blood and treasures. The Soviet leader might reason that huge losses, especially when suffered by enemy countries, would serve his purposes best; he might begin by deciding just what losses he would be willing to accept for his own population—a decision that would considerably simplify his planning.

[20] See Gerhart Niemeyer and John S. Reshetar, Jr., *An Inquiry into Soviet Mentality* (New York: Praeger, 1956).

The formulation of Soviet strategy is also affected by the political character of persons occupying the highest positions in the Soviet Union—"adventurer," "reformist," or "centralist." As the 1964 ouster of Khrushchev demonstrated, precipitate shifts may occur from one type of leadership to another. Khrushchev was both the "adventurer" who put the Soviet missiles into Cuba and the "centralist" who restored the very cult of personality for which he had castigated Stalin. Generally, the men who are most likely to succeed to leadership in the Kremlin are, by necessity, strong-willed, ruthless, adroit, and zealous; for in order to have consolidated their power, they must have enlisted the support of the military, the intelligence services, and the terror apparatus. So long as Communist dictatorship endures, aggressive personality types are likely to rule the Soviet Union.

Communist China: Thorny Alliance

Although the United States is confronted by increasing difficulties in Africa, Southeast Asia, and Western Europe, these complications cannot compare with those the Soviets have encountered in their relations with Communist China. The Soviet Union is engaged in an ever-widening dispute with its erstwhile ally, and both are vying for leadership within the Communist-dominated portions of the world. The ties that bind the two power centers are being pulled apart by ideological conflict and by a tug of war between Russian national interests and renewed Chinese chauvinism. It is difficult, perhaps even impossible, for the Kremlin to shed the ideological rationalization that has given successive Soviet regimes a semblance of legitimacy. The leaders of Russia and China share some strands of the ideological heritage of Marxism-Lenism, and both seek to displace the still prevailing global political, social, and economic structure by some variant of Communism. But the Soviets have a peculiarly Russian objective, which is usually unstated: The great Russians will be the "older brothers" of all other nations in the future Communist system. From the Chinese point of view, a future world Communist order should have at its center the Chinese, who regard themselves as the true heirs of Marx, Lenin, and Stalin.

The roots of the Sino-Soviet controversy have been traced to widely varying origins. Some students contend that the source of the conflict is ideological and that it came about once the Chinese concluded that the Soviet world view in the post-Stalinist period was fundamentally in error and could not be reconciled with the "correct" Peking interpretation of present and future revolutionary forces.

In November, 1965, the Chinese Communist publications *Renmin Ribao* and *Hongqi* printed a long, policy-delineating editorial that dismissed the possibility of cordial relations between the Soviet Union and China:

> The relation between the Khrushchev revisionists and ourselves is certainly not one in which "what binds us together is much stronger than what divides us . . . on all the fundamental issues of the present epoch the relation is one of sharp opposition; there are things that divide us and nothing that unites us.[21]

This official statement suggests that Peking regards the conflict as irreconcilable unless the "revisionists" now in command in Moscow should one day come to see the world through the ideological lens of the Chinese leaders. Because the article was written primarily for domestic Chinese consumption, it may have been overdrawn, for as Philip Mosely observed:

> Between Moscow and Peking there is at bottom no real difference in basic doctrine, but mainly a disagreement over the uses to which Communist power should be put. Each remains committed to promote the "national liberation" of oppressed peoples. Each remains free to choose the time, occasion and extent of that assistance, in accordance with its own appraisal of interests and risks.[22]

The Sino-Soviet dispute has also been attributed to a conflict of national interests and thus to old-fashioned power politics. The dream of the present leaders of the Chinese mass society is to gain on a global scale the hegemony that China once held in Asia. Prior to Communism, the Chinese sought in both Christianity and democracy the key to the restoration of Chinese grandeur. These having failed, Mao Tse-tung adopted Marxism-Leninism as the action concept most capable of putting China in its rightful place at the center of a new world order. The compatibility between the Marxist dialectic and the yin and the yang of ancient Chinese philosophy made it easy for the Chinese Communist leaders to absorb Marxism-Leninism and, in

[21] *Peking Review,* November 12, 1965, p. 12.
[22] Philip E. Mosely, "Soviet Policy in the Developing Countries," *Foreign Affairs,* October, 1964, p. 97.

their ideological contest with the Russians for leadership of the world Communist movement, to employ skillfully the tools of diamat.

Better than anyone else, the Soviet leaders know the depth of their differences with the Chinese Communists; the Russians have been careful not to exacerbate these disputes, since they do not wish an open break with Peking. But the Soviets will not be free to devote their prime attention to the ideological rivalry with China as long as Western capitalism exists in all its variant forms. The United States remains the chief Soviet antagonist because of its power and its successful way of life, which is completely inimical to Communism. Seen in this perspective, the Soviet ideological dispute with China is an argument over which means to employ in destroying capitalism. The ideological dispute is unlikely to spark open conflict between Communist China and the Soviet Union as long as the United States continues to be the ideological opponent they would each like to overpower. It is also unlikely that either Communist power anticipates major aggression by the other, for it is obvious to both that Moscow should have little difficulty over the next few years in dealing with any significant Chinese threat.

The Chinese population (estimated at more than 700 million and growing at a rate of 2 per cent annually), still largely agrarian, is living close to the subsistence level. But although one out of two of China's people is illiterate, the country boasts a highly intelligent and educated managerial and scientific class. Its densely populated cities hold practically the entire administrative and intellectual elite. Potentially, China could become one of the most productive nations on earth, but most mainland Chinese are still largely unfamiliar with modern technology—nuclear progress notwithstanding. China produces only 10 million tons of steel, little electric power, only 150 million tons of coal, and lacks accessible oil.

An accurate assessment of the military power of Communist China is difficult. Large numbers of soldiers, imbued with the fatalism of the culture and the fanaticism of the ruling ideology, represent a considerable strength. It is likely that they would fight valiantly and could seize the territories adjacent to the mainland, but their logistic capabilities would be strained by sustained efforts even against India. The operations against the offshore islands in 1958 were suspended, for example, because of lack of ammunition. When the Soviets stopped delivering aircraft, they condemned the Chinese Air Force to a period of obsolescence; and when Soviet aid was withdrawn, the debut of the first Chinese nuclear bomb was probably delayed by several years. As of 1966, China was a second-rate military power; the Chinese nevertheless managed to impress the world with their allegedly formidable war potential.

To develop significant strategic military strength, China would have to expand its economy at a sensational rate. In 1966, China was more than three times as populous as the Soviet Union and had a gross national product of approximately $60 billion, or one-fifth that of the Soviet Union. To keep pace with population growth, China must annually invest more capital than is available. Although a crash industrial program was launched in the late 1950's to achieve economic growth, the economy regressed. The channeling of the economy's major resources into industrial programs had helped to bring on a serious food shortage—a catastrophe that temporarily slowed the pace of industrialization and led the Chinese Government to give higher priority to increasing the agricultural production. The Peking regime subsequently issued stern warnings that it would be twenty to thirty years before the Chinese people obtained a decent living standard. The great "cultural revolution" that convulsed China in 1966 may set back Chinese economic aspirations even further.

An estimate of Peking's capabilities for developing modern weaponry calls for a review of the Chinese approach to nuclear weapons. Even after the Soviets exploded their first nuclear device in 1949, the U.S. near monopoly of nuclear weapons seemed permanent. Shortly thereafter, when the Chinese Communists gained control of the mainland, it became clear that a nuclear capacity was a prerequisite for any nation aspiring to be a great power, and the Chinese began to work on such a capability. As early as 1947, the U.S.S.R. had been extracting uranium ores from a part of Sinkiang over which it had gained indirect but effective control. The Chinese permitted them to continue mining the ores as a *quid pro quo* for aid in atomic research and development; and when the U.S.S.R. showed signs of achieving parity with the United States, the Chinese felt secure under the umbrella of Soviet nuclear power. There is little doubt, however, that even before withdrawal of Soviet technicians from nuclear projects in China, the Chinese had lost full confidence in the efficacy of Soviet nuclear protection. With their loss of confidence in Soviet willingness to come to their aid with nuclear weapons, the Chinese coincidentally lost some of their fear of a U.S. nuclear attack.

Since attaining nuclear capability—largely by their own power and resources—the Chinese have modified their strategic outlook. They are now working on intermediate-range missiles that will give credibility to their nuclear force; and by the time they have amassed a stock pile of bombs, they will probably have the means for medium-range delivery. The Chinese also have the world's third-largest submarine force, which before many years may be able to launch missiles directly on U.S. cities (provided the Chinese gain the requisite skill in naval warfare). In addition, the Chinese will doubtlessly acquire tactical nuclear weapons to counter the threat of similar U.S. weapons. Until these developments take place, the mere fact that the Chinese have nuclear capability gives them new leverage for power plays in Asia. Chinese Communist ambitions will not be pursued in other areas of the world until China acquires a significant nuclear delivery system.

Meanwhile, the Chinese Communists have publicly endorsed the strategy of a "people's war" as enunciated by their Minister of Defense, Lin Piao. Lin Piao asserts that "war is a great school required for the building of communism" and that "peaceful coexistence is rubbish." The Communist road to victory will be by way of a people's war—a protracted war modeled on the strategy that the Chinese used against the Japanese thirty years ago under Mao Tse-tung. This strategy parallels Mao's pattern of seizing power in the Chinese countryside and moving in to encircle and finally capture the cities. But now the world is to be the stage:

> Taking the entire globe, if North America and Western Europe can be called "the cities of the world," then Asia, Africa, and Latin America constitute "the rural areas of the world." . . . In a sense the *contemporary world revolution also presents a picture of the encirclement of "cities" by the "rural" areas.* In the final analysis the whole cause of world revolution hinges on the revolutionary struggle of the Asian, African and Latin American people who make up the overwhelming majority of the world's population.[23]

[23] From the text of the Lin Piao article "Long Live the Victory of the People's War: In Commemoration of the 20th Anniversary of Victory in the Chinese People's War of Resistance Against Japan," as printed in English in

The people's war strategy established principles as well as political guidelines for conducting conflict. It played down the efficacy of nuclear weapons in general and U.S. nuclear forces in particular:

> U.S. imperialism relies solely on its nuclear weapons to intimidate people. But . . . nuclear weapons cannot be used lightly. The U.S. . . . has been condemned by the . . . whole world for . . . dropping bombs on Japan. If it uses nuclear weapons again, it will become isolated in the extreme. Moreover, the U.S. monopoly of nuclear weapons has long been broken. . . . If it threatens other countries with nuclear weapons, U.S. imperialism will expose its own people to the same threat.[24]

The Chinese effort to denigrate nuclear weapons while their own nuclear capability is minor is reminiscent of the political-psychological tactics that the Soviets employed when their nuclear capability was in its infancy. It is also noteworthy that the Soviets pursued an aggressive political policy even during the period of American nuclear monopoly. Perhaps the aggressive concepts contained in Lin Piao's manifesto will be even more openly applied as the Chinese Communists' nuclear stock pile and delivery systems grow.

Despite divergencies in style and methods, both the Soviet Union and Communist China have revolutionary objectives in common. Ultimately, they must neutralize, circumvent, or dismantle U.S. military power or alter American intentions to halt Communist expansion. Both the Soviet Union and Communist China seek to exploit unrest in the underdeveloped world. The Soviets, in their spheres of interest, encourage "national liberation movements." "People's war" is the Chinese version of expansion through subversion and lower-level armed conflict.

The Soviets, at least for the time being, want to reduce the risk of nuclear warfare. The Chinese talk as if they are more willing to risk a nuclear showdown; they might even want to provoke one between the United States and the Soviet Union. Both Communist giants would like to seize key parts of the world without provoking military opposition from the United States. But the balance of world power will not change decisively so long as Western Europe's re-

the official Red Chinese *Peking Review*, September 13, 1965, p. 24. (Lin Piao is Vice-Chairman of the Central Committee of the Communist Party of China, Vice-Premier of China, and Minister of Defense.

[24] *Ibid.*, p. 26.

sources do not fall into Communist hands. Should the Communist powers attempt to seize control of Western Europe or Japan, the United States might decide to invoke its strategic power to thwart the policy of either the Soviet Union or Communist China.

Thus far, the Communist powers have taken minor risks and have moved cautiously from one limited conquest—or setback—to another. They are likely to continue this strategy for the sake of maintaining the forward momentum of the revolution and strengthening the morale and prestige of the Communist movement. So long as NATO is capable of preventing a Communist conquest of Europe, however, a strategy of this kind might never accomplish the Communist world revolution.

The chief obstacle to any kind of Communist world domination, the United States, could be eliminated by means of direct military attack. This kind of strategy is beyond the reach of Communist China for many years to come. From the Soviet point of view, such a strategy would become feasible only if the United States were to drastically reduce its military capabilities. Strategically impotent as they are, the Chinese see the United States, despite its overwhelming nuclear power, impaled on the horns of a dilemma. At what stage in a crisis can the United States initiate a military action (such as a naval blockade) and, at the same time, satisfy American public opinion, obtain the support of its allies, ensure a minimum of opposition from the so-called uncommitted powers, and forestall U.N. censure? At what stage of difficulty in a war being fought with conventional weapons can the United States employ tactical nuclear weapons with sufficient justification to satisfy the same political blocs and, further, to risk a nuclear response from the Soviet Union? Such psychological deterrents to U.S. action may have compensated the Chinese for their loss of faith in the U.S.S.R.'s nuclear protection. Although, for the near future, Communist China would like to take advantage of any opportunities for expansion, the stepped-up U.S. military commitments in Vietnam during 1965 and 1966 not only may have restrained Chinese ambitions but may have partially triggered the "cultural revolution" in China.

From the Soviet point of view, a strategy of direct attack on the United States would be feasible only if this country failed to maintain its relative strategic advantage. Although competent observers argue that the Soviets have already written off the option of direct military action against the United States, the evidence supporting such statements is inadequate. In any judgments about Soviet strategic intentions, growing Soviet military capabilities must be given greater weight than Soviet pronouncements. Soviet leaders may not wish, even under favorable circumstances, to risk war with the United States. The key task of American strategic design is to *ensure* that the Soviets wil not adopt such a course of action. The nuclear confrontation between the United States and the Soviet Union—be it nuclear war or the psychological exploitation of nuclear weapons—provides the framework within which all American foreign policies must be conceived. The nuclear capabilities that Communist China gains will modify the framework.

The Soviet Union will probably not choose to embark on a military struggle with the United States unless it can comfortably maintain Communist rule at home as well as fend off blows from its main Communist rival. If China cannot be kept under control, the burden of one more adverse factor may force the Soviets to revise their timetable for world revolution or to abandon the concept altogether.

5

The Soviet Dilemma

Scholars may argue whether ideological or nationalist forces play
the predominant role in the dispute between the Soviets and the
Chinese, but the important fact now is that the dispute will not be
settled until their main common enemy, the United States, is either
checkmated or eliminated. Each Communist power meanwhile keeps
a careful eye on its ideological and "nationalistic" rival while carrying
on its sometimes competitive and sometimes complementary efforts to
undermine the power and influence of the United States. Although
the Soviets and Chinese both focus their expansionist policies on the
United States, the timing of their strategies is basically different. To
put it simply: The Chinese can afford to wait. Once the Chinese,
one-fourth of the human race, acquire the full range of modern technology, the Chinese Communist influence in world affairs will become more and more potent. The Russian Communists, however,
placed by geography and history between a resurgent Western Europe
linked to the United States and a potentially powerful China, must
make their bid for world leadership within a definite time span. The
practical problem confronting Soviet leaders is to split the West
before the rising power of Communist China forces them to divert
major strategic resources eastward.

But this is more easily said than done. The Soviets know that
Western cohesion weakens in an atmosphere of peaceful coexistence
and that it diminishes even faster if a superficial *détente* exists between Washington and Moscow. The presence of a bellicose Communist China on the world stage may even strengthen the belief of
many Westerners that the Kremlin worries far more about improving
the Soviet economy and reducing world tensions than about world

revolution. There is little evidence, however, that the Soviet leaders have abandoned their revolutionary heritage. To the contrary:

> Mr. Khrushchev's successors now seem to have made up their minds that the immediate task is to restore their country's political and military prestige as well as to reassert its authority within the communist movement. But the latter, they have apparently concluded, cannot be achieved now while Russia is open to the Chinese charge of "collusion with the United States." Hence the Russian counteroffensive now developing on both fronts.[1]

The Soviets face a number of difficult and mostly unpleasant policy choices. They can attempt to neutralize the United States as rapidly as possible by a variety of stratagems so that, in turn, they can settle their dispute with Peking in the Stalinist manner. At the expense of their own ego, they can resume cooperation with Peking by suppressing matters of ideological contention. Finally, they can seek a genuine *détente* with the West—which might culminate in a common alliance against Communist China. Only the first of these alternatives offers the Soviets any possibility of attaining their revolutionary goal—a Communist world with Moscow at its center.

Soviet Military Might: Means to Success

The precondition for ultimate Soviet success in the dual struggle with the United States, the leader of the West, and Communist China, the Soviet's rival for leadership of the world Communist movement, is more adequate military power. Now and for the near future, the Soviet Union is vastly superior to Communist China in almost every attribute of power. Despite the intensity of their rivalry and the acrimonious nature of their public debates, there is every reason to believe that for a long time the Chinese will be reluctant to provoke the Russians into military action. Soviet military power in relation to that of the United States has been until recently far less formidable:

> Some people are beginning to argue that there is only one superpower, America, and that Russia is not in the same league. The Americans have more missiles. . . . The American's conventional forces are more

[1] "Friends with Nobody," editorial in *The Economist*, December 18, 1965, p. 1297.

mobile. . . . The combination, so the argument runs, will compel the Soviet Union to accept the rules of coexistence in their full rigour—no support for revolution anywhere where it hurts, by either side.[2]

If the Soviets are to reject such restrictive rules for coexistence and engage successfully in revolutionary activities, they must, if they can, improve their strategic power position relative to the United States. For the past three years they have been pushing hard to do just that.

The London Institute for Strategic Studies, which has the reputation for being a reliable unofficial compiler of military information, stated in its 1965 report that the U.S. missile advantage had slipped from 4:1 to 3:1. A crude projection of trends in Soviet ICBM strength can be obtained by comparing the institute's estimates for 1963, 1964, and 1965.[3]

ESTIMATES OF SOVIET ICBM STRENGTH

Type of ICBM	1963	1964	1965
First generation, soft	100	135	140
Second generation, stable	. . .	. . .	. . .
Liquid fuel, hardened	Some	65	140
Total	100	200	280

Rate of increase: 1963–64, 100 per cent; 1964–65, 40 per cent
Estimated total by 1970: 1,075

The above table illustrates the 1965 deployment rate of Soviet ICBM's; but it does not include the 700 to 1,000 MRBM's and IRBM's that the Soviets have emplaced against Western Europe, the Far East, the Middle East, and Africa, which, by virtue of geopolitical factors, must be reckoned as strategic missiles. It also does not include missiles that would be launched from Soviet submarines. The estimates show that by the end of 1964 the Soviets had doubled their 1963 missile force and, more importantly, had begun deployment of second-generation missiles, which accounted for one-third of the total ICBM's in 1964. By 1965, their force had increased by 40 per cent and the number of second-generation missiles had tripled.

[2] *Ibid.*

[3] *The Military Balance 1963–64; 1964–65; 1965–66* (London: Institute for Strategic Studies), yearly reports.

If this rate of increase were to continue until the end of 1969, the Soviets will have 1,075 hardened second-generation ICBM's. By 1970, the Soviets will have created a hardened, invulnerable second-generation missile force almost equal in size to the U.S. Minuteman I and II force currently programmed. Unless the United States builds more missiles, its superiority in strategic offensive missiles will have vanished. An ever expanding, highly accurate[4] Soviet force of ICBM's, carrying high-yield warheads, will give the Soviets a considerable counterforce capability.

The Department of Defense occasionally releases estimates of the current status of U.S. and Soviet missile forces. On May 24, 1966, United States officials reported a continued superiority of more than 3:1 over Soviet long-range nuclear missiles despite an "expected modest increase" in Russian capability. The brief announcement contained no specific figures; however, informed sources indicated that the number of Soviet land-based strategic missiles is "somewhere around 300."[5]

Reasonable projections of future Soviet missile strength that are based on open sources probably differ from classified estimates and from what is periodically disclosed to the American people. Department of Defense releases generally play down the Soviet strategic threat, although occasionally this practice is violated.[6]

The Pentagon has been progressively upgrading its estimates of

[4] Pavel F. Batitsky, Soviet First Deputy Chief of Army Staff, stated that the "precise accuracy" of Soviet missiles was proven by 1965 firing tests in the Pacific.—*New York World Telegram*, February 18, 1966, p. 3.

[5] *Baltimore Sun*, May 25, 1966, p. 1.

[6] On June 2, 1966, "Dr. Finn J. Larsen, Deputy Director of Defense Research and Engineering, at a dinner meeting in Washington only hours after a Defense Dept. conference with President Johnson, twice referred to Soviet ICBM strength as being close to the U.S. level. Any gap he said was 'modest.'" This report appeared in the June 6, 1966, issue of *Technology Week* (p. 10). A week later, in the same magazine, Arthur Sylvester, Assistant Secretary of Defense for Public Affairs, stated that reports about Soviet strength being "close to the U.S. level" were totally without foundation. Instead he reaffirmed an official Department of Defense statement that the United States has a 3:1 or 4:1 superiority over the Soviet Union in the number of operational intercontinental ballistic missiles. In this same issue of *Technology Week* (June 13, 1966), Larsen modified the statement attributed to him at the June 2 dinner to conform with Sylvester's.

Soviet strategic strength. Gradually these higher estimates have seeped into the public press. According to one source:

> The Russians have doubled their missile force in the past two years—to almost 400 land-based ICBM's and 130 submarines. They now have the capability, it is reported, to turn out 300 to 400 missiles a year. If they desired, they could catch up with the U.S. by 1970 and be well ahead by 1972.[7]

There has also been a rapid decline in total deliverable megatonnage:

> Military men say that, by 1972, U.S. missile power may be down to 5,000 megatons, while the Soviets could easily go to 10 times that. Says one expert:
> "Consider the total megatonnage in the warheads of Russian missiles zeroed in on our cities and missile sites. Then consider the much lesser megatonnage in our missiles. Then compare the total destruction patterns, magnetic-flux patterns, incendiary patterns and fall-out patterns of both—and you will understand why we are so concerned."[8]

During a 1965 military parade in Red Square celebrating the anniversary of the Bolshevik Revolution, the Soviets displayed a mobile 115-foot three-stage ICBM rocket of the type that orbited the Vostok spaceship. The Soviet news agency Tass called it an "orbital missile" that could deliver a "surprise blow on the first or any other orbit on the earth."[9] The U.S. Government professed to be uncertain whether this announcement violated the October, 1963, United Nations resolution, in which was stated the "expressed intention of the United States and the Soviet Union not to put nuclear weapons in orbit."[10] There are a number of potential uses for an orbiting bomb; however, the United States has never seen much value in either an orbital missile or a mobile ICBM as compared with other strategic offensive weapons.

---

[7] "Is Russia Winning the Arms Race?," *U.S. News & World Report,* February 6, 1967, p. 36.

[8] *Ibid.,* p. 37.

[9] *The New York Times,* November 8, 1965, p. 6.

[10] "The initial reaction was to consider both as familiar Soviet propaganda moves like other experimental weapons put on display at similar shows. These induced U.S. authorities to believe that supersonic bombers, giant transports and various new missiles were to be produced in quantity."—*Washington Post,* November 18, 1965, p. A-10.

The Soviet Union has a clear superiority in medium- and intermediate-range ballistic missiles. The initial inventory of fixed Soviet MRBM's and IRBM's reached 750 by 1960. Soviet MRBM's have a range up to 1,000 nautical miles, the IRBM's up to 2,200. All these missiles are deployed within the U.S.S.R., and they can strike all of Western Europe as well as North Africa. A large number of Soviet mobile launchers, called Scamps, capable of launching missiles into Western Europe from the Soviet Union, were deployed in 1965.

The future role of manned bombers has been as heatedly debated in Soviet circles as in the United States. The present manned-bomber force of the U.S.S.R. is almost exclusively jet or turboprop. The Soviet Mach 2 Bounder represents a considerable expenditure of resources and indicates an abiding Soviet concern with manned aircraft. To complement its land-based missiles and aircraft, the Soviet Union has a submarine force with a missile-launching capability.

In the area of strategic defense, the Soviets claim to have developed a successful ABM system, which is already believed to be deployed to defend the Leningrad-Moscow-Kiev industrial heartland. There is reason to suppose that the Soviets can develop an even more effective ABM designed for the interception of missiles before they re-enter the atmosphere. Work on a terminal defense ABM, perhaps comparable to the Nike-Zeus Sprint, may be in progress. The Soviets obtained much technological data on the development of the ABM as a result of their 1961 and 1962 operational nuclear-test series.[11]

The Soviet institutional bias toward defense is well known. Public sources give evidence of the implications for U.S. security of the

[11] "Missile systems for offense or defense are extremely complex, yet must function not only under the ideal laboratory conditions in which they are usually tested, but also under the most adverse conditions—those of nuclear war.

"I know of simpler systems which have not performed as expected—or which have actually failed—when proof tested in environments which are far better understood than that of a hostile nuclear situation.

"Technical people have had this experience not once but many times. That the exact nuclear environment for missiles, missile sites, and reentry vehicles probably cannot be completely duplicated even without treaty restrictions is not an argument for no atmospheric tests whatever. We can obtain a much better understanding of the situation with nuclear experiments in the atmosphere than without them."—Dr. John Foster, cited in U.S. Congress, Senate, Report of the Committee on Foreign Relations, *The Nuclear Test Ban Treaty*, 88th Cong., 1st Sess., Executive Report No. 3, 1963, p. 15.

Soviet development of an ABM system.[12] The Soviets also apparently believe that strategic superiority requires a combination of offensive and defensive forces. They recognize that the power of a nuclear offense cannot be exploited unless a defense against hostile nuclear attack is first created. If they deploy an ABM system and the United States does not, the Soviets will sooner or later attain strategic superiority. They are apparently not worried about provoking an ABM race. For if both sides should achieve a relatively effective ABM, the kind of accurate, high-payload offensive forces that the Soviets are now building should give them an over-all advantage sometime during the 1970's—unless, of course, the United States accelerates the development and deployment of comparable missiles. On February 2, 1967, Air Force Secretary Harold Brown, in hearings before the U.S. Senate, stated:

> Militarily there is no question that the threat is much more severe. Whether their intentions are as severe is a separate question, but militarily they have a very formidable missile force. They are building missiles very fast. . . . The capability for our military forces to survive an attack and assure the destruction of the Soviet Union is maintained. But we have to keep working hard to continue to maintain it. If we stand still and they add to their threat, then they will erode our capability to deter war.[13]

Even if both sides acquire equivalent offensive and defensive capabilities, the Soviets might still be ahead. In such circumstances, stability would be re-established at the top level of the strategic spectrum, which would make it safe for the Soviet Union to pursue revolutionary strategies further down the conflict ladder.

The Soviets, aware of the U.S. manned-bomber capability, are increasing both the number and the quality of their ground-to-air missiles, such as SA-2 and SA-3, which are already far more extensively deployed than those of the United States. In addition, they are expanding their early warning systems and are maintaining a large inventory of manned supersonic-speed interceptors. Soviet

---

[12] In particular, see Hanson W. Baldwin, "Soviet Antimissile System Spurs New U.S. Weapons," *The New York Times,* February 5, 1967, p. 1.

[13] Hearings Before the Committee on Armed Services and the Subcommittee on Department of Defense of the Committee on Appropriations, U.S. Senate, 90th Cong., 1st Sess., on S. 666 (Washington, D.C.: Government Printing Office, 1967), p. 875.

surface-to-air missile sites, radar sites, and interceptor aircraft are manned by approximately 750,000 men.

To complement their active defense measures—ABM's, antiaircraft missiles, and interceptor force—the Soviets have instituted a civil-defense program, which is an integral part of the Soviet military posture. The U.S.S.R. already has fallout shelters that can accommodate about one-half of the Soviet urban population. Soviet shelters are hardened to about 25 pounds per square inch (psi) and are designed to take advantage of the protective cover of the postattack rubble. In some cities, subways have been constructed with a series of powerful blast doors that provide excellent shelters at depths of more than 150 feet. Population evacuation has become a basic part of the Soviet civil-defense doctrine and would probably be undertaken preceding, and in conjunction with, a threatened Soviet first strike.

The Soviet Navy, of the hunter-killer variety, is assigned the role of destroying aircraft carriers and nuclear submarines. As previously stated, the large Soviet submarine fleet would supplement land-based missiles and manned aircraft in thermonuclear attacks against the United States. The total U.S.S.R. submarine force is estimated at nearly 400, thirty or more of which carry missiles. At least twenty of the thirty are nuclear-powered, and the number will increase considerably over the next decade.

The Soviets have long excelled in land forces. By the mid-1960's, there were indications that the Red Army was being reduced in actual numbers, although its over-all combat effectiveness was perpetuated by means of continuing innovations in tactical nuclear weapons. The strength of the Soviet Army during this period was estimated at 2.2 million men, organized into 140 divisions.[14] In a February, 1965, press conference, Marshal Sokolovskii announced that the total number of men in the Soviet armed forces had been reduced to 2.4 million; but the fact that neither *Pravda* nor *Izvestia,* the two leading Soviet newspapers, carried the news conference suggests that the figure might have been cited for foreign news consumption and was simply a psychological gambit in the Cold War. Sokolovskii's figure did not include security and border troops, which are under the control of other government agencies and number between 250,000 and 500,000

[14] *The Military Balance 1964–65* (London: Institute for Strategic Studies, 1964), p. 4.

men. Sokolovskii's announced armed-force reduction may have been another indication that the "modernists" had gained the upper hand over the "traditionalists" in the debate over the composition of Soviet armed forces.

Tomorrow's strategic balance will turn on whether the Soviets are able to exploit military technology to the point where they clearly out-run the United States in key areas of the elusive offensive-defensive race. Mose L. Harvey has stated that the best way for the Soviets to break the circles of difficulties encompassing them is "to pour more re-sources into the effort to build Soviet strategic power"; by following this course, the Soviet Union

> . . . can hope to make its own breakthroughs without major risks. A shift in the strategic balance would bring new leverage against the United States; relieve the pressure on many domestic problems; restore Soviet prestige vis-à-vis Communist China; and furnish new momentum to the campaign to influence the developing countries. The heady lure before Moscow is the possibility of a repeat on a more enduring scale of the breakthrough in missilery and space technology represented by the first ICBMs and Sputnik. . . . Of all the things the new rulers can do, the one that poses the least number of problems is to pour more resources into the effort to build Soviet strategic power.[15]

To be most productive, however, these resources must be poured into one or another kind of strategic mould that would give them some discernible long-term advantage. The design of Soviet strategic forces for the 1970's was probably already framed by the mid-1960's. Yet even if the United States accurately assessed Soviet military capabili-ties in 1966, it could not predict the Soviet Union's strategic posture for the 1970's. However, a range of Soviet alternatives can be pos-tulated from what was known in 1966 about Soviet military doctrine and capabilities. For the past several years, Soviet military writing has emphasized nuclear strategy, the quest for military superiority, and the advantage of technological surprise. Soviet military capabili-ties increasingly match the thrust of Soviet military doctrine. Bearing this in mind, the following alternatives set some reasonable bound-

---

[15] "The Post-Khrushchev Soviet Leadership: Dilemmas and Alternatives," *Orbis*, Winter, 1965, p. 758. (Mose L. Harvey, presently director of the Center for Advanced International Studies, University of Miami, was formerly a mem-ber of the Policy Planning Council, Department of State, and the leading authority on Soviet affairs in the Bureau of Intelligence and Research, Depart-ment of State.)

aries for probable designs of future Soviet strategic forces. Any one of these strategic directions could provide the framework for the R&D and procurement that would advance Soviet efforts to achieve military and technological superiority.

The Persistent Strategy

The *persistent strategy,* one of three hypothetical Soviet strategic postures, is consistent with the 1945–66 rate of the introduction of advanced weapons into the Soviet inventory. It is also consistent with Soviet attitudes toward military security that originated in imperial Russia and have subsequently persisted in the Soviet Union. The traditional Russian determination to defend national frontiers against land invasion has been extended to include defense against vertical attack. The essentially conservative persistent strategy provides for the steady incorporation of advanced weapons and step-by-step force improvements. Since the economic resources of the Soviet Union are directed toward the service of the state, there is no economic reason why this strategy could not be continued. By 1970, the effectiveness of the Soviet force would be greater than it is at present owing to an increase in hardened missile sites, which could ride out a first strike, and to a steady numerical increment in both offensive and defensive weapons.

At the present time, the Soviets are allocating more funds to strategic offensive and defensive forces than is the United States. Their allocation to strategic defensive forces—surface-to-air missiles, warning and control radar systems, interceptor aircraft, and antiballistic-missile defenses—is on approximate parity with allocations to their offensive forces. Their inherent bias toward defense has provided the Soviets with a base posture that they may exploit in the future; but finding the right strategic offensive-defensive combination is a complex, sophisticated problem. By the progressive development of its 1966 forces, the Soviet Union may stumble on a combination that could yield strategic superiority. Because of the geographical position of the U.S.S.R., the Soviet strategic offensive forces are not limited to weapons of 5,000-mile range. Sufficient (750) IRBM's have been deployed to give the Soviets overwhelming nuclear supremacy against NATO forces in Europe. Soviet counterforce targets in the NATO area consist of thirty-five to forty soft targets—the bulk of the NATO nuclear delivery systems. In the event of a conflict, the net result of the 750 missiles directed against Western Europe would be the strategic neutralization of that area.

Up to the mid-1960's, the bulk of Soviet expenditures on strategic defensive forces has gone into surface-to-air missile forces, and an increasing effort has been expended on all-weather interceptors and long-range fighter interceptors, plus the early-warning and control radar complexes needed to make the system effective.

With this base and with approximately the same rate of total expenditure, the Soviets can invest heavily in ballistic-missile defenses. They can also reduce expenditures on IRBM's and turn more of their attention to ICBM's, either maintaining or augmenting their military space budget, which, within their current economy, can easily be increased at the rate of 2 to 4 per cent a year.

Within further break-throughs or significant increases in their present budget, the Soviets could soon match the United States in number of ICBM's and at the same time continue with their ABM and shelter programs. If the United States continues to delay both its ABM and civil-defense programs, those two Soviet defense efforts could upset the present balance. And if in 1970 the U.S. population were to remain defenseless, there would be a re-evaluation as to which side possessed strategic superiority. A massive first strike directed mainly against counterforce targets in the United States might permit the Soviets, with their shelters and ABM's, to ride out a U.S. second strike and thus might open up a "win" option for the Soviet Union.

Because technological break-throughs may occur unpredictably, it is not improbable that by 1970 the Soviets may have an ABM system or a space program that is unforeseen at this time.

Should the Soviet Union not wish to chance the residual damage that a U.S. retaliatory strike might inflict on the U.S.S.R. regardless of Soviet ABM's, the leaders in Moscow may seek an alternative route. The realm of space has been an area of abiding Soviet technological interest and one of the few areas in which they have an impressive record of successes. The Soviet people have experienced a split in international Communism; their agriculture policies have proved unsuccessful; and they have been forced to buy food from the capitalists. From the viewpoint of maintaining the confidence of the Soviet people, their rulers would be reluctant to risk being surpassed by the United States in space achievements. The launching of sputnik and subsequent space spectaculars may be only a small manifestation of what the Soviets might be able to do in the future.

The Soviets also may visualize the translation of technological supremacy in space to strategic military supremacy and may consider using space systems for a variety of military purposes. A space-based anti-ICBM, utilizing laser or other devices to destroy missiles shortly after launch, could become an effective defense system, which, if the Soviets could perfect and deploy it, would drastically change the strategic picture.

Under a persistent strategic posture, a major strengthening of Soviet strategic capability would take place by 1970. More high-yield warheads would be assigned for countervalue targeting; a substantial fleet of Polaris-type submarines would be assembled; and a moderate manned-bomber force, equipped with improved air-to-ground missiles, would be maintained. The strategic-force–conventional-force ratio would favor the first of these, although there would be a steady improvement in weapons for conventional Soviet forces.

The Soviet IRBM force deployed against Western Europe would be maintained at a high level. At present, little of this force is hardened, but it is believed that by 1970 the Soviets may have a new hardened or mobile system of intermediate-range missiles (1,000 to 2,200 nautical miles) and could phase out or redeploy the older, softer system. Through 1970, a high percentage of the Soviet IRBM force might be either mobile or hardened and, unless there is some radical change, maintained at a level superior to that of NATO.

An ABM defense deployment would probably be easier for the Soviet Union than for the United States because of the more concentrated configuration of Soviet cities—U.S. cities, such as the Maine-to-Virginia megalopolis, are sprawling and almost contiguous. Providing ABM cover for a U.S. city would probably be more costly than for a comparable Soviet city.

Pursuing a persistent strategy for 1970 and beyond would pose no greater difficulties for the Soviets than those they now face, such as the present problem of choosing between allocations for the military or the consumer sectors of the economy. At minimum, the persistent strategic posture would enable the Soviets to continue a political-psychological offensive, including support of "wars of national liberation" behind the shield of an effective deterrent force. Strategic forces would probably be employed only in a crisis that threatened the very existence of the Soviet state and the survival of the Communist Party in the U.S.S.R. Should the Soviet leaders consider that such a condition existed, or were about to exist, a pre-emptive war against the United States would probably be initiated by covertly positioned ballistic- or cruise-missile submarines and by global-range missiles. This mode of attack, as any other, would require careful planning, excellent security, a salvo-launch capacity, and very high-yield weapons to destroy or neutralize U.S. hardened ICBM sites, bomber bases, and centers of political decision and command and control.[16]

The Restrained Strategy

If Soviet leaders become convinced that the U.S.S.R.'s military course during recent years has been too risky and expensive and if they recognize that economic restraints are not permitting them to pursue both internal development and world revolution simultaneously and effectively, they may adopt a *restrained strategy*. Such a strategy would mark the revival of the Leninist idea that the struggle between Communism and capitalism will continue to ebb and flow for an entire historical epoch. If this concept were to predominate, a generation would have to be spent in overcoming the many current obstacles to Soviet expansion—U.S. strategic superiority, the Soviet agrarian crisis, the Sino-Soviet dispute, and the resurgence of Western Europe.

Leninist dogma proclaimed that the ultimate victory against capitalism might be long in coming and must be pursued with patience. According to Lenin, the Communist struggle against established society is "a hundred times more difficult, prolonged and complicated"[17] than ordinary wars. This dogma was viewed more optimistically in the few years after the launching of sputnik, when it appeared that the socialist millennium might be close at hand. The anticipation of an imminent revolution, however, was probably revised as a result of the Cuban missile crisis. Since the fall of 1962, the Soviets have

[16] As a variant, such an attack would deliberately spare a sizable portion of the country and hold it hostage in an attempt to prevent the remaining U.S. Polaris fleet from being used against the U.S.S.R.

[17] Nikolai Lenin, *Left-Wing Communism: An Infantile Disorder* (New York: International Publishers, 1940), p. 77.

probably taken a longer view of the ultimate victory over capitalism and have entered a period of more restrained action. Soviet strategic thinking in 1966 was more in the line with Lenin's words of 1915: "The revolution may, and probably will, consist of long battles lasting many years, of several onslaughts with intermissions."[18] If this is the case, the Soviet leaders may conspicuously adopt a posture that would induce a long *détente* with the West and eschew aggressive penetration into non-Communist areas. Announced Soviet force cutbacks, which are not necessarily true, could be designed to induce U.S. unilateral disarmament by "mutual example."

There are those who believe that the gradual decline "in the revolutionary orientation of the Soviet leaders" may permit "some optimism concerning a future adjustment with the West."[19] If the Soviet leaders were interested in achieving a genuine nuclear *détente* with the West, a restrained strategy might be an attractive preliminary stage for them. The postwar record of Soviet behavior in the world arena, however, should make us extremely cautious in interpreting Soviet motivations for adopting a restrained strategic posture.[20] Unfortunately, the present *détente* may be, as W. W. Rostow suggests, merely "the third round"[21] in the protracted conflict, in which the Soviets have temporarily given up the initiative to the West until they can establish a relative strategic superiority. From this point of view, it might be advisable to establish criteria by which the United States can judge a Soviet commitment to peace and to the settlement of the issues still outstanding in the East-West conflict. According to Rostow, these issues are:

> . . . the problems of self-determination and security in Central Europe, the problems of inspection and arms control, and the commitment of the Communists to seek to advance their cause by techniques of sub-

[18] *Ibid.*
[19] See, for example, Zbigniew Brzezinski, "Threat and Opportunity in the Communist Schism," *Foreign Affairs*, April, 1963, p. 519.
[20] Harvey Averch, *Strategic Ambiguity, Asymmetry and Arms Control: Some Basic Considerations* (Santa Monica, Calif.: The RAND Corporation, 1963), RM-3426-PR. This study concludes that, given current U.S. strategic superiority but Soviet advantages in budget flexibility and intelligence, "on the basis of arms control agreements and information provided by inspection, it is difficult to distinguish between a case in which the United States seeks stable deterrence and the Soviet Union seeks superiority, and a case in which both sides seek stable deterrence."
[21] W. W. Rostow, "The Third Round," *Foreign Affairs*, October, 1963.

version and guerrilla warfare, not only in the developing areas but elsewhere as well. On the basis of statements and policies emerging from Moscow, there is no reason at the moment to believe that we are on the eve of great final settlements of these fundamental issues. . . . We see no signs that peace will suddenly break out and the Cold War come to an end.[22]

If ever the Soviets were to demonstrate *over a sustained period* their readiness to come to terms with the United States on these issues, which are so fundamental to the security of the West, there would be justification for believing that the adoption of a restrained posture by the Soviet Union may be indication of a genuine desire for world peace.

Meanwhile, the difference between the persistent and restrained strategies is *not* that the first is a strategy of nuclear war with the United States whereas the second is not. From 1957 until the time of the Cuban crisis, Soviet nuclear power was used as an instrument of intimidation and blackmail in support of an overtly expansionist Soviet political strategy—for example, the Berlin crisis of 1958–61. The threat was not that the Soviets would attack the United States but that any clash between the nuclear superpowers would automatically culminate in general war. So, too, it is a difference in Soviet political stance that distinguishes a restrained strategy from a persistent strategy. The former would help convince the West that the Soviet Union has given up its expansionist political goals and earnestly seeks a stable *détente*.

A restrained posture for 1970 would reflect a cautious and limited approach on the part of the Soviets. The military-force levels of the restrained strategy in comparison with the persistent would be: (1) a smaller force of well-protected strategic nuclear missiles; (2) increased tactical nuclear forces; (3) reduced conventional forces. Quantity of weapons would be sacrificed for qualitative improvement, although strategic and defensive capabilities against ground and/or air missile attack would still be formidable. The Soviets would try to modernize all forms of weaponry but would avoid a race toward parity with the United States in actual numbers of strategic weapons. The full nuclearization of the reduced Soviet Army and the development of strong ABM defenses could bring the cost of a restrained posture

[22] "United States Tasks on the World Scene," *The Department of State Bulletin*, December 16, 1963, p. 928.

almost to the level of the persistent. Although a restrained posture would call for fairly low force levels, it would in no way be a step toward unilateral Soviet disarmament.

This strategy would be an attempt to prevent thermonuclear war with the United States at all costs. The U.S.S.R. could achieve a restrained posture by eliminating the potentially offensive characteristics of its present forces or by reducing its risk-taking activities or both (cutting back soft missiles and bombers). Soviet Army divisions in Germany could be decreased so that the overt threat of Soviet aggression would not weigh on Western Europe. Soviet Army forces, however, could be heavily armed with low-yield, short-range tactical weapons so that the defense of Soviet-held territory would be guaranteed. Under this strategy, the Soviets would field a small, versatile, and survivable strategic force that, in addition to strong active and passive defenses, would include ICBM's with very large warheads, bombers, Polaris-type submarines, and IRBM's. Sufficient forces would be deployed against Communist China to prevent Chinese attacks on the U.S.S.R. If the Sino-Soviet dispute continues and particularly if it becomes more acrimonious, it will be difficult for the Soviets to contemplate substantial arms reductions in any category, but they may be attracted to arms control agreements that would facilitate transferring some of their deployments from West to East.

With the relatively few missiles that the Soviets would possess under this projected posture, they would not be able to adopt a successful first-strike attitude even if the United States were in an extremely weak position. Only against significantly reduced current and projected U.S. forces would the restrained posture have any substantial war-waging potential, since counterforce targeting would be impossible for the Soviets.

The features that would commend a restrained posture to the Soviets would be its capacity to lull the United States into making force-level cuts commensurate with those apparently undertaken by the Soviets. This characteristic Communist practice is designed to trade tactical time for strategic advantage. A substantial force build-up under the guise of a *détente* might be a subsequent feature of this posture. Admittedly, surveillance techniques have improved much since the Japanese were able to build a powerful force under the eyes of the United States, but hard intelligence is often obscured by wish-

ful thinking. If the political leaders of the United States were convinced that the Soviets sincerely wanted a *détente*, it is possible that
even reliable intelligence data indicating a Soviet build-up might be
set aside:

> We may do ourselves a disservice if we discount the possibility of
> changes in the international environment and give *too much* weight to
> such factors as whether or not the Soviet-American strategic balance
> might be upset 15 years hence by weapons systems that the Soviet
> Union might develop as a result of successful evasion of some agree-
> ment under consideration today.[23]

This sentence seems to imply that we should anticipate beneficial
changes in the international environment (for example, the dissolution
of the international Communist system and the mellowing of Communist ideology) that would offset possible Soviet evasions of disarmament agreements.[24]

The restrained posture, then, would be molded by political, economic, and military curbs. It would be a cautious and deliberate program of consolidation and retrenchment. From a technological point
of view, the securing of a relatively small deterrent force would be
moderately simple. Economically, this posture would be the least
costly; politically, the most prudent; and militarily, the least risky. It
would also redound to the Soviets' moral image.

Since this strategy would be deliberately nonprovocative, its positive gain would be a probable decrease in U.S. and Western forces.
Meanwhile, the Soviets could proceed with a careful, low-key campaign cultivating allies and conducting cadre training in Asia, Africa,
and Latin America—either in competition or in cooperation with the
Chinese Communists. The Soviets would be willing to take advantage
of opportunities as they arose, but would not actively promote conflicts
outside their borders. This kind of long-term strategy might prevail for
at least a generation, although a major drawback is that it might erode
the *élan* of the world-wide Communist movement.

[23] William C. Foster, "New Direction in Arms Control and Disarmament,"
Foreign Affairs, July, 1965, p. 594.
[24] When asked by letter whether this interpretation might be correct, Ned-
ville E. Nordness, public affairs adviser of the United States Arms Control and
Disarmament Agency, replied (October 5, 1965): "Your interpretation of the
sentence quoted in your communication is correct, but since you have not put
a time element in your interpretation, I think perhaps you have gone a little
further than Mr. Foster had intended in his article."

Of all projected Soviet postures, the restrained has the greatest subterfuge potential. Substantial technological advances, especially in the area of space weapons and even in multiple-warhead vehicles, could be effected even within the bounds of the nuclear-test ban; great strides could be made in the area of delivery systems without a single thermonuclear detonation. The surprise revelation of a Soviet technological break-through would go far toward eroding the confidence of our allies in an extended U.S. deterrent and would put the Soviet Union in an excellent position to extract concessions from a disillusioned Europe. This Soviet force posture, paradoxically, would have the greatest potential for long-range threat because superficially it is nonthreatening. Whereas a persistent or a coercive posture conveys no illusions about Soviet insincerity, the restrained posture capitalizes on an apparent Soviet desire for peace.

The Coercive Strategy

Two factors could lead the Soviets to a *coercive* posture. Soviet exploration in technology may produce weapons that, if deployed in sufficient quantity, could secure military advantage over the United States and a victorious termination of the Cold War. Furthermore, the Soviet leaders may come to believe that continued "peaceful coexistence" could sap the dynamics of revolutionary Communism.

If Soviet leadership is still committed to Communist ideology, it will adhere to its operational code eschewing adventurism[25] but encouraging boldness. Ideologically, the failure of the Party (and hence its leaders) to exploit a decisive opportunity is a criminal betrayal of the revolution. If technology can open up the vista of victory to one side, it can do so for the other. But since success will go to the side that first discovers and develops the means for technological superiority, there is compelling reason for the Soviet leadership to adopt a strategy of ultimate supremacy. This may have already been decided.

Statesmen in the West should take care not to project their own hopes for a *détente* onto Soviet officials. Soviet leaders' endeavors to convey the impression that they favored a prolonged *détente* did not

[25] V. I. Lenin said in 1917 that "this work must be carried on . . . without running ahead of events, without hastening to consolidate organizationally what has not yet been perceived . . . [and] comprehended."—*Pravda*, April 29, 1917, as quoted in Nathan Leites, *A Study of Bolshevism* (Glencoe, Ill.: The Free Press, 1953), p. 373.

interfere with their support of North Vietnam or their backing of
Nasser in the 1967 Middle East crisis. Contemporary Soviet officials
keep in mind Lenin's stricture, which was pronounced in 1921 but is
no less valid today: "Sentimentality is no less a crime than cowardice
in war."[26]

The obvious aim of a coercive strategy would be to achieve strategic
superiority over the West and overcome once and for all the imbalance that existed during the Cuban missile crisis. Under this more
flexible posture, the Soviets would be likely to launch probing actions
on the lower rather than the higher level of the force spectrum and
would not have to fear general nuclear war. Moreover, they would
gain control of escalation and be prepared to fight effectively at several
different levels of violence. Survivability, by means of passive defense
and active air and missile defense, would be of prime importance for
both military and civilian industrial centers. If by 1970 Soviet technology were able to produce a missile with an accurate target-location
capability of 1,500 feet (which is quite likely), the number of offensive missiles necessary for this Soviet posture would be greatly decreased, and the vulnerability of the U.S. missile force would correspondingly increase—with the possible exception of the Polaris as a
second-strike force.

A coercive posture would require that the Soviets possess an effective system of command and control as well as a capability for highly
accurate target location. Hardened ICBM's would probably form the
backbone of the coercive force. ICBM's and bombers directed at the
United States would complement the IRBM missiles aimed at Western Europe. Cities would not be the preferred targets, for the greater
number of Soviet missiles, improved in accuracy, could instead be
used against military targets. The Soviets could also launch a combined fallout attack on command and control centers and population
to unbalance U.S. strategic forces and demoralize the U.S. population. But to fight a prolonged war and thereby enhance their bargaining powers, the Soviets would need an extensive and sophisticated
ABM system, which, along with passive defense measures, would
help preserve the population and make victory meaningful.

[26] V. I. Lenin, *Selected Works* (New York: International Publishers, 1937),
IX, 267. This injunction was offered by Lenin in a speech at a Congress of
Political Education Departments on October 17, 1921.

The coercive posture possesses a considerable degree of military flexibility, which, in turn, would buttress Soviet political gambits. With a coercive strategy, the Soviets would add to their threats and posturings the ability to wage and possibly to "win" a nuclear war. Yet, at the very least, it would provide effective deterrence, allowing them to engage in limited operations without fear of precipitating all-out war.

In order to surpass the United States strategically, the Soviet Union must conduct some of their development activities on a clandestine basis, for the United States would surely react to any Soviet advances that are divulged. It is doubtful, however, that complete secrecy is possible, for the evasion of detection depends on such factors as sites with reload capabilities or rapid deployment of a large number of prefabricated ICBM's. Experience has shown, moreover, that certain Soviet technological gains have been counterproductive; that is, they induce maximum effort on the part of the United States—as was the case after the Soviet launching of sputnik in 1957.

A coercive posture would entail greater economic sacrifices than either the persistent or the restrained would. Although the cost problem would not prove insuperable, many civilian needs would have to be neglected. Technological obstacles would center around perfecting and deploying an ABM system and developing a missile with a target-location ability that is sufficiently accurate for effective counterforce.

If put to a test, a coercive posture would enable the U.S.S.R. to destroy enough missile sites and command posts to impair seriously, if not forestall, U.S. retaliation. Europe could then be taken relatively intact unless the British and French decided to employ their national deterrent forces. If the Europeans did not react, the Soviets would not have to strike simultaneously at the Continent, for U.S. failure to retaliate would make that move unnecessary. If the Soviets possessed the capability not only to check the United States strategically but also to wage effective land warfare, U.S. guarantees for Western Europe would mean almost nothing. The chief hazard of this strategy is that it would light the fire under the U.S. effort to maintain strategic superiority—provided the Soviet coercive strategy were detected in time.

Interplay of Inhibiting Forces

"Faced with the unknown future," wrote General de Gaulle some thirty years ago, "the human mind seeks a refuge in what has already happened. The human being seeks from the evidence of yesterday and today the rules that should guide him tomorrow."

Barring a Soviet commitment to arms control, major economic reverses, or insurmountable intrabloc difficulties, the future trend of Soviet armament is likely to be upward in both numbers and sophistication. Even the most modest posture may be flexible enough to allow the Soviets to take advantage of any sizable decrease in U.S. strategic forces, and we can count on the Soviets to watch strategic trends in the United States very closely and to capitalize on any gaps that might be detrimental to this country.

Unless unforeseen circumstances (the premise on which both the restrained and the coercive strategies as postulated here are based) arise, the persistent strategy seems to provide the most likely design for future Soviet security efforts. The Soviets may wish, however, to convey the impression that they have taken a restrained posture, plainly because if they cannot induce the United States to reduce its strategic forces, they have little or no chance of making the world revolution succeed.

By pursuing a persistent strategy, the Soviets have been advancing from a somewhat precarious defensive posture to an effective deterrent capability. They are now undoubtedly preparing to gain at least partial superiority—the first step having been the development of an antimissile system. By following its present course, the Soviet Union could eventually be in a position to adopt a coercive strategy, provided that the United States fails to modernize its own forces or otherwise reduces its military strength. Of course, the Soviets may be overtaken by events within the U.S.S.R. and the Communist bloc or by a vigilant and determined United States.

The limitations of our knowledge about the Soviet Union are such that we cannot be certain whether, within the broad boundaries suggested for the Soviet military effort, a restrained, persistent, or coercive strategy is currently being pursued. Because of the secrecy that shields the Soviet Union, major military efforts can be undertaken without the cognizance of the outside world,[27] unless the Soviet leaders decide otherwise. The West, therefore, is forced to rely on past experience with the U.S.S.R. as a guide in assessing the present capacity of the Soviets to deceive or confuse their antagonists.

From the time of Catherine the Great to the present, Russian leaders' successes at deception have been legion. In 1945, for example, it was "the general impression in the West that Stalin just didn't understand these new weapons,"[28] such as atomic bombs, and their effect on military doctrine. As we now know, the contrary was true. At that time, the Soviets had actually begun their effort to equal and overtake the United States in thermonuclear-warfare capability. In 1946, "the Soviet budget for research and development in these categories was trebled."[29] This effort followed the conclusion of a war in which the Soviets suffered 18 million to 30 million casualties and devastation on a scale unknown even to the defeated powers of Germany and Japan. Slightly more than a decade afterward, the Soviets possessed ICBM's, sputniks, supersonic aircraft, and thermonuclear weapons. As each of these systems came into being, the outside world was surprised again.

Although a few years ago Soviet budget figures indicated a decline in military expenditures,[30] denoting a restrained strategy, the subsequent steady build-up of missiles and the introduction of new aircraft into military inventories (which are both in line with normal developments in the state of the art) mark a persistent strategy. Despite serious uncertainties concerning Soviet R&D efforts,[31] such indicators, com-

[27] It is extremely difficult for U.S. military and political leaders to comprehend how a major Soviet military effort such as placing missiles in Cuba could have gone so far without being detected.

[28] Philip E. Mosely and Marshall Shulman, *The Changing Soviet Challenge* (Racine, Wisc.: The Johnson Foundation, 1964), p. 18.

[29] *Ibid.*

[30] Timothy Sosnovy, "The Soviet Military Budget," *Foreign Affairs,* April, 1964, p. 487.

[31] Senator Ellender asked Dr. John Foster, Director of Defense Research, whether he knew "enough details about the money being spent by Russia on the same efforts that we are putting forth." Dr. Foster replied, "Sir, I am sure we are making every effort we can, but all of us would love to have a statement from Russia similar to the unclassified statements that we make available here. . . . I have some information, but I do not have enough detail."—Hearings Before the Committee on Armed Services and the Subcommittee on Department of Defense of the Committee on Appropriations, *op. cit.,* 1968, p. 539.

bined with stated or known Soviet capabilities in space, an ABM system, and thermonuclear weapons, may point in the direction of a
coercive posture. We simply do not now know which pattern the Soviet
Union is pursuing in designing its strategic forces.

Several times during the past two decades, the Soviet Union has
sought to convince the West that it wants a genuine *détente*. The
present period of avowed *détente* has been the longest. Yet, on the
eve of the Twenty-third Congress of the CPSU, held in early April,
1966, the Kremlin circulated a 10,000-word letter to Eastern European
Communist parties in refutation of Peking's charges that the Soviets
had become "revisionists." About Communist operations, it said:

> The success of the struggle of the working class for the victory of rev-
> olution will depend on the extent to which it and its party learn to em-
> ploy all forms of struggle, peaceful and nonpeaceful, legal and extra-
> legal, and on whether they are prepared for the swiftest and most sur-
> prising replacement of one form of struggle with another.[32]

What this seems to imply is that the Soviets' acquisition of strategic
superiority might terminate a policy of *détente*.

The Soviet leaders' understanding of the correlation between politics and war in the nuclear age will influence their decisions on the
design of Soviet strategic forces. The relationship between nuclear
weapons and politics was candidly discussed by Soviet Lieutenant
Colonel E. Rybkin in an article in the Russian journal *Communist
of the Armed Forces,* September, 1965.[33] The article conceded that,
owing to the nature of a nuclear conflict, the possibility of gaining
political aims in a nuclear war is greatly reduced. Therefore, "the
centre of gravity in the efforts of policy to guide strategy are trans-
ferred to peacetime."[34] This insight suggests that the Soviets perhaps
conceive of manipulating strategic doctrines and power to influence
the strategic thinking and action of the opponent.

Rybkin disagrees with those in both the West and the Soviet Union
who believe that general war cannot be "won" in any meaningful
sense. To the contrary, Rybkin argues that "to affirm that victory in a

---

[32] Reprinted in *Die Welt,* March 21, 1966, p. 6.
[33] As published in *Survival* under the title "War and Policy," January, 1966,
pp. 12–16.
[34] *Ibid.,* p. 16.

nuclear war is impossible is not only theoretically incorrect but politically dangerous";[35] and he continues:

> Victory in war is determined not merely by the character of weapons but by the *relationship of forces* of the combatant sides. A quick victory may be gained over the aggressor [defined in Communist doctrine as the "imperialist" United States], thus averting further destruction and tribulation. It is possible that new means of war, capable of reliably parrying the enemy's nuclear strikes, will be developed. . . .
>
> *A priori* denial of the possibility of victory is harmful because it leads to moral disarmament, disbelief in victory, fatalism and passivity.[36]

Nuclear weapons have obviously complicated the strategic dilemma that confronts Soviet political leaders. For them to accept the concept that there can be no victor in a nuclear conflict would almost be tantamount to abandoning the belief that Communism will inevitably triumph under all circumstances.

Soviet strategic problems are compounded by the fact that the Soviet Union faces for the first time in the nuclear age two adversaries rather than one. Although Moscow and Peking have a common problem—how to break out of the flexible wall of containment erected by the United States—neither has found a solution. Occasionally, this wall has been breached, but only at great risk and cost to the Communist powers. To reconcile themselves to the hegemony of the United States, they would have to relinquish whatever justification they claim for the hardships that both have imposed on their subjects.

Since the Soviet Union and the United States, separately or together, can effectively block the fulfillment of Chinese dreams of world leadership, the effective nullification of the power of the U.S.S.R. and the United States must be the prime concern of top-level Chinese policy-makers. Looking toward the future, Chinese policy-makers and planners must seek to ensure that the two will never combine forces against Communist China. Peking would also want, if possible, to precipitate a conflict between the United States and the Soviet Union in which the two would neutralize or destroy each other. That the Soviet Union might wish to ignite a United States–Communist China conflict is another possibility not to be discounted.

[35] *Ibid.*
[36] *Ibid.*

Both Washington and Moscow are aware of Peking's aspirations; and within the next decade, both the Soviet Union and the United States will monitor Communist China's nuclear developments. Eventually, the Chinese Communists may loom far larger in Soviet strategic calculations than the United States. For at least the next ten years, however, the strategic interplay between the United States and the Soviet Union will be more crucial for either nation than will the maneuvers of Communist China.

The Chinese Communists are severely limited in their economic and technological resources. If they try to move too fast too soon to acquire weapons, they will not be able to build up an economic base and will subsequently find it difficult, if not impossible, to achieve solid great-power status. On the other hand, if a slower-paced, more reasonable, and more integrated technological-economic development is going to interfere with other Chinese Communist ambitions, they may attempt another "great leap forward." If the Chinese Communists choose the more orderly and efficient course, the time period in which the Soviets can attempt to splinter the West may be prolonged.

The Soviet leaders must know that as long as U.S. power remains superior and is linked with Western Europe, they will not be able to escape from their strategic dilemma: too much to do and too little time in which to do it. On the other hand if U.S. leaders act on their estimates of Soviet intentions rather than on the implications of the constantly growing Soviet strategic military capabilities, the Soviets may be relieved of the dilemma.

6

Arms Control: Cooperation
or Competition?

Should the United States strive for a nuclear *détente* with the Soviet Union regardless of the impact of such a search on U.S. strategic superiority and the Free World's security? This central political and strategic issue confronting the United States has so far been complicated by implications that the Soviets intend to compete with the United States no matter what U.S. policy might be. The question of arms control, then, turns on whether Soviet leaders will become convinced that the gains of a continued technological arms race are less alluring than the lower costs of a genuine agreement on arms control.

The U.S. search for a *détente* with the Soviet Union has thus far been a one-sided courtship. According to James Reston, who interviewed Soviet Premier Kosygin in December, 1965:

> Soviet officials do not converse with foreigners: they compete. There is no searching for understanding in conversation as we understand it in the West, no effort at accommodation of the mind, not even the slightest hint or suggestion that the Soviet Union has ever done anything that was in any way wrong or even unwise, imprudent or intolerable. Their idea of give and take in a talk is simple: you give; they take.[1]

Lacking hard evidence that the Soviet Union is prepared to seek a legitimate *détente* with the West, how far should the United States venture in seeking verifiable arms control agreements that could safeguard both peace and freedom?

Disarmament or Partial Measures?

In U.S. strategic planning, considerations of arms control already influence the design deployment, and use of military forces and weapons. Paradoxically, the man credited with modernizing the

[1] *The New York Times,* December 8, 1965, p. 46.

armed forces of the United States has also been at the forefront of the U.S. arms control effort. Arthur M. Schlesinger, Jr., wrote of him:

> Next to the President, McNamara . . . probably did more than any-one else to sustain the disarmament drive. With his sense of the horror of nuclear conflict, his understanding of the adequacy of existing stock-piles, his fear of nuclear proliferation, his analytic command of the weapons problem and his managerial instinct to do something about an irrational situation, he forever sought new ways of controlling the arms race.[2]

By 1960, arms control ideas were beginning to influence the strategic situation. But now, in the minds of some, the situation is—or should be—reversed:

> If, in the past, it was argued that arms control policy was a part of mili-tary policy, it may now be argued that strategic weapon policy is an adjunct to arms control efforts. If, in the past, arms control seemed more urgent, it now seems more feasible and, in the long run, no less vital. This is a time for renewed, subtle, and coordinated efforts to keep the competition within bounds.[3]

No one can quarrel with this objective. Since the days of the Baruch Plan, which called for an international atomic authority, this country has persistently sought agreements with the Soviet Union for balanced arms reductions to be completed under an effec-tive system of international controls. Between 1959 and 1962, Soviet and U.S. proposals for general and complete disarmament (GCD) were the subject of intensive debate.

Most governments, however, do not regard total disarmament as a realistic policy goal for the near future.[4] During 1964, the Geneva

[2] Arthur M. Schlesinger, Jr., *A Thousand Days* (Boston: Houghton Mifflin, 1965), p. 504.
[3] Jeremy Stone, *Containing the Arms Race* (Cambridge, Mass.: M.I.T. Press, 1966), p. 20.
[4] The major technical obstacle to GCD is the scientifically insuperable prob-lem of devising adequate inspection safeguards against the danger of hidden nuclear stock piles sequestered from past production. The strategic problems of GCD include the intelligence and information on which disarmament is to be based; the infeasibility of controlling fast-changing weapons technology by means of traditional diplomatic agreements; the military asymmetries between the major powers, which compound the difficulties of devising preliminary steps

talks of the Eighteen Nation Disarmament Committee (ENDC) were devoted primarily to partial measures rather than to total disarmament. At the ENDC Conference in the summer of 1965, most states preferred to use the limited time available for discussing a nonproliferation treaty or a comprehensive nuclear-test ban instead of debating about GCD.

Leading U.S. strategic analysts have preferred to approach the arms problem by way of arms control rather than total disarmament.[5] The term "arms control" embraces many different measures, including formally negotiated agreements, informal tacit arrangements, unilateral initiatives, and reciprocal actions. The over-all concept implies some form of restraint on a nation's armaments policy; in this sense, the principle of civilian supremacy over the military has traditionally constituted an application of arms control in the United States.

The growing arms control community within the West (especially in the United States and the United Kingdom) has generated a large set of "safety" proposals. Some of the suggested measures are: (1) a nuclear-test ban, partial or complete; (2) the disengagement or reduction of forces and the banning of certain weapons systems in a prescribed geographical zone in Central Europe; (3) a freeze on the production of fissionable materials for weapons use; (4) a freeze on the production of strategic delivery vehicles; (5) a freeze on the deployment of nuclear weapons in Central Europe; (6) improvements in command, control, and communications systems; (7) the destruction of obsolete bombers; (8) the phase-out of manned aircraft; (9) a moratorium on antimissile systems; (10) aerial inspection, exchange of observers, and other safeguards against surprise attack; (11) the demilitarization of outer space; (12) the establishment of an emergency communications link between adversaries;

---

in the early stages of disarmament; the dangers of destabilization incurred by reducing the level of deterrent forces too far or too fast; the dangers of rapid remobilization and rearmament in a disarmed world, since it may not be possible to apply timely sanctions to a potential aggressor.

[5] These include Amron H. Katz, Herman Kahn, Thomas C. Schelling, Henry A. Kissinger, J. David Singer, Fred Ikle, James E. King, Jr., Robert R. Bowie, Morton H. Halperin, Clark C. Abt, George E. Pugh, John B. Phelps, Herbert S. Dinerstein, Jeremy Stone, Donald G. Brennan, James E. Dougherty, and others.

(13) an agreement to "ban" nuclear weapons entirely or to refrain from the initial opening use of these weapons; (14) the build-up of a flexible, conventional capability to lessen recourse to nuclear weapons in the defense of Europe; (15) the development of methods for terminating nuclear war on the least disadvantageous terms; (16) a treaty to prevent the proliferation of nuclear weapons; and (17) reductions in military budgets.[6]

The Arms Control Spectrum

Proposals for arms control have been authored by an expanding body of scholars searching for means of outlawing or curbing the use of nuclear weapons. Among them is Anatol Rapoport, whose opposition to present U.S. nuclear strategy is based on the contention that "our civilization is now so organized that it is possible for unspeakable crimes to be committed without anyone involved in these crimes being an 'evil person' in the accepted sense."[7] Consequently, he argues that the physical systems—the strategic offensive forces— that make those crimes possible should be dismantled through disarmament:

> I find that the most formidable obstacles to disarmament are created by the strategists who place their strategic considerations above the needs of humanity as a whole, and who create or help maintain an intellectual climate in which disarmament appears dangerous or unrealistic. . . . It so happens that American strategists have made a much greater impact on the general intellectual climate than have those of any other country. . . . For this reason, I chose the mode of thinking of American strategists as my principal target.[8]

[6] U.S. policy-makers have officially subscribed to some of them, especially Nos. 1, 3, 4, 8, 10, 11, 12, and 15. In a New Year's letter to the Soviet Government, President Johnson included the subject of arms control: "Arms control remains especially urgent, nothing can contribute more to the hopes of mankind for the future. During the months ahead I hope we can work for practical agreements to this end. We can and should move to limit the spread of nuclear weapons; to achieve a verified worldwide comprehensive test ban; to make a cut-off of fissionable material production for weapons coupled with measures to safeguard the peaceful uses of nuclear power; and to agree on a verified freeze in existing offensive and defensive strategic nuclear delivery systems."—*The New York Times*, December 31, 1964, p. 7.
[7] Anatol Rapoport, "The Sources of Anguish," *Bulletin of the Atomic Scientists,* December, 1965, p. 34.
[8] *Ibid.,* p. 35.

Rapoport has derived many of his insights on international behavior from experimental games such as "chicken" and "prisoner's dilemma."[9] The first is the analogy of two juveniles racing their cars toward each other on a narrow road, both traveling the median strip. Which will lose his nerve first and swerve to avoid a collision? Will neither? Or will one "chicken out" too late to avoid a collision fatal to both? Rapoport suggests that any nuclear confrontation between the United States and the Soviet Union will be of this macabre and insane character.

In "prisoner's dilemma," two prisoners who have been charged with the same crime are held incommunicado and asked to confess their crime. Although both would get a lighter sentence if *neither* confessed than if *both* confessed, either of the two—not knowing what the other might do—is better off by confessing. Thus, through the dilemma of uncertainty, they are both led to confess in spite of the fact that they could have improved their fate by "cooperatively" refusing to confess.

As a means for quickly comprehending the structural characteristics of a situation, games can be quite useful. But for the rich realities of the contemporary international system, the basic flaw in this methodology is that excessively simple game models cannot duplicate problems confronting the leaders of major power blocs. Rapoport's games have some specific disadvantages:

1. For real events, there is no known method for assigning numbers to mirror the costs and gains in a particular situation.

2. Nonzero-sum games of the "chicken" type have no mathematical solution. The nature of the solution is determined by the mathematical definition of rationality that is chosen. Yet, for situations involving fatal decisions, there is no consensus on what constitutes rationality.

3. Such games fail to take into account the nonrational elements of choice, and so their assumption of rationality—"rules of decision" that will always be followed—is not realistic.

4. The assumption that there are only two alternatives in the de-

[9] For a lucid critique of Rapoport's game experiments, see Albert Wohlstetter's "The Non-Strategic and Non-Existent," in Kathleen Archibald, ed., *Strategic Interaction and Conflict* (Berkeley: University of California, Institute of International Studies, 1966), p. 107.

cision structure is basically faulty. (This is not true of games in general but is true of "prisoner's dilemma" and "chicken.") In real life, many decisions must usually be made simultaneously and the factors leading to one of these decisions cannot be scaled from most to least threatening or most to least escalatory. Moreover, each decision usually opens up a range of responses and is not a simple choice of "act" or "don't act."

5. These games are also based on the assumption that results follow inevitably from decisions and that both participants know the nature of these results. In the complexities of the real world, this rarely, if ever, happens.

6. Finally, Rapoport's game world, in which players seek imaginary rewards, is completely insulated from the emotions and stress of a crisis environment. From such laboratory lessons, it is difficult to draw guidance for the actions of President Johnson, Premier Kosygin, and Chairman Mao Tse-tung.

Although Rapoport condemns the system in which statesmen and their strategic advisers operate as well as the modes of thought they employ, he rarely castigates individuals in the system. Since Rapoport attributes evil to weapons and systems and rarely to human intentions, he logically approaches but does not quite come to the conclusion that the war against Hitler was a mistake:

> It is conceivable to me that even the conquest of the world by the Germans (if it were unresisted) would have left some hope, for example, of an eventual dissolution of the Herrenvolk empire by inner social and psychological stresses. It is not unreasonable to suppose that the actual number of deaths and the amount of physical suffering would have been smaller if no resistance were offered to the Germans.[10]

It was inevitable that some of the intellectual believers in pacifism would come to this position; for many of them (Bertrand Russell, for one) advocate policies that frankly urge the West to

[10] Rapoport, "The Sources of Anguish," p. 36. He adds this qualification: "In short, I find it possible to believe that, many things considered, on the whole humanity might have been better off if World War II had not been fought (especially if the present state of the world turns out to be a prelude to a holocaust surpassing all the Nazi horrors). However, this is only a surface belief, arrived at by admitting the plausibility of certain arguments. Emotionally, I still justify in retrospect World War II and my participation in it. I still derive satisfaction from the knowledge that the Axis was smashed, not tamed, and that for a while at least the master race was humiliated."

accept Communist rule submissively rather than risk a nuclear war to prevent it. They reason—and probably correctly—that some ten to twenty generations later, Communism would be disarmed by "inner social and psychological stresses." This long view of history, however, gives little comfort to those who would have preferred not to live under Hitler's tyranny or under present-day Communist totalitarianism and who would like their children to escape a similar fate.

Those who are not unilateralists or pacifists also question the value of strategic superiority. Thomas C. Schelling, who is a tough-minded advocate of arms control as opposed to disarmament, has suggested that superior military power may contribute very little to the kind of diplomatic bargaining that occurs in the contemporary nuclear world:

> "Bargaining power," "bargaining strength," "bargaining skill," suggest that the advantage goes to the powerful, the strong, or the skillful. It does, of course, if those qualities are defined to mean only that negotiations are won by those who win. But, if the terms imply that it is an advantage to be more intelligent or more skilled in debate, or to have more financial resources, more physical strength, more military potency, or more ability to withstand losses, then the term does a disservice. *These qualities are by no means universal advantages in bargaining situations; they often have a contrary value* [italics added].[11]

To make this point more explicit, Schelling contends:

> When a person—or a country—has lost the power to help himself, or the power to avert mutual damage, the other interested party has no choice but to assume the cost or responsibility. "Coercive deficiency" is the term Arthur Smithies uses to describe the tactic of deliberately exhausting one's annual budgetary allowance so early in the year that the need for more funds is irresistibly urgent.[12]

Whether the economic analogy of "coercive deficiency" would apply in a nuclear confrontation between the U.S.S.R. and the United States if the U.S.S.R. were clearly ahead in strategic superiority is questionable.

[11] Thomas C. Schelling, *The Strategy of Conflict* (Cambridge, Mass.: Harvard University Press, 1960), p. 22.

[12] *Ibid.*, p. 37. (Thus an agency that deliberately exhausts funds in May can get emergency appropriations to tide it over to July as part of a calculated plan to increase its annual budget.)

Morton Deutsch takes a more ambivalent view of the issue of U.S. superiority and accepts as reasonable the proposition that:

> Western military *inferiority* might tempt the Communists to exploit their military superiority. This proposition, however, does not necessarily imply that the attempt to attain a clear-cut Western military superiority is desirable. Obviously, if the Communists were unwilling to settle for a position of military inferiority, our attempt to achieve military supremacy would only lead to a continuing intensification of the arms race.
>
> To argue against the reasonableness of the policy of military supremacy does not imply that we should accept a position of military inferiority.[13]

Taking an unequivocal view, Sidney Hook, a distinguished humanist who has rejected totalitarian Communism, argues: "We must retain the deterrent. Those who scoff at it ignore the plain fact that the deterrent has preserved the peace. The only thing that can tame Communist fanaticism, Russian or Chinese, is fear of failure, and the deterrent has kept that salutary fear alive."[14]

These conflicting views reflect a range of perceptions about the world, the future, and power and values in the nuclear age. There are no hard data supporting any one of them. Empirically, the only evidence is that no nuclear war has occurred during the few short years in which the United States has enjoyed strategic advantage.

Arms control and disarmament advocates differ in their stances. Some contend that U.S. policy-makers have little choice but to seek an agreement for total disarmament with the Soviets. Others argue that the United States should not hold out for high reliability in inspection systems because they deem the perils of continued weapons competition greater than the dangers of an inefficiently policed disarmament treaty.[15] Some assert that the risks inherent in unilateral disarmament are preferable to those posed by a continua-

---

[13] Morton Deutsch, "Producing Change in an Adversary," in *International Conflict and Behavioral Sciences,* ed. Roger Fisher (New York: Basic Books, 1964), pp. 147–48.

[14] In *Prospects for Arms Control,* ed. James E. Dougherty, with John F. Lehman, Jr. (New York: Macfadden-Bartell, 1965), p. 157.

[15] Seymour Melman declares that "the gains that could be obtained for the security of humankind by relaxation of the arms race are so substantial as to be well worth the risks of successful evasion that may be involved in concluding disarmament agreements."—*Inspection for Disarmament,* ed. Seymour Melman (New York: Columbia University Press, 1958), p. 4.

tion of the arms race.[16] At one extreme, some well-intentioned men have concluded that the abolition of weapons will *ipso facto* lead to the abolition of war, and they therefore urgently recommend disarmament at any price—unilateral disarmament if necessary.[17] Those who hold this position tend to equate "peace" with lack of conflict and advocate policies channeled toward the termination of conflict. They take this stand regardless of the effect such policies might have on the preservation of values such as freedom of choice or justice. Unilateral disarmament on the part of the United States would, of course, presuppose a policy of surrender to any power that still retains the means to wreak destruction on this country (without having to fear any consequences to itself). In such a case, pacifists such as Rapoport and Russell offer the recourse of passive resistance. But it is more likely that Americans subjected to Communist control by unilateral concessions would actively resist—a course that would have fatal consequences for a great many people.

Those who recommend marginal steps toward disarmament hold with the pacifists that the very existence of nuclear weapons makes their use (accidental or provoked) inevitable. They believe that the United States and the Soviet Union have interests in common, the foremost of which is to avoid war. They see mutual distrust as the basic factor separating the two nations and making agreement on disarmament impossible. According to this school of thought, the break-through must be initiated by one party (the United States); it must demonstrate its good faith by reducing its forces without waiting for an agreement by the other party (the Soviet Union). (Such unilateral initiatives have also been termed the "experimentalist" approach to disarmament.) The program would be carried out in stages, each stage being announced in advance, and the Soviet Union would be expected to reciprocate. Whether or not further unilateral-disarmament steps should be contingent on commensurate steps by the Soviets brings on a divergence of views. Amitai Etzioni, an advocate of "gradualism," maintains that unilateral disarmament should proceed by carefully devised stages and that each stage

[16] Erich Fromm, "The Case for Unilateral Disarmament," in *Arms Control, Disarmament and National Security*, ed. Donald G. Brennan (New York: George Braziller, 1961).

[17] See, for example, H. Stuart Hughes, *An Approach to Peace, and Other Essays* (New York: Atheneum, 1962).

should be conditional on the other side's reciprocation: "A second round of concessions is not initiated until the first round has been reciprocated. But no negotiations are held to assure reciprocation or to determine its scope."[18]

Other experimentalists, who believe in the intrinsic value of unilateral disarmament, would carry the experiment to its conclusion regardless of whether the Soviets reciprocated or not. Thus Mulford Sibley writes:

> If . . . preliminary agreements were not forthcoming within a reasonable period (six months, for example), the government would proceed with its planned unilateralist policy. . . .
> Once launched there would be no hope for success apart from a continuing determination to see things out to the finish and never go back to the prison house of nuclear deterrence.[19]

Underlying the proposals of the experimentalists is the assumption that the differences that have divided East and West for the past twenty years are no longer obstacles to peace. The sources of the Cold War, whatever they may have been, are no longer important. Each superpower is equally responsible for the struggle in which both are locked; and, incidentally, some Western writers assign far more blame to the United States.

Uri Bronfenbrenner is of the opinion that past and present tensions and stresses in Soviet life provide fertile ground for the growth of antagonistic feelings toward, and fears of, the West: "Is the defensive intent of our rearmament as unmistakable to the Russians as it is to us? Our own difficulties in attempting to appraise dispassionately the meaning of Russian acts and intentions should suggest the possibility of Soviet misinterpretation."[20] Presumably, the same fundamental fears and desires motivate both Americans and Russians. Neither John nor Ivan has the slightest interest in going to war, but each may be convinced of the other's warlike

[18] Amitai Etzioni, *The Hard Way to Peace: A New Strategy* (New York: Crowell-Collier, 1962), p. 95.

[19] Mulford Sibley, *Unilateral Initiatives and Disarmaments* (Philadelphia: American Friends Service Committee, 1962), pp. 19–28, cited in Robert A. Levine, *The Arms Debate* (Cambridge, Mass.: Harvard University Press, 1963), p. 57.

[20] Uri Bronfenbrenner, "Secrecy: A Basic Tenet of the Soviets," *The New York Times Magazine*, April 22, 1962, p. 7.

intent.[21] The United States–Soviet conflict, according to such interpretations, is based upon misunderstanding of each other's policies and intentions; and we Americans must therefore take the initiative in developing mutual trust.

Dimensions of Military Stability

A common theme of the arms control debate is that both the United States and the Soviet Union would find it mutually advantageous to seek a "stable military balance" or "stable arms deterrence." This would be reached by creating "invulnerable strategic forces" at some finite level of offensive power sufficient to deter aggression but incapable of destroying each other's urban-industrial centers.

Arms control experts do not agree on what separates military stability from military instability. According to Lewis F. Richardson, a proponent of the instability theory of the causes of war, mutual fears fanned by mutually stimulating arms races lead to conflict. Richardson relies on a combined psychological-mathematical methodology to demonstrate this thesis.[22]

Without subscribing to the proposition that every increase in international tensions brings an increase in strategic instability,[23] J. David Singer argues that the arms-tension relationship should be considered in predominantly reciprocal terms. Stability cannot be equated with the absence of tensions, nor instability with their presence. Stability is a function of many complex factors, including quali-

[21] Charles E. Osgood, *An Alternative to War or Surrender* (Urbana, Ill.: University of Illinois Press, 1962), pp. 72–73.

[22] Lewis F. Richardson, *Arms and Insecurity: A Mathematical Study of the Causes and Origins of War* (Chicago: Quadrangle, 1960) and *Statistics of Deadly Quarrels* (Chicago: Quadrangle, 1960). Using such devices as "friendliness-hostility curves" and "reaction coefficients," as well as crude data concerning the arms race of 1908–14 and 1929–39, Richardson concludes that arms races can produce exponential increases in military expenditures and in international tensions until an explosion point (or "system boundary") is reached. He does not insist that war is always the inevitable result of military technological competition.

[23] J. David Singer, *Deterrence, Arms Control and Disarmament* (Columbus, Ohio: Ohio State University Press, 1962), p. 169. Inis L. Claude, Jr., also refers to the "circular problem, in which causes and effects, policies and instruments of policy, revolve in a cycle of interaction and are blurred into indistinguishability."—*Swords into Ploughshares* (New York: Random House, 1956), p. 298.

tative and quantitative aspects of weapons systems, the flow of intelligence about such systems, and the assessments that are made by each side of its own interests and objectives as well as of the interests, objectives, intentions, and behavior of the other side. A tension-ridden world might prove to be highly stable if the side committed to defend the existing order and the processes of peaceful change enjoys a sufficient margin of military superiority to deter war. Conversely, a world that seems deceptively free of tensions could suddenly become unstable if an expansionist state, tempted by a technological break-through or by the other side's complacency, should decide to threaten a strategic attack. Such a potential move is ignored by authors who have attempted to apply Richardson's theory to the present confrontation between the United States and the Soviet Union.[24] They overlook the fact that in military capabilities, the United States requires a large safety margin over the Soviets simply because U.S. second-strike policy concedes to the adversary the choice of place, time, and method of presenting a nuclear challenge.

The idea of stability in the field of military strategy is vastly complicated by political and psychological factors. The notion of stable balance implies some sort of parity of forces. The United States has sought to reach agreement with the Soviet Union on limiting the number of strategic delivery vehicles (or the total number of strategic missiles, whether offensive or defensive) to be retained by each side.[25] But any scheme of mathematical equality does not take into account strategic asymmetries favoring one side or the other.

Agreements and Negotiations

Some of the ideas developed by the arms control scholars have been incorporated into proposals advanced for negotiations by the United States. Since mid-1963, the United States and the Soviet Union

---

[24] See, for example, Kenneth Boulding, *Conflict and Defense: A General Theory* (New York: Harper & Brothers, 1962), pp. 25–40; and Karl W. Deutsch and J. David Singer, "Multipolar Power Systems and International Stability," *World Politics*, April, 1964.

[25] In his message to the opening session of the Eighteen Nation Disarmament Committee Conference in Geneva, January, 1964, President Johnson proposed the exploration of "a verified freeze of the number and characteristics of strategic nuclear offensive and defensive vehicles."—*Washington Post*, January 19, 1964.

have formally agreed to three arms control measures: the installation of the Moscow-Washington "hot line" for emergency communications, the 1963 test-ban treaty, and the United Nations resolution prohibiting orbital bombs or weapons of mass destruction in outer space. Early in 1964, President Johnson unilaterally ordered a 25 per cent cutback in the production of fissionable materials in the United States. This was followed in April, 1964, by two simultaneous announcements: The U.S. would further reduce the production of plutonium by an additional 20 per cent between 1966 and 1968; and the U.S.S.R. would cancel the scheduled construction of two plutonium-producing reactors.

The synchronism of the announcements may have created an unwarranted impression of a bilateral arms control accord, which did not conform to the apparent facts of the situation. In view of repeated U.S. assertions that some kind of on-site inspection is needed to verify a cessation in nuclear production, those who claim that the Soviets are reducing their production of fissionable material rely more on the veracity of Soviet declarations than on any concrete proof. In fact, there is some evidence that Soviet production of fissionable materials has expanded rather than diminished.[26] But there is little evidence that the Soviets have slowed down the pace of their advanced weapons research and development in the interest of arms control or arms stability. Nevertheless, the United States has continued to cut back its production of fissionable materials for nuclear weapons:

> On or about July 1, the Atomic Energy Commission will shut down another of its large plutonium production reactors at Hanford, Washington. This will bring to five the number of production reactors that have been closed by the United States since 1964. In contrast to the earlier shutdown, however, the Administration played the latest move in . . . low key, with no direct appeal to the Soviet Union to follow the example of the United States.[27]

Arms control appears to hold much less interest for Soviet policymakers than it has held for their American counterparts in recent years.[28] With the testing of thermonuclear warheads of fifty mega-

[26] See Senator Henry M. Jackson's statements to this effect in the Chalmers Roberts column, *Washington Post*, November 24, 1965, p. 7.

[27] *The New York Times*, January 25, 1967, p. 9.

[28] See the Introduction by Herbert S. Dinerstein, Leon Gouré, and Thomas W. Wolfe to the English translation of *Soviet Military Strategy*, ed. V. D. Sokolovskii (Englewood Cliffs, N.J.: Prentice-Hall, 1963), p. 77.

tons and larger in the fall of 1961, Soviet policy-makers moved in a
direction diametrically opposed to the one prescribed by the overwhelming majority of U.S. arms control analysts. Soviet arms
strategists generally avoid the use of such terms as "overkill," "stability," "parity," "finite deterrence," and "avoidance of cities," for, if
anything, they are interested in achieving deterrence by making the
prospect of a nuclear exchange as devastating as possible.[29]

In international negotiations, Soviet diplomats repeatedly branded
arms control as a capitalist deception on the grounds that it pre-
supposed the continued existence and manipulation of armaments
rather than their total abolition.[30] Since 1962, the Soviets have begun
to show a greater interest in certain partial arms control measures
that are consistent with their own objectives. At the 1964 conference
of the Eighteen Nation Disarmament Committee, the Soviets proposed measures that might reduce their military disadvantages or
effect political discords in the Western alliance.[31]

In view of the Soviets' ability to surprise the West with technological achievements, the present Soviet attitude toward arms control
requires some scrutiny. Thus far, the Soviets have rejected any international inspection of their own territory. From time to time, for
purposes of diplomatic bargaining, Soviet negotiators have paid lip
service to the principle of international inspection; but there is no

---

[29] "The Government which puts the bigger force in the first blow will more
quickly pave the way to victory."—Lieutenant Colonel E. Rybkin, "On the
Nature of World Nuclear-Rocket War," *Kommunist vooruzhennykh sil* (*Communist of the Armed Forces*), September, 1965, p. 54; unpublished English
translation by Harriet Fast Scott.

[30] See S. Yefimov, "Disarmament or the Arms Race?", *International Affairs*,
February, 1962, p. 3.

[31] On January 28, 1964, Semyon Tsarapkin, Soviet delegate at the ENDC
talks in Geneva, proposed these nine collateral measures for discussion: (1)
withdrawal of foreign troops from the territories of other countries; (2) reduction of the total numbers of the armed forces of states; (3) reduction of military
budgets by 10–15 per cent; (4) conclusion of a nonaggression pact between
NATO and the Warsaw Pact countries; (5) establishment of denuclearized
zones, especially in Central Europe but also in other regions of the world; (6)
prevention of the further spread of nuclear weapons, particularly to Germany;
(7) measures to prevent surprise attack (specifically, an exchange of observers
between the two opposing groups) provided that this can be linked to such
measures as the reduction of foreign troops in Europe and an agreement not to
station nuclear weapons in East and West Germany; (8) elimination of bomber
aircraft; and (9) prohibition of underground nuclear tests, with reliance on
national detection capabilities rather than on international inspection.

tangible evidence that the U.S.S.R. was any closer to accepting actual international inspection in 1966 than it was in 1946.

U.S. arms control policy-makers and analysts, worried about Soviet sensitivities on the subject of "espionage by inspection," are currently in favor of relying more heavily on "nonintrusive" forms of verification, such as satellite reconnaissance.[32] Yet, as a matter of fact, the Soviets connect all forms of inspection with intrusion:

> All too often, Americans echo the linkage, using "intrusive inspection" for inspection proper and "nonintrusive inspection" for monitoring. A standard definition of intrusion is "forcing of oneself into a place without right of welcome, the act of wrongfully entering onto property of another." Inspection is defined in lexicons as "the act of examining officially"—and officially means "with authority, with sanction." "Intrusive inspection" is a contradiction in terms and "nonintrusive inspection" a tautology. Both expressions should be banned from U.S. discourse.[33]

But verification without inspection is not sufficiently reliable given the risks resulting from possible violations. Great advances have been made in orbital surveillance, but the Soviets are as aware of its limitations as is the United States. They might consider this type of surveillance less objectionable than "intrusive" methods of inspection only because it is less damaging to Soviet strategic secrecy.

The absence of any inspection provision in the ban on orbital bombs in space was a cause for some misgiving, and the November, 1965, Soviet statement that it possessed an orbital bomb was no consolation. From 1960 to 1963, whenever arms control strategists discussed the possibility of a prohibition against orbital weapons, most of them took it for granted that such a prohibition would entail prelaunch inspection. Nevertheless, the U.N. resolution of October, 1963, contained nothing more than a verbal pledge of mutual self-restraint. Because of the danger of satellite weapons and the difficulties of policing a ban on such weapons, President Johnson announced on September 17, 1964,[34] that the United States had developed two antisatellite systems.

[32] See Leonard S. Rodberg, "Graduated Access Inspection," *Journal of Arms Control*, April, 1963; and Lincoln P. Bloomfield, "The Politics of Administering Disarmament," *Disarmament and Arms Control*, Autumn, 1963.
[33] Charles Burton Marshall, *Cuba: Thoughts Prompted by the Crisis* (Washington, D.C.: Washington Center of Foreign Policy Research, 1963), p. 19.
[34] *The New York Times*, September 18, 1964, p. 1.

Whatever apprehensions the United States may have about Soviet orbital bombs, in December, 1966, President Johnson announced that a treaty had been agreed upon by the United States and the Soviet Union and other members of the United Nations to ensure that outer space will be used solely for peaceful purposes.[35] The President described this treaty (ratified April 20, 1967, by an 88-to-0 Senate vote, after perfunctory debate) as "the most important arms control development since the test-ban treaty in 1963." Unlike the test-ban treaty, however, the treaty on outer space was not preceded by years of public discussion and was passed with almost no debate.

Many of the regulations of the treaty that govern the exploration and the use of space are desirable, such as those making the moon off limits for military activity and those dealing with "freedom of scientific investigation," the health and welfare of astronauts, and the legal responsibilities of states for their space activities. However, certain of the space treaty's articles should have received closer scrutiny. For example, the term "outer space," which is introduced in the first article and which is employed frequently throughout the treaty, is nowhere defined. In the future, the boundaries between inner and outer space could become very obscure, for already the X-15 aircraft climbs to more than 50 miles above the earth's surface.

Article III states that parties to the treaty shall carry on their space activities "in accordance with international law, including the charter of the United Nations." Yet, who has determined what principles of international law, if any, apply to outer space except those embodied in this treaty? Unless these principles are clearly spelled out, certain presumed principles of international law might someday be invoked against American space activities.

The most crucial article of the proposed space treaty is Article IV, which follows:

> States parties to the treaty undertake not to place in orbit around the earth any objects carrying nuclear weapons or any other kinds of weapons of mass destruction, install such weapons on celestial bodies, or station such weapons in outer space in any other manner.
>
> The moon and other celestial bodies shall be used by all states parties to the treaty exclusively for peaceful purposes. The establish-

[35] For text of treaty, see *The New York Times,* December 9, 1966, p. 18.

ment of military bases, installations and fortifications, the testing of any type of weapons and the conduct of military maneuvers on celestial bodies shall be forbidden. The use of military personnel for scientific research or for any other peaceful purposes shall not be prohibited. The use of any equipment or facility necessary for peaceful exploration of the moon and other celestial bodies shall also not be prohibited.

This article prohibits weapons of mass destruction from being orbited, installed on celestial bodies, or stationed otherwise in space, but it does not prevent other military weapons from being carried into space. For example, a laser beam emitted from a space station may prove to be a feasible way of shooting down reconnaissance satellites. With respect to the prohibited weapons, there are no inspection provisions in the treaty to make certain that they will not be employed. The only effective method that could be relied upon to prevent weapons of mass destruction from being carried by a space vehicle is a system of prelaunch inspections reciprocally conducted by the space powers. Long-range surveillance systems that would reduce the possibilities of space "cheating" may be developed. As of now, however, there is no known method of external surveillance for detecting the presence of a nuclear warhead at long distance. On a matter of such security importance, some type of inspection system is necessary, and it should be a highly reliable one. Article IV also prohibits the testing of any type of weapon or the conduct of military maneuvers on celestial bodies. At the same time, the treaty paradoxically permits the use of military personnel for scientific research and other peaceful purposes.

Article XVI states that any party to the treaty may withdraw from the treaty one year after written notification of its intent to withdraw is given. The test-ban treaty required only three months' notice. In view of the possible exploitation of space for military advantage, shorter withdrawal time would have been equally desirable for the space treaty.

As previously mentioned, in 1964 President Johnson proposed a verified freeze on the nature and number of strategic nuclear offensive and defensive vehicles. The proposal, which at first glance seems to present a sensible approach to the limitation of armaments, exemplifies the difficulties met in assessing implications of arms control for the strategic posture of the United States. It is based on the position that there can be no substantial disarmament until production of strategic weapons is brought to a halt, for it is senseless to dismantle some weapons while others of equal or greater destructive power are still being manufactured.

In describing the purpose of the freeze, the Canadian representative at the Eighteen Nation Disarmament Committee meeting stated that "between the phase of building up armaments and the hoped-for phase of reducing armaments, there has to be a point of time at which you stop—like changing the movement of a motorcar from forward to backward.[36] The U.S. delagate, William C. Foster, clarified the President's proposal by saying that it should include strategic missiles, aircraft, and antiballistic-missile systems. The immediate objective of the freeze would be to maintain at constant levels the quantities of strategic nuclear vehicles held by the United States and the U.S.S.R. The agreement would provide for a suitable number of missile tests without warheads to check on the reliability of missile systems over a period of time, and it would permit the production of replacements on a 1:1 basis without making it possible for either side to increase an established force level.

The freeze would also forestall the development and deployment of significant new types of strategic vehicles. Halting efforts to improve strategic vehicles (to carry larger warheads) would thus spell the end of not only the quantitative but also the qualitative arms race. It is not clear, however, to what extent the freeze would be related to the U.S.S.R.'s so-called bomber-bonfire proposal, which was frequently discussed at Geneva during the 1964 negotiations: The Soviets were arguing that all manned bombers were obsolete and hence should be abolished.[37] At the present time, the destruction of all bombers would appreciably reduce the total megatonnage-delivery capability of the United States and thus represent a radical step toward U.S. disarmament.

Antiballistic-missile Defense: To Ban or to Build?

President Johnson's suggestion that the freeze should include antimissile systems appears to be in line with the view of some arms

[36] *Department of State Bulletin,* March 2, 1964, p. 351.
[37] *Washington Post,* January 29, 1964, and March 20, 1964.

control specialists that defense is provocative. A report prepared for the 1965 White House Conference on International Cooperation reflected such views and recommended that the United States and the Soviet Union should agree—"explicitly or tacitly—to a moratorium of at least three years on new development . . . of systems for ballistic-missile defense"[38] As of 1967, no Geneva agreement had been reached on any of the various freeze proposals.

The case against U.S. deployment of an ABM system was formulated by Jeremy Stone in his book *Containing the Arms Race*. Stone's major assumption is: "If the probability of war is sufficiently low and the cost of defenses sufficiently high, if the value placed on a stable strategic situation is sufficiently high and the need for further improvement in our strategic superiority sufficiently low, it might be well to consider ways of preventing or inhibiting, by treaty or otherwise, the development or procurement of defenses."[39] In support of this assumption, Stone argues that "active defense seems impotent compared to the powers of the strategic offense; . . . the development of a very effective defense is likely to be pernicious, destabilizing, and dangerous."[40] He also contends that "defenses are at present expensive, and no one expects them to be very effective." Furthermore, it is easier to inspect defenses under some kind of arms control arrangement.[41] Stone believes the deployment of an ABM would precipitate a qualitative or quantitative arms race in offensive weapons[42] and that an ABM would "impede progress toward arms limitation or reductions."[43]

Richard B. Foster, a strategic analyst who focuses on the offensive-defensive interaction, charged that the kinds of arguments advanced by Stone and others were "invalid for six principal reasons":

First, they are based on an assumption that there is, at present, an "arms race" between the United States and the Soviet Union. Second, they fail to take fully into account publicly expressed Soviet attitudes to-

[38] National Citizen's Commission on International Cooperation, *Report of the Committee on Arms Control and Disarmament*, prepared for the White House Conference on International Cooperation, 1965, as reprinted by the United Nations Association of the United States of America.

[39] Stone, *op. cit.*, p. 25.

[40] *Ibid.*, p. 21.

[41] *Ibid.*, p. 25.

[42] *Ibid.*, p. 55.

[43] *Ibid.*, p. 57.

ward BMD. Third, they ignore the fact that in the next two decades there will be an increasing Nth Country threat to both the U.S. and the U.S.S.R., which, given long lead times, the two major powers must take into account now in their strategic planning. Fourth, in maintaining that BMD would be destabilizing, they disregard some of the basic elements constituting strategic stability. Fifth, they take inadequate account of the probable impact of changing technology on the future strategic offensive and strategic defensive force structures of both the U.S. and the U.S.S.R. Finally, they ignore the prospects of BMD for enhancing, rather than disrupting, arms control agreements.[44]

Most of the arguments advanced by Stone, Wiesner, and others against the deployment of an ABM by either the United States or the Soviet Union have been frequently conveyed to the Kremlin to no avail. As the *Washington Post* reported:

> United States officials expect the Soviet Union to begin deploying an anti-missile missile system in one or two years despite U.S. attempts to discourage the plan.
> This assessment has been reached on the basis of new intelligence received in the two months since Secretary of Defense Robert S. McNamara reaffirmed the U.S. decision not to push "all-out" for a counterpart American system.
> The United States made indirect approaches to the Russians, according to informed sources, in an unsuccessful effort to dissuade them from going through with their anti-missile plans.[45]

Even Stone conceded: "In this sense, the ultimate decision whether or not we should buy a defensive system is likely to be made by the Soviets."[46] Paradoxically, the fact that the Soviet Union has already deployed an ABM has not led to a U.S. decision to deploy an ABM system of its own. Such a decision, however, may be made belatedly and reluctantly by the United States in the near future.

The argument that ABM systems are infeasible for technical and practical reasons has not been widely advanced since 1961; if such systems were really impracticable, there would be no apparent need for an agreement to ban them. According to Freeman J. Dyson of the Institute for Advance Study at Princeton University, the race

---

[44] Richard B. Foster, *The Impact of Ballistic Missile Defense on Arms Control Prospects* (Menlo Park, Calif.: Stanford Research Institute, 1966), SSC-RM-ISR-1, p. 1.

[45] *Washington Post*, April 21, 1966, p. 1.

[46] Stone, *op cit.*, p. 38.

between offensive and defensive technology is an incessant one. "If at any time the offense stood still and committed itself to a fixed 'finite deterrence' system, the defense could . . . find means to nullify the offense."[47]

Since the Chinese Communists tested their first nuclear weapon in October, 1964, the argument that the United States should deploy a ballistic-missile defense system to neutralize a future nuclear threat from Peking has gained currency. The argument has merit but is misleading insofar as it conveys the impression that Communist China poses the threat against which the ABM should be developed and deployed. On the contrary, an ABM is more urgently needed to counter the growing Soviet ICBM arsenal. Because the United States would not raise the first strike against the Soviet Union, it can be argued that the United States needs to possess an ABM capability—a defense vital for surviving a missile attack by the Soviet Union.

If the United States should outstrip the Soviet Union in developing and deploying antimissile missiles, the U.S. deterrent would probably remain as effective for the next fifteen or twenty years as it has been for the last fifteen. Conversely, if there is a reduction in strategic missiles, combined with a "go slow" policy in the development and deployment of antimissile weapons in the United States and an accelerated program in the Soviet Union, the U.S. deterrent will undergo major devaluation.

Whether or not we can, or should, reach a freeze agreement with the Soviets on ballistic-missile defense is a question that illustrates the role of the Pentagon in arms control. The Soviets are acquiring a capability for a ballistic-missile defense; it may become an extensive capability. If the United States does *not* deploy an ABM, the relative *status quo* at the time of a freeze agreement would put this country at a strategic disadvantage. On the other hand, if the United States sought to persuade the Soviets to dismantle their ABM's, the Soviets would undoubtedly not concur unless the United States relinquished something of comparable strategic value in exchange. Lacking a deployed ABM system, our diplomatic bargaining position has already been weakened.

[47] "Defense Against Ballistic Missiles," *Bulletin of the Atomic Scientists,* June, 1964, p. 14.

The fear of destabilization may be a factor in U.S. reluctance to deploy an ABM system or initiate an adequate civil-defense program. Presumably, destabilization ensues from changes made in the strategic-force structure, either offensive or defensive—changes that tend to upset the balance of forces existing at any given time. Soviet strategists seem to devote little time to such sophisticated arguments. Apparently, they do not regard defense capabilities as either provocative or destabilizing, believing instead that a government should provide for the defense and safety of its people and property. Soviet General Talenskii has written:

> It is said that the international strategic situation cannot be stable where both sides simultaneously strive toward deterrence through nuclear rocket power and the creation of defensive antimissile systems.
> I cannot agree with this view either. From the standpoint of strategy, powerful deterrent forces and an effective antimissile defense system, when taken together, substantially increase the stability of mutual deterrence, for any partial shifts in the qualitative and quantitative balance of these two component elements of mutual deterrence tend to be correspondingly compensated and equalized.[48]

During a February, 1967, visit to London, Premier Kosygin held a press conference in which he reiterated long-held Soviet views on disarmament in general and ABM defenses in particular. When asked whether a build-up of a Soviet antimissile defense system was a new step in the arms race, Kosygin responded as follows:

> It seems to me that the system that warns of an attack is not a factor in the arms race. On the contrary, it is a factor that reduces the possibility of the destruction of people.
> That is why I think it is a mistake to look at this question the way some people do.
> According to some theories that are gaining ground in the world, the question is posed in the following way: Which is cheaper, to destroy man, that is, to have an offensive weapon that destroys people, cities, entire states, or to have a weapon that prevents such destruction?
> According to these theories, the cheaper system should be adopted. As you know, in some countries they figure in arming the country how much it costs to kill a person—$1,500,000 or $100,000.

[48] "Antimissile Systems and Disarmament," *Bulletin of the Atomic Scientists,* February, 1965, p. 28.

The antimissile system probably costs more than an offensive weapon. But these questions are unrelated.

You see, there are other ways of solving this problem, more serious ways that would really help mankind.

You know that we favor altogether a ban of nuclear weapons and nuclear stockpiles. We are ready to do so not because we have little of them, but probably because we have a lot of them. And we think that mankind has no need for nuclear weapons.[49]

This expression of Soviet military doctrine on the advantages of a defensive system, combined with the propagandistic Soviet position that all nuclear weapons should be abolished (without any system of verification), should give pause to those who believe that the Soviets can be persuaded to give up the ABM system they have already developed. In short, unless the Soviet Union is willing to make mutual concessions and—in Walt Rostow's phrase—"bite the bullet of inspection," overlapping interests in the realm of disarmament remain a theory and not a fact.

Prospects for Arms Control

No sweeping judgment can be made about particular arms control measures either contributing to or detracting from U.S. national security. Some forms of arms control may be desirable; other forms may not. Measures that genuinely reduce the possibilities of war by accident, strategic miscalculation, or uncontrolled escalation are worth pursuing.[50] Much can be accomplished in this area through our own unilateral decisions based on intelligent military planning. The creation of highly reliable systems of command, control, and communications; the development of credible decision-making arrangements among the Western allies; and the ability to communicate unambiguously our defensive intentions to the adversary—these are directions much more persuasive than downgrading the quality of military technology on which the Western deterrent depends.

The greatest danger that arms control poses to U.S. security lies in the possibility that a series of partial measures may generate a

---

[49] *The New York Times*, February 10, 1967, p. 13.

[50] For an excellent proposal combining arms control measures with the means of enhancing their effectiveness, see John R. Raser's "Weapons Design and Arms Control: The Polaris Example," *The Journal of Conflict Resolution*, IX, No. 4 (December, 1965).

euphoric atmosphere of *détente*. This could slacken the national R&D effort long before it has been definitely established that the Soviet Union subscribes to ideas of arms control compatible with the West's. Perhaps no single measure, whether unilateral or bilateral, will jeopardize totally the national security; but a number of factors taken together—the test-ban treaty, an agreement to destroy obsolete bombers, a freeze on strategic delivery vehicles, a modest reduction of military budgets—might very well superimpose subtle restraints that could seriously affect U.S. efforts in weapons development. A vague "feeling" that the arms race is leveling off is no substitute for proof that both sides are throttling down their efforts in the field of advanced weapons technology.

If the United States really wants to reach sound reciprocal arms control agreements with the Soviet Union, it should face the records of history, for rarely has disarmament been a symmetrical undertaking. More often than not, arms control measures have been negotiated under some kind of duress or threat of sanction rather than by a mutual desire to disarm.

In this light, arms control can more usefully be an adjunct of defense planning. For example, invulnerable offensive systems force the opposite side to develop a capability for retaliating effectively, thereby reducing the danger posed by hidden stock piles in violation of disarmament agreements. Consequently, the problem of hidden stock piles—of crucial importance a decade ago—has become less important as a result of the Department of Defense decision to create a relatively invulnerable strategic-missile force.

Paradoxically, the intensified U.S. effort to reach a series of arms control agreements with the Soviet Union has been prompted by new uncertainties growing from the recent period of offensive-missile ascendancy. A few years ago, a general nuclear war was universally assumed to be irrational, since it would inevitably become a mutually suicidal exchange. By the mid-1960's, however, the certainty of mutual annihilation was transformed into uncertainty.[51] New technological developments made possible a two-fisted posture—both an effective ABM defense and a discriminating offensive strategy. Thus,

[51] Richard B. Foster, Stanford Research Institute, is acknowledged as the source of this insight.

the certainty of mutual destruction could be transformed into the possibility of a decisive advantage. But the uncertainties related to recent technological advances are more difficult for some U.S. policy-makers to cope with than was the "mutual-suicide" phase, for in the latter it was often taken for granted that the United States and the Soviet Union would, out of self-interest, eventually disarm. Other U.S. policy-makers seem to want to reach arms control agreements before the unsettling effects of the technological revolution of the mid-1960's are too widely understood.

Unfortunately, there is no easy way of safely putting a nuclear Pandora back into her box. Despite the hot line, the communication gap between Moscow and Washington is as wide as it ever was. Premier Kosygin told James Reston in December, 1965: "The next few years will set the pattern for the next 10 to 15 years. One prospect is for the arms race and the increase in military budgets.

"It is the United States which is setting the military tone and whipping up military psychoses. It is of your doing, this generating of tensions in the world."[52]

Such views dampen the prospects for a meaningful arms control agreement between the United States and the Soviet Union, but negotiations will continue despite the slim chance for their success. The two chief items on the arms control agenda for 1967 were the space treaty, already discussed, and the anti-proliferation treaty, whose implications will be discussed in the next chapter.

Otherwise, arms control as well as disarmament efforts appeared to be in the doldrums. The impasse was typified in the announcement of the British journal *Disarmament and Arms Control* that it was suspending publication:

> At present there are no new ideas coming forward and very little comment on the old ones. . . . The sort of people who write in this journal have done all they can. Furthermore, Soviet cooperation at the editorial level has not been forthcoming, nor has distribution in Eastern Europe. With China, no meaningful contact has been established at all. So it continued for three years as an international journal for the exchange of ideas among Western and neutral countries.[53]

[52] *The New York Times,* December 8, 1965, p. 20.
[53] Letter to subscribers of *Disarmament and Arms Control* from Wayland Young, editor, March 21, 1966.

Despite the current drought in arms control ideas, there still appears to be far greater intellectual activity directed toward achieving security by arms control than toward gaining security by sound strategic analysis. National security remains a problem, and the endeavor to reconcile arms control measures with the desiderata for retaining United States strategic superiority continues.

7

NATO in the Face of *Détente*

The Soviet Union seeks the fruits of expansion while minimizing the risks of nuclear war. The United States looks for a way to defend itself and its allies without resorting to nuclear conflict. But this difference need not stifle the search for arms control agreements to ease the arms race. Those who believe that the United States and the U.S.S.R. share an overriding interest in avoiding nuclear war also hold that relations between the two nuclear superpowers are being transformed from a competition to a cooperation. Even if the contention were true under all circumstances, there is still that significant difference in approach. In a sense, then, the current strategic debate is an exploration of the extent to which Soviet–U.S. cooperation is feasible in nuclear matters.

Today, although few analysts maintain that the Soviets will ever launch a calculated nuclear attack against the United States,[1] there is little evidence that either the United States or the Soviet Union is as yet willing to relinquish the threat of nuclear conflict, which safeguards their respective vital interests. The North Atlantic Treaty Organization provides a guarantee to the Europeans and a warning to the Soviets that the United States is prepared to use its strategic power to foil Communist ambitions in Western Europe. NATO links the security of Western Europe with that of North America.

The Soviet Union has long sought to divide the Atlantic Alliance and ultimately would like to break the links between the United States and Western Europe. Of all the forces nurturing an alliance, the most important is the protection that the alliance can provide. If the effectiveness of deterrence is demonstrated, if each challenge can be met as it occurs, and if resolve can be communicated to ally and

---

[1] It would be imprudent, however, to ignore the possibility. See Chester Ward, "The 'New Myths' and 'Old Realities' of Nuclear War," *Orbis*, Summer, 1964, pp. 255–91.

adversary alike, then allies' confidence in the alliance—a precondition for cohesion—will be met.

Despite NATO's remarkable initial success in achieving its founder's objectives, some of its members began to question the relevance of the alliance to their security needs as the strategic gap between the United States and the Soviet Union narrowed. Relations among the members of NATO are incredibly complex, and many factors are responsible for NATO's current disarray, particularly the Europeans' strong desire to move from dependence on the United States to partnership with it. Yet, at the risk of oversimplification, the heart of the discord within NATO appears to be the fear that the United States would not fulfill its treaty obligations in the event of a Soviet attack upon Europe if to do so might result in the destruction of American cities. In fact, many Europeans believe that the U.S. endeavor to achieve a nuclear *détente* with the Soviet Union is an attempt to escape from this country's explicit pledge to defend Western Europe with nuclear weapons. Because of the fundamental relation between U.S strategy and alliance cohesion, the future of NATO depends to a great extent on the strategic decisions of U.S. policy-makers. Many thorny political and economic issues confront the NATO allies, but the strategic facet of transatlantic relations bears most directly on world security and peace.

NATO's Discord over Deterrence

Since NATO's own conventional-force strength has always been inadequate to the task of meeting a Soviet attack, U.S. forces in Europe have served as an assurance that the United States would strike the Soviet Union if a massive Soviet attack were launched against Western Europe. Despite periodic calls over the years for enhanced conventional forces, European nations have not raised troops capable of parrying a Soviet thrust into Western Europe without calling on the aid of U.S. strategic power.

After the Soviets acquired intercontinental ballistic missiles, progressive changes took place in the U.S. strategic position vis-à-vis the Soviet Union. Top U.S. officials frequently, often publicly, reappraised the U.S. role in the defense of Europe, naturally provoking concern among Europeans, who had almost taken for granted the U.S. commitment to defend them with nuclear weapons.

One of General de Gaulle's first orders of business after his return to power in 1958 was to announce that France would build its own nuclear deterrent force.[2] To many Americans, the French desire for a national deterrent force seemed quixotic. France, with but a handful of Mirage bombers and a small stock pile of nuclear weapons, could not hope to deter the Soviet Union. President de Gaulle justified French efforts to acquire a nuclear deterrent by expressing doubts that the United States would risk its own destruction to come to Europe's defense. After 1961, U.S. preference for increased conventional capabilities in Western Europe strengthened de Gaulle's position, for most European members of NATO do not see the necessity for large ground forces but instead regard a strong nuclear deterrent as the best assurance against Soviet attack.

President Kennedy outlined his administration's approach to NATO strategy in a speech in Ottawa on May 17, 1961. After declaring that the military balance of power had been altered since the founding of the alliance, he offered the following military advice to NATO: "First, we must strengthen the conventional capability of our alliance as a matter of the highest priority. Second, we must make certain that nuclear weapons will continue to be available for the defense of the entire treaty area." One analyst, in commenting on European reactions to changes in U.S. strategy, suggested:

> It was doubtful that the nonnuclear buildup, on which the President and his advisors set great store, would receive enthusiastic support. And the Administration's known aversion to any further diffusion of nuclear weapons was unlikely to win any popularity contests among government leaders in France, Germany and Italy.[3]

In the Ottawa speech, President Kennedy proposed a solution for the NATO nuclear dilemma that was essentially the same as that of the Eisenhower Administration: "We look to the possibility of eventually establishing a NATO sea-borne missile force, which would be truly multilateral in ownership and control, if this should be desired and found feasible by our allies once NATO's nonnuclear goals have been achieved."

The Kennedy Administration simultaneously disparaged the na-

---

[2] The French nuclear program had its origins, however, in the Fourth Republic.

[3] William Kaufman, *The McNamara Strategy* (New York: Harper & Row, 1964), pp. 104–5.

tional nuclear forces that France and Britain were striving to develop or maintain. Secretary of Defense McNamara claimed these forces were almost valueless for deterrence, since a major antagonist could take a variety of measures to counter them. "Indeed, if a major antagonist came to believe there was a substantial likelihood of it being used independently, this force would be inviting a pre-emptive first strike against it."[4] Despite the advice of the United States, both France and Great Britain continued to develop their national nuclear forces. The United States assisted the efforts of the British but not those of the French. In December, 1962, the United States announced plans to abandon development of the Skybolt air-to-surface missile by which the British strategic bomber force would have been given a long lease on life. In its place, the United States offered to equip a British nuclear-submarine force with Polaris missiles. Subsequently, the multilateral-nuclear-force concept (MLF) was shifted from submarines to surface ships.

Western Europeans did not react favorably to the proposals of the Kennedy Administration and rejected its call for more conventional capabilities. Moreover, they appeared to doubt the sincerity of U.S. proposals for greater European participation in nuclear forces; the MLF seemed to offer the illusion of control over nuclear weapons without the substance. Few European countries, with the exception of the Federal Republic of Germany, showed any marked interest in the MLF. When the United States practically abandoned interest in the concept in 1965, the prospects for any kind of combined NATO or Western European deterrent became dim.[5]

[4] Robert S. McNamara, commencement speech, University of Michigan, Ann Arbor, Michigan, June 16, 1962, cited in Department of Defense news release No. 980-62.

[5] The ironic finishing touch to the MLF was the U.S. offer to cosponsor a resolution put forward by the Soviet Union in the General Assembly that was generally considered to be directed against the U.S.-proposed Western multilateral nuclear force. The resolution would have the Assembly urgently request all countries "to refrain from all actions which may hamper the attainment of an agreement" against the spread of nuclear weapons. U.S. Deputy Ambassador James M. Nabrit, Jr., told the Assembly's steering committee: "We find much to commend in this draft resolution, and my delegation would not only be able to support it but we would also be able to cosponsor it, and we hope that members of the committee would also be willing to consider cosponsorship."—*New York Herald Tribune,* Paris, September 26, 1966, p. 3.

In advocating a multilateral force, the United States was motivated partly by political reasons; originally, the MLF was designed not to meet a military need but to discourage European national nuclear forces. Washington found itself in the position of insisting that its existing nuclear forces were capable of deterring an attack against Western Europe while concurrently advocating the development of the MLF. This inconsistency was not overlooked by most Europeans, particularly General de Gaulle.

The French criticism of U.S. strategy for NATO was presented by Premier Georges Pompidou before the French National Assembly in April, 1966.[6] In summary, he stated that one of the few important steps ever taken by the NATO Council was the adoption in the mid-1950's of a strategic doctrine calling for immediate atomic retaliation against any major aggression from the East. This concept, which since then had been the official NATO strategy, was unilaterally being discarded by the United States in favor of a strategy of flexible response. The French therefore assumed that the United States was adopting a flexible response to lessen its own risk of war in the event that a conflict were to erupt in Europe. It appeared that by attempting to limit the area of initial combat operations, the United States was trying to spare the territory of the only conceivable aggressor, the Soviet Union, as a way of safeguarding its own territory. Such an idea was based on the assumption that a war in Europe could remain localized between the Atlantic and the eastern Polish frontier. But this area, the core of Europe, would be doomed to destruction. Thus, for the Europeans, the danger of this lay in the fact that the Soviets could seize Western Europe without fearing retaliation.

The French have never believed that the conventional forces of the alliance, which alone were integrated, could be sure of halting an attack from the East. The often-repeated U.S. preference for employing a conventional defense for Western Europe has been another primary source of European anxiety. According to Premier Pompidou:

[6] The full text of the statements by Premier Georges Pompidou before the French National Assembly on April 13 and April 20, 1966, supplied by the French Embassy, Service de Presse et d'Information, 972 Fifth Avenue, New York, N.Y.

Such a strategy risks dooming us [the French] to atomic bombardment first, to invasion next. It occupies the integrated general staffs with planning operations of the most superannuated type, in which we would indeed risk being defeated. Does it not perpetuate the error committed by William II in 1914, made by Hitler in 1939, which is to imagine that a war in Europe can be "localized" and that once the immediate objectives were attained, the conflict can be negotiated and halted?[7]

Since tactical atomic weapons are under American control, whether they would be used to stop a major aggression at the border between West and East Germany is also widely debated in Europe. Aware of European apprehensions on this issue, American officials stress the number of warheads stock-piled in Western Europe: "Secretary of Defense Robert S. McNamara told a North Atlantic Treaty Organization working party today that the United States now had about 7,000 nuclear warheads in inventory for NATO forces in Europe. This, he said, is an increase of more than 100 per cent since 1961."[8] But the European members of NATO, knowing that these weapons are under tightly centralized U.S. control, are far less concerned about numbers of warheads than about the willingness of the United States to use these weapons in a critical emergency.

The French want the United States to apply to all of NATO the same deterrence concept that guides the U.S. strategic confrontation with the Soviet Union. The rationale behind deterrence is that the best guarantee against aggression is the would-be aggressor's conviction that he would suffer intolerable retaliatory losses. This strategy justifies maintaining both the U.S. and the French nuclear forces, but unfortunately the rationale for U.S. and French cooperation on a deterrence concept for NATO has yet to be devised.

U.S. Defense of Europe: A Withering Guarantee

In the summer of 1963, President Kennedy assured all of Europe that regardless of the vulnerability of this country to nuclear attack, our strategic forces could be counted on to answer a Soviet attack against Western Europe. Secretary McNamara was reported to have said at the December, 1964, NATO ministerial meetings that "the United States could not make a distinction between a nuclear threat

[7] *Ibid.*
[8] *The New York Times,* September 24, 1966, p. 1.

to Europe and one to America, nor permit the loss of Western Europe in a 'limited' war."[9] But according to Herman Kahn, the situation will change:

> Eventually the U.S. deterrent will decline too much. One or two years ago it was very difficult to convince Americans that Paris was not just like Boston. When President Kennedy went to Berlin and said, "Ich bin ein Berliner," he meant it. It would be difficult for President Johnson to make that comment; he certainly could not say, "Je suis un Parisien." People would laugh at him. In two or three years, given the defense establishment we are procuring, it is going to be very hard to say, "I am a Londoner."[10]

Nevertheless, the United States continues to underscore its commitment to NATO by discouraging the nations of Western Europe from acquiring their own nuclear force or from pooling their efforts to develop a force. Particularly in its opposition to national nuclear forces, U.S. nuclear strategy has been influenced by the desire to prevent nuclear proliferation. The United States officially argues that its strategic force can protect Europe because of the margin of strategic superiority it presently holds over the Soviet Union.

In a number of statements, however, U.S. leaders have indicated that the United States is not prepared to engage in nuclear war over European issues. President Johnson, as well as Presidents Kennedy and Eisenhower, has stated that nuclear war is utterly irrational and hence "impossible." What reconciles these seemingly contradictory statements is the U.S. concept of deterrence, which is almost, but not quite, divorced from war-waging. For a number of reasons, the United States was unable to avoid intervention in World Wars I and II, although it had made no previous commitments. Now pledged to intervene on the European continent, the United States avows to honor its nuclear guarantee even if that means catastrophe for itself; yet, the United States, as well as its European allies, does not anticipate having to fight a nuclear war. This ambivalence causes the United States some difficulties with the Europeans. Although relying on deterrence, the United States has the nagging fear that deterrence might fail. Consequently, in dealing with the Soviets, the United

[9] *The New York Times*, December 17, 1964, p. 2.

[10] Herman Kahn, "Arms Control and Current Arms Environment," in *The Prospects for Arms Control*, ed. James E. Dougherty, with John F. Lehman, Jr. (New York: Mcfadden-Bartell, 1965), p. 47.

States tends to be too apprehensive—or so it appears to many Europeans—lest disagreement grow into a war calling for U.S. protection of Europe.

This paradox strengthens General de Gaulle's misgivings about the U.S. guarantee. He does not fear that the U.S. would refuse to honor its guarantee in the event of Soviet nuclear aggression, for, like U.S. leaders, he is convinced that the Soviets are effectively deterred. Rather, he seems to fear the extent to which the United States might bargain away European interests in its anxiety to prevent nuclear war. The Soviet Union plays on the American fear of a European nuclear war by insisting that war would inevitably result if European disputes, particularly over Berlin and the reunification of Germany, were not settled to Soviet satisfaction. Increasingly, the United States has been more willing than Germany or France to try to negotiate these issues. In fact, most of President Kennedy's difficulties with President de Gaulle and Chancellor Adenauer were a consequence of U.S. discussions with the Soviets during the Berlin crisis of 1961.[11] The Europeans may not be more stubborn than the United States in defending Europe's vital interests, but they define those interests somewhat differently. It is natural that European governments should want to make their own evaluation of their vital interests and, if necessary, at least in the case of France, to develop a nuclear force to protect those interests.

Although in 1965 U.S. strategy appeared to exclude a first-strike posture, McNamara assured U.S. allies at the December, 1964, NATO ministerial meeting that the American nuclear guarantee was unchanged. McNamara apparently was assuming that a Soviet nuclear strike against Europe would be done hand in glove with an attack on the United States—an assumption undoubtedly valid when the U.S. guarantee was backed only by SAC bombers and vulnerable missiles. But the guarantee could not be expected to ring as true after the United States began concentrating on obtaining an exclusive second-strike capability.

[11] "The Atlantic solidarity upon which partnership had to be based repeatedly was strained by the pursuit of other, conflicting objectives—felt to be of overriding importance—such as maintenance of the U.S. nuclear monopoly in the West and unilateral negotiations with Russia."—Robert Kleiman, *Atlantic Crisis* (New York: W. W. Norton, 1964), p. 127.

At the end of 1966, the United States still postponed the decision to deploy an ABM system. If the Soviet Union continues to develop and deploy ABM's, the credibility of the U.S. nuclear guarantee will further decline. This may occur even if the United States and the Soviet Union both acquire antimissile defense systems. Then the United States might have to help the Europeans develop an effective antimissile system suitable to the needs of Western Europe. Otherwise, the limited military utility of the British nuclear force, the French *force de dissuasion,* or any other possible Western European deterrent will have no practical value.

> Europe cannot defend itself against all likely dimensions of threat in the future without an intimate association with the United States. Nor can the United States maintain an effective global deterrence against the Communist bloc without being equally involved in the defense of Europe. . . . The purpose of perfecting NATO's defenses is much less one of staving off an attack, since none appears imminent, than of denying the Communist bloc any profitable political returns from renewed adventuring. Such denial can hasten the transformation of Soviet policies toward the West which is already under way.[12]

The Price of Nonproliferation

To compound the crisis facing NATO, the Soviets have seized upon the West's desire for a nonproliferation agreement and the Western allies' divergence of political interest, the latter making it virtually impossible for the allies to reach agreement on, and to share in, nuclear-weapons control and strategy planning.

The *Committee Report on Arms Control and Disarmament* of the National Citizens' Commission on International Control, chaired by Jerome Wiesner, treats the subjects of *détente* and the NATO alliance thus:

> The search for détente and the loosening of the ties of the Pact in the East has implications for the Western Alliance. The military element in Western relations must not be viewed as central, and accordingly should be given less emphasis. . . .
> The most important contribution that arms restrictions can make

[12] Timothy W. Stanley, *NATO in Transition: The Future of the Atlantic Alliance* (New York: Praeger, 1965), p. 402.

toward peace in Europe lies in measures that signal and encourage détente and help to perpetuate and solidify whatever degree of relaxation can be achieved.[13]

The Educational Committee to Halt Atomic Weapons Spread, which included twelve Nobel laureates, Jerome B. Wiesner, and other notables, chose the eve of Chancellor Erhard's September, 1966, visit to Washington to urge the President to remove "the chief obstacle to a treaty with the Soviet Union" by preventing "the imminent spread of nuclear weapons to nonaligned and neutral powers." The obstacle was defined as "the unresolved issue of U.S. sharing of ownership and control of atomic arms with West Germany through the North Atlantic Treaty Organization."[14] Obviously, Wiesner and his colleagues assigned a higher foreign-policy priority to a *détente* with the Soviet Union—to be advanced by a nonproliferation treaty— than to the preservation of NATO alliance cohesion.

Following Chancellor Erhard's visit, the *Washington Post*, in an editorial entitled "Germany in the Alliance," took a more realistic view:

> No one familiar with the intricacies of the nuclear issue in the alliance could have expected the Germans to respond publicly to demands that they renounce any role in determining the strategy by which they are defended. The thought that this is all that is holding up a nuclear nonproliferation treaty is too naive and simplistic a reading of Soviet objectives in pillorying Germany and attempting to divide the West. . . . It ought to be clear by now that any German decision respecting nuclear participation must be voluntary. That is the only role compatible with equality in the alliance.[15]

Most students of the problem concede that solutions to the nuclear question within NATO should not include the creation of new nuclear forces. One plan envisaged is for the United Kingdom and France to pool their national nuclear forces and place them under control of the Western European Union. Since the Federal Republic of Germany is a member of the Western European Union, it too might eventually participate in a nuclear consortium. If the United States were to share more of its technological know-how with its Eu-

[13] *Committee Report on Arms Control and Disarmament*, prepared for the White House Conference on International Cooperation in 1965, reprinted by the United Nations Association of the United States of America, pp. 22–23.
[14] *The New York Times*, September 15, 1966, p. 1.
[15] *Washington Post*, September 29, 1966, p. A-20.

ropean allies, it might possibly promote such a European nuclear
force. However, the prospects for this happening are slim. Moreover,
many American experts, including Wiesner, oppose the creation of
such a tight European force and would prefer instead

> . . . the "Select Committee" that the Secretary of Defense . . . sug-
> gested in 1965. Such a committee would provide for more involve-
> ment of our Western European allies, especially Germany, Great
> Britain, France (if she so desires) and Italy in the detailed business
> of planning for the Alliance's strategic force. To accept this solution
> the European members of NATO would have to agree that "the U.S.
> nuclear forces *are* the Alliance strategic force."[16]

It is this idea that French Premier Pompidou so forcibly rejected
in his speech to the French Assembly in April, 1966. By that approach, Europe would remain a security ward of the United States;
but many Europeans believe that their dependence on the nuclear
guarantee of a non-European power can lead only to the growing
insecurity of Europeans. They are not worried now about the United
States not using its nuclear weapons should the Soviets launch a
major attack on Europe, because they believe such an attack highly
improbable. They are more concerned about ambiguous military
probes made for political gain. For the defense of the opposing Warsaw Pact area is highly centralized under Soviet command, and the
Soviets have carried on a regular process of modernizing the military
forces of their allies.

The strategy preferred by the United States for defending Europe
against lesser threats would rely primarily on conventional weapons
as long as possible and would keep atomic weapons far back of the
line of combat. The German and French governments, however,
would like the Soviets to face NATO's atomic power as soon as possible and thus to be discouraged from venturing any kind of aggression. As long as NATO remains intact, the European nations may
eventually obtain recognition of their own interests in the alliance
despite the U.S. near monopoly on nuclear forces. However, should
the United States and the U.S.S.R. sign a nonproliferation treaty
that excludes a European nuclear force, the chance of strengthening
NATO could be lost, and the Soviets would gain an indirect voice in
the organization of Western defense. If the people of Western Eu-

[16] *Committee Report on Arms Control and Disarmament, loc. cit.*

rope ever come to believe that the United States has more in common with its Soviet adversary than with its European friends and their security—the heart of alliance policy—NATO would fade away.

U.S. Strategy and NATO's Welfare

Government officials stress the U.S. guarantee to Western Europe and, as evidence of its reliability, point to the troops and the multitude of nuclear weapons stationed on NATO territory.[17] At the same time, the United States deliberately plays down the use of nuclear weapons with the intent of halting their spread. It is claiming on one hand that nuclear weapons are important and on the other that nuclear weapons are not really very useful against most of the threats we might face in Europe. Although both arguments have application, no strategy exists to reconcile them as compatible propositions. Thus, any U.S. effort to freeze the existing nuclear equation by signing a nonproliferation pact implies some kind of working political relationship between the United States and the U.S.S.R., which would destroy the *raison d'être* of NATO.

If NATO should fall by the wayside, the present NATO allies may look elsewhere for their protection. Before permitting such a condition to develop, we should understand that it is the U.S. guarantee that makes it possible for the industrially advanced nonnuclear powers to eschew the acquisition of nuclear weapons. In trying to halt the spread of nuclear weapons through a U.S.-U.S.S.R. agreement, we may instead stimulate their proliferation by having removed the main bulwark for countries such as Germany and Japan—namely, a reliable long-term nuclear commitment from the United States. The Soviets, of course, are aware of this factor and are doing what they can to block it from discussions concerning an antiproliferation treaty.[18]

In sum, an antiproliferation treaty could increase the world-wide security obligations of the United States and provide the Soviet Union with a tool capable of wrecking both the heart and the struc-

[17] See Stanley, *op. cit.*, 262.

[18] "Premier Aleksei N. Kosygin called tonight for a ban on the use of nuclear weapons against countries without such weapons on their territory. Western diplomatic sources said the proposal was new and represented a Soviet attempt to win more support for a treaty against the spread of nuclear weapons."—*The New York Times*, February 3, 1966, p. 1.

ture of NATO. Nevertheless, it is impossible to predict whether the United States will ultimately place a *détente* with the Soviet Union above its role in the Western alliance. In every crisis between the United States and the Soviet Union or Communist China, the Communists have had one common objective: to demonstrate the inability of the United States to defend its own interests or those of its allies. Thus far, the determination of the United States, backed by its ability to withstand a wide range of Soviet threats through strategic superiority, has shielded many nations. Consequently:

> *For the United States to show unsureness and unsteadiness in its perception of the continuing Soviet threat is especially disturbing.* Despite the remarkable recovery of the Western European allies, they do not have, separately or jointly, the strength to counter Soviet pressures. *For the United States to toy with the idea of rapprochement, therefore, is to tempt its allies into unilateral exploration of the possibilities of transforming their relations with the Soviet Union and thus to create new opportunities for Soviet diplomacy to achieve what Soviet arms and pressures have been unable to win* [italics added].[19]

There are many signs indicating that 1966, the year of the French withdrawal from NATO, marked the end of the era of transatlantic cooperation. Even as staunch an advocate of close European-American security ties as Konrad Adenauer viewed the future with deep pessimism. In an interview with C. L. Sulzberger, Adenauer stated: "Europe, after all, is really the most vital area for the U.S.A., neither Latin America nor Asia. If you ignore us there is a chance Russia will succeed in gaining control over both Germany and France. Then we shall all be lost"[20]

During 1966, influential Europeans frequently intimated their lack of confidence in American leadership, strategic wisdom, and sense of political direction. Their disenchantment can be traced to many causes, the most important being the unsuccessful U.S. effort to impose a conventional strategy on NATO and President Kennedy's handling of the Cuban missile crisis. The impact of the effort to force NATO to adopt a conventional strategy was discussed earlier.

---

[19] *The Atlantic Alliance: Basic Issues,* a study submitted by the Subcommittee on National Security and International Operations to the Committee on Government Operations, U.S. Senate (Jackson Committee), 89th Cong., 2nd Sess., 1966, p. 6.
[20] C. L. Sulzberger, *The New York Times,* August 17, 1966, p. E8.

Regarding the second, many perceptive and important European leaders profess the conviction that the *quid pro quo* for the withdrawal of Soviet missiles from Cuba was the withdrawal of U.S. missiles from Greece and Turkey. Although these soft missiles were to be removed in the spring of 1963, their withdrawal gave the impression of unseemly haste. The results of the Kennedy-Macmillan meetings in Nassau, which immediately followed the Cuban crisis, undermined the belief in the consistency of American security commitments and contributed to De Gaulle's decision to veto Britain's application for Common Market membership. As many Europeans interpreted these events, the United States appeared willing to sacrifice European security arrangements in order to safeguard its own. In the eyes of the French, this attitude was magnified by the effectuation of the test-ban treaty in 1963 by the United States and the Soviet Union.

From Cuba and Nassau in 1962 to the negotiations in Brussels and Moscow in 1963, U.S. military collaboration with the European NATO allies progressively deteriorated. France has since all but severed its connections with NATO. Subsequently, the United States has sought to create a NATO triumvirate with Great Britain and the German Federal Republic, but because of economic weakness, Britain can do little to replace the gap created by the withdrawal of France. In fact, Britain may find it necessary to make substantial reductions in its forces assigned to NATO in Germany.

Only the United States and the Federal Republic of Germany have, in recent years, taken seriously their military obligations to NATO; and the Federal Republic remains the most important ally of the United States in Western Europe. Yet, by its insistence on vast German purchases of conventional armaments and its inability to resolve NATO nuclear problems, the United States has damaged the nexus between Bonn and Washington. The Federal Republic has already begun to strengthen its ties with the Eastern European countries. Should its confidence in the U.S. security guarantee be diminished, the Federal Republic might be tempted to turn to the Soviet Union for a settlement of German reunification. A German-Soviet agreement on Central European problems, without the participation of the United States, would serve neither U.S. nor Western European interests. A straw in the wind was the June, 1966, statement of Dr. Reiner Barzel, majority leader in the Bundestag and deputy chairman of the ruling Christian Democratic Party. Dr. Barzel proposed that

> ". . . Moscow be offered the right to keep troops in a re-unified Germany, the right to increasing amounts of trade with and technology from it, and the opportunity to participate in a new Germany's politics through a legal Communist party."[21]

Although Dr. Barzel's speech was subsequently disowned by his party, some of his ideas to establish new relationships with the East have been pursued by Chancellor Kiesinger's government.

If the West Germans become disillusioned with NATO, they might very well cut themselves adrift from the moderate political moorings that NATO has provided them since 1955. If this happens, the West Germans might begin to oscillate unstably between two poles—neutralization or unilateral nuclearization—each another potential path toward reunification.

Under the constant U.S. pressure, Bonn has apparently abandoned whatever aspirations it may have had to participate in any kind of a future European nuclear force. But even Willy Brandt, a Social Democrat and Foreign Minister in the coalition West German Government, has "expressed concern that a treaty to bar the spread of nuclear weapons might impose a technological handicap on Germany in developing the peaceful uses of atomic energy."[22]

In a February, 1967, visit to London, Soviet Premier Kosygin stated that "we will probably soon reach unanimous agreement to ban [the spread of] nuclear weapons."[23]

The fact that the Soviets regard the eternal denuclearization of Germany to be the main objective of the antiproliferation treaty was baldly asserted by Kosygin: "As far as the Federal Republic of Germany is concerned, I must tell you that, whether it likes it or not, the document must be signed because we will not allow the Federal Republic of Germany to have nuclear weapons."[24]

The problems that plague the major NATO powers have also affected the attitudes of the smaller countries. The smaller member

[21] Max Frankel, *The New York Times*, June 16, 1966, p. 1.
[22] *The New York Times*, February 9, 1967, p. 12.
[23] *The New York Times*, February 10, 1967, p. 13.
[24] *Ibid.*

nations of NATO are unwilling to increase their defense contribution and, in view of the disunion in NATO, perceive little need for forces at the existing levels. With NATO on the verge of becoming a nominal alliance, the dismantling of its effective forces is likely to continue.

If in 1970 the United States is less able to provide for the defense of Europe than it was in 1967, pressure for the dissolution of NATO might conceivably intensify in both the United States and Western Europe. Chances are that the Europeans, rightly or wrongly, will continue to interpret U.S. behavior from lessons deeply embedded in their own history—namely, that nation-states have frequently been willing to sacrifice others to protect their own heartland. It is possible that those political factions advocating accommodation with the Communist world might gain greater influence in Europe and the United States. The Atlantic Alliance would then be a source of considerable risk to its members. If Americans become unwilling to use nuclear weapons except to defend the continental United States, a more satisfactory alternative for the Europeans might be found in neutralism.

The further disintegration of NATO may open many opportunities for Moscow to attract Germany and France into its sphere; and, willy-nilly, other European countries will follow suit. If Western Europe should fall under Soviet hegemony, the Soviet Union would be more powerful economically and perhaps militarily than the United States.

If the United States is to play any role in the eventual achievement of a European political settlement ensuring the future security of the peoples of the Atlantic Alliance, it must hold a recognized margin of strategic superiority over its adversary. Then Europeans would have more reason to reassess the contributions that national nuclear programs actually make to their security, and the United States could argue with persuasion that its strategic posture rendered independent European military nuclear forces unnecessary, since any force that the Europeans could build would be costly and would not significantly increase their security.

8

U.S. Strategy in Crisis

For better or worse, the United States cannot escape the dilemma of power. If the United States is to have the option of introducing constructive changes into the existing world order—changes that could render the military technological race unnecessary—it must ensure its own and the world's security during the process of change.

Today, because of U.S. strategic superiority—the capstone of U.S. and world security—nuclear war is highly improbable. We may assume that as the Soviet Union nears the U.S. strategic position and gains leverage, the balance of power will become more unstable and the probability of general international instability will be greater. The risks to the American people of a nuclear war and the political consequences to the United States of a loss of strategic superiority are so great that, to lessen these dangers, we must be prepared to maintain, over a period of time, a relatively high level of national defense.

Tomorrow's military capabilities will be the product of today's management of technology and of decisions reflecting today's surmise of the future. As weapons systems become more complicated, greater lead time is required to conceive, design, test, and produce them. Not only time but also considerable courage and resources are needed to create a strategic posture capable of coping with a calculated Soviet quest for political dominance through superior technology. Rather than resting on past performance, we must recognize that "we are in the dark about the future of science and technology, still more so about the long-term military and political future."[1]

The U.S. strategic capability must not only deter a nuclear war but also ensure survival of the United States in the unlikely contin-

[1] Albert Wohlstetter, "Technology, Prediction and Disorder," *Bulletin of the Atomic Scientists,* October, 1964, p. 15.

gency that deterrence fails. In 1960, Paul H. Nitze, who was to become Secretary of the Navy in 1963, succinctly expressed the comprehensive nature of future military superiority:

> I fear that one nation, which devotes itself intelligently and persistently to the problem of how to win a war through a rational military strategy geared to a consistent political aim, may well develop a strategic doctrine, tactics, training, and deployments that will give it a decisive *advantage against the side that devotes itself solely to deterrence of war through military means that cannot be adapted to any sensible military strategy if deterrence fails* [italics added].[2]

And in 1961, he suggested:

> If deterrence fails and we are involved in a general war, I can see no reasonable aim for our military strategy other than substantially to disarm the enemy while preserving our own essential core as a nation capable of exercising policy and thereby leaving the enemy no practical choice but to accommodate himself to our political will.[3]

For the eventuality that strategic military actions are necessary, the United States must structure a force capability that would limit damage by utilizing the range of means necessary to defeat a hostile force. Implicit is the requirement that the enemy force must be intercepted either at its source, en route, or by terminal defenses. Whether or not such defensive capabilities can be created is open to question. Many argue against making the effort at all, since they would like to halt military technological competition. But can it be stopped at this point? Regrettably, this aspect of the confrontation may be, for the present, a force unto itself, intrinsic to industrial civilization and the existing world-wide state system.

Three Strategic Designs: Counterforce, Damage Limiting, and Finite Deterrence

The composition of U.S. forces for the mid-1970's hinges on our decision-makers' predilections toward alternative strategic concepts, varying methods of coping with strategic and technical uncertainties, as well as admitted Soviet and Chinese Communist advances in

[2] "Power and Policy Problems in the Defense of the West," *Proceedings of the Asilomar National Strategy Seminar*, Asilomar Conference Grounds, Monterey Peninsula, California, April 25–30, 1960, p. 11.

[3] "Political Aspects of a National Strategy," *Armed Forces Management*, September, 1961, pp. 25–51.

weaponry. The Johnson Administration, following guidelines initiated by President Kennedy, has tried to acquire flexible means for dealing with the various forms of conflict, from counterinsurgency to general nuclear war. Prior to the Cuban missile crisis, a counterforce concept had been given serious consideration as the best way of achieving flexibility at the upper end of the conflict spectrum; but during 1962, Secretary of Defense McNamara became convinced that counterforce was technically infeasible. He advised the House Armed Services Committee in January, 1963, that "it would become increasingly difficult, regardless of the form of the attack, to destroy a sufficiently large proportion of the Soviets' strategic nuclear forces to preclude major damage to the United States, regardless of how large or what kind of strategic forces we build."[4]

U.S. strategy rapidly evolved into what Secretary McNamara termed in 1964 a "damage limiting" strategy. In the Secretary's words: "Such a strategy required a force considerably larger than would be needed for a limited 'cities only' strategy."[5] The purpose of the damage-limiting strategy is "to deter a deliberate nuclear attack upon the United States and its allies by maintaining a clear and convincing capability to inflict unacceptable damage on the attacker, even were that attacker to strike first."[6] In the event a nuclear war comes about through accident or miscalculation, the damage-limiting strategy seeks to limit damage to our population and industry. The U.S. ability to deter war will issue from its capability to wreck the aggressor's society—a capability McNamara termed "assured destruction." The assured-destruction force, designed to strike the enemy's major urban areas, is essentially a large countervalue force.[7]

[4] *Statement of Secretary of Defense Robert S. McNamara Before the House Armed Services Committee on the Fiscal Year 1964–68 Defense Program and 1964 Defense Budget* (mimeo.), January 30, 1963, p. 29.

[5] *Statement of Secretary of Defense Robert S. McNamara Before the House Armed Services Committee on the Fiscal Year 1965–69 Defense Program and 1965 Defense Budget* (mimeo), January 27, 1964, pp. 31–32. This strategy was reaffirmed in the 1966 hearings. See *The New York Times*, January 26, 1966, p. 1.

[6] *Statement of Secretary of Defense Robert S. McNamara Before the House Armed Services Committee on the Fiscal Year 1966–70 Defense Program and 1966 Defense Budget* (mimeo.), February 18, 1965, p. 38.

[7] As Secretary McNamara stated: "Based on the projected threat for the early 1970s and the most likely planning factors for that time period, our calculations show that even after absorbing first strike, our already authorized

Theoretically, other components of the 1967 U.S. strategic posture will reduce damage on the United States by (1) striking the enemy's offensive forces, (2) defending against incoming delivery vehicles, and (3) protecting the American people against nuclear radiation through fallout shelters. The problem is to determine the optimum combination of forces for these tasks.

By 1965, the Defense Department had established three somewhat pessimistic guidelines for damage limiting:

> First, against the forces we expect the Soviets to have during the next decade, it would be virtually impossible for us to be able to provide anything approaching perfect protection for our population no matter how large the general nuclear war forces we were to provide, including even the hypothetical possibility of striking first. . . .
>
> Second, since each of the three types of Soviet strategic offensive systems (land-based missiles, submarine-launched missiles and manned bombers) could, by itself, inflict severe damage on the United States, even a "very good" defense against only one type of system has limited value. . . .
>
> Third, for any given level of enemy offensive capability, successive additions to each of our various systems have diminishing marginal value. . . . *Beyond a certain point each increment added to the existing forces results in less and less additional effectiveness.* Thus, we should not expand one element of our Damage Limiting forces to a point at which the extra survivors it *yields per billion dollars spent are fewer than for other elements.* Rather, any given amount of resources we apply to the Damage Limiting Objective should be allocated among the various elements of our defense forces in such a way as to maximize the population surviving an enemy attack. This is what we mean by a "balanced" Damage Limiting force structure.
>
> The same principle holds for the Damage Limiting force as a whole. . . . Accordingly, the question of how much we should spend on Damage Limiting programs can be decided only by carefully weighing the costs against expected benefits [italics added].[8]

What emerges from analyzing defense policy and actions is a Department of Defense commitment to maintain a sizable assured-destruction force to deter war (a strong finite-deterrence posture, really)

---

strategic missile force, *if it were directed against the aggressor's urban areas, could cause more than 100 million fatalities and destroy about 80 per cent of his industrial capacity.* . . . Beyond the 200 largest urban areas, the amount of population and industrial capacity located in each additional increment of 200 cities falls off at a rapidly declining rate" [italics added].—*Ibid.*, pp. 42–43.

[8] *Ibid.*, pp. 39–40.

and an intellectual acceptance of the desirability of damage-limiting forces. Thus far, the Defense Department has been reluctant to invest substantially in any of the components for the damage-limiting mission.

Because there is some similarity between an assured-destruction capability and the forces required for finite deterrence, it is argued by some that damage limiting is merely a halfway station on the route to a resurrected finite-deterrence strategy. The objective of finite deterrence is to *prevent* the outbreak of nuclear war rather than to fight such a war. A large portion of the scientific community, many intellectuals interested in military affairs, most European strategists, and some leading American military officers support finite deterrence. These proponents oppose strategic-defense measures and recommend that the United States rely on an invulnerable second-strike force capable of striking the attacker's cities.

The common denominator of all three of these strategic designs is the deterrence of nuclear war.[9] Central to the concept and workability of deterrence is the notion of credibility. The burden of maintaining the credibility of the deterrent rests with its possessor rather than with those he seeks to deter. The more the deterrent possessor speaks about credibility without acting to improve it, the less credible the deterrent appears. And the greater the effort expended in improving the credibility of an existing strategic deterrent, the smaller the effort expended in developing new systems to meet future needs.

If the deterrent possessor chooses to rely primarily on but one element of deterrent posture, such as the assured-destruction capability, then he is obviously unable to counter the many options available to his adversary. On the other hand, the options that might be exercised

[9] Joseph I. Coffey has put forth the idea that in the United States "many of those who support deterrence through predominance do so because they are convinced that Communism can be contained or rolled back only through the application of superior power—a 'means and ends' relationship. . . . Most of those who advocate or support finite deterrence do so on the basis that the Communists are not inherently aggressive. . . . Those who espouse Limited War, coupled with a policy of 'stable strategic deterrence,' seemingly do so on the basis that the Communists are opportunistic, rather than either malevolent or quiescent by nature. Whether these views reflect emotional biases, value judgments, or differing 'cost-risk-benefit' outcomes, logical analysis should help one recognize the extent to which various theories of deterrence are based upon such views."—"Strategies and Realities," *U.S. Naval Institute Proceedings,* February, 1966, pp. 40–41. Reprinted by permission.

by an aggressor can be limited if the goal of defense planning is a *war-waging strategic posture* designed to deter war. In point of fact, war-waging capability provides by far the most credible deterrent.

So long as deterrence is the U.S. strategic policy, both the United States and its adversaries will have to calculate which side has the advantage. Secretary McNamara's annual report to the U.S. Congress sets forth this country's military posture, which is geared to an assessment of present and future Soviet and Chinese Communist forces and to the maintenance of a credible deterrent.

The calculations that are the underpinnings of the annual posture statement are complex and are influenced by many assumptions and uncertainties regarding a variety of future situations. The following crude simplification may help to explain the crucial variables. The credibility of a given deterrent force depends on the survival and arrival on target of X number of retaliatory missiles and bombers plus an active and passive defense capability to limit damage. Excessive losses to the retaliatory forces or inadequacies in the latter components could severely negate the credibility of a deterrent force. Precise Soviet targeting, increased missile accuracy, and high-yield warheads are some of the possible means for achieving a high degree of damage to U.S. strategic offensive and defensive forces The employment of a Soviet ABM to destroy incoming U.S. ICBM's, attrition resulting from component or warhead unreliability, or the effects of electromagnetic pulse (EMP) radiation would greatly reduce the retaliatory forces X by a factor Y. The resulting difference $X - Y$ in the strategic retaliatory megatonnage could conceivably be absorbed by the Soviets, especially if they possessed an effective ABM.

In a hypothetical nuclear conflict the United States, lacking an ABM system, would find itself with a high casualty rate, severe physical damage, an inability to cope with follow-on Soviet ICBM strikes, and an insufficient number of surviving forces to penetrate Soviet defenses and destroy essential targets in the Soviet Union. The net result would be a deterrent force lacking credibility.

Strategic superiority can conceivably exist when the superior force has certain deficiencies; however, the U.S. claim to strategic superiority often is not matched by actions that could correct acknowledged deficiencies in its posture—for example, no defense against incoming missiles and insufficient fallout shelters. In 1966, Secretary McNamara reiterated:

> We should not now commit ourselves to a particular level of Damage Limitation against the Soviet threat—first, *because our deterrent makes general nuclear war unlikely,* and second, because attempting to assure with high confidence against all reasonably likely levels and types of attack is very costly, and even then the results are uncertain. Our choices should be responsive to projections based upon the observed development of the Soviet threat and our evolving knowledge of the technical capabilities of our own forces [italics added].[10]

Nevertheless, even in the Department of Defense there is a nagging though rarely expressed fear: What happens if our deterrence fails? But the Department of Defense continues to act on the assumption that U.S. deterrence will *not* fail. It is a comfortable assumption grounded on the following analysis: Once two powers acquire sizable inventories of nuclear weapons and a range of offensive delivery systems, each becomes vulnerable to almost any nuclear attack that might be launched by the other. Consequently, deterrence will work because of the peculiar logic of the nuclear situation. Even if great effort is expended to calculate the advantage that one side or the other might gain by developing new defenses, more precise targeting, or better command and control, such military "improvements" cannot guarantee a decisive advantage to one or the other side in an actual nuclear exchange. Hence, there is no point in further straining the economy with war-making facilities that might not change the strategic equation.

A less convenient assumption: The adversary's capabilities should be constantly reassessed lest the United States suffer a technological Pearl Harbor. In the face of mounting technological uncertainties, some experts believe that the search for the ever more effective offensive-defensive weapons balance should be unrelenting and that such continuing research and development should guide U.S. strategic planning. These strategists can find no realistic ground for assuming that failure-proof deterrence will be maintained by some

---

[10] *Statement of Secretary of Defense Robert S. McNamara Before the House Subcommittee on Defense Appropriations for Fiscal Year 1967–71 Defense Program and 1967 Defense Budget* (mimeo.), February 23, 1966, p. 56. (Subsequently referred to as the *McNamara 1966 Posture Statement.*)

invisible hand. In their view, truly effective deterrence is achieved through calculated weapons selection made in relation to an adversary's weapons decisions. Within this context, it is useful to note how specific problems about the composition of U.S. strategic forces are being approached. According to Secretary McNamara's 1966 posture statement:

> It seems to me that there are seven major issues involved in our FY 1967–71 programs for the general nuclear war forces: The first five are related primarily to the threat projected in the latest intelligence estimates. The last two are associated with the more remote possibility of a much more severe threat. These issues are:
>
> 1. Should a manned bomber force be maintained in the 1970s; if so, what aircraft should be selected for the force?
> 2. To what extent should qualitative improvements (in range, payload, etc.) be made in the MINUTEMAN force?
> 3. Should an anti-ballistic missile system be deployed; if so, when and what type?
> 4. Should we produce and deploy a new manned interceptor?
> 5. What should be the future size and scope of the Civil Defense program?
> 6. Should development of new penetration aid packages for the POLARIS and MINUTEMAN missile forces be accelerated?
> 7. Should development of the POSEIDON missile be accelerated?

The philosophy underlying current Pentagon approaches to strategic forces is capsuled in the Defense Secretary's answers to these major issues. With regard to the first and second questions, he has agreed to maintain a somewhat reduced manned-bomber capability, supplemented by 210 FB-111 (TFX) aircraft, and to proceed with a Minuteman III. Although the utility of the TFX as a strategic bomber has been debated, Secretary McNamara so far has refused to go ahead with another advanced manned bomber or to develop a new series of large ICBM's. To questions three and four, he has answered negatively, except for declaring himself willing to consider future deployment of a "light ABM" against a possible Chinese threat. Regarding civil defense, he has given no clear answer. For the rest, he has taken positive steps to develop penetration aids and to accelerate development of Poseidon. The effect of these decisions has been to continue the stress on improvements in offensive missiles earmarked for the assured-destruction mission and to do almost nothing to improve the U.S. damage-limiting capability.

The damage-limiting concept signifies theoretical recognition that the offensive-defensive balance has become paramount in strategic planning. It provides for the design of a strategic posture from which the United States could again move, if it chose, in the general direction of counterforce. Because of some technological advances in the past several years, a counterforce strategy may theoretically be more feasible now than it was when the concept was first developed, in the early 1960's. The U.S. adoption of a second-strike policy should make an effective defense the essential prerequisite of both a damage-limiting and a counterforce posture. The difference between these two strategic designs is primarily one of scale or quantity of both offensive and defensive systems. In comparison, a counterforce posture calls for a greater number and mix of strategic offensive forces capable of penetrating the adversary's defenses and destroying his fixed residual offensive weapons. There are further differences in the weapons systems, force levels, reconnaissance, and command and control mechanisms associated with the damage-limiting, counterforce, and finite-deterrence strategies.

A Frame of Reference

Contemporary U.S. strategy, influenced in large measure by new technology, is a product of the military debates of the late 1950's. By the end of 1966, the adequacy of U.S. forces was being questioned, particularly on the basis of a number of belated disclosures made by the Defense Department concerning the Soviet deployment of an ABM system and a marked increase in the rate of Soviet deployment of ICBM's.

On November 10, 1966, Defense Secretary Robert S. McNamara said that "there was 'considerable evidence' that the Soviet Union was building and deploying an anti-ballistic missile system, probably requiring an increase in the United States offensive capacity." The Secretary added that "the Administration would probably recommend to Congress that the United States begin production and deployment of the Poseidon missile, a large submarine-launched missile with greater power than the Polaris missile to penetrate sophisticated defense systems."[11]

While finally conceding that the Soviet ABM deployment was al-

[11] *The New York Times*, November 11, 1966, p. 1.

ready under way, Secretary McNamara did not at that time disclose the equally startling information that the Soviets were also building and deploying ICBM's far faster than the U.S. had previously estimated. On December 6, he announced: "Evidence now suggests that the Soviets in mid-1968 will have more ICBM's than were predicted for that time period by intelligence estimates in 1965."[12] Secretary McNamara then made these points:

> Even if the new intelligence estimate for mid-1968 proves accurate, the United States, without taking any actions beyond those already planned, will continue to have a substantial quantitative and qualitative superiority over the Soviet Union in ICBMs at that time.
>
> The United States has as many ICBMs today as the latest national intelligence estimate gives the Soviet Union several years hence.[13]

On the same day that this statement was published, *The New York Times* reported that qualified U.S. sources estimated: "Antimissile missile facilities are being constructed all over Russia, not just around Moscow and Leningrad. They are being positioned athwart natural access avenues that American land-based and sea-based missiles must traverse to attack key military and industrial targets."[14] The following day: "United States officials said they may not try to maintain indefinitely the present numerical superiority in long-range missiles over the Soviet Union. . . . Above all in strategic importance, they said, the United States will maintain its capability to penetrate Soviet defenses."[15] A few days later, perhaps the same or other U.S. officials alleged that the Soviet Union appeared to be making only an "experimental" deployment of an antiballistic-missile system and that because of the growing demand for consumer goods among the Soviets, Moscow would be cautious about making a full ABM deployment.[16]

Thus the stage was set in Washington to resume overtures to the Soviet leaders to head off a costly renewal of the arms race. Subsequently, "Mr. Rusk said at a news conference that the United States

12 *Washington Post,* December 7, 1966, p. 1.
13 *Ibid.*
14 *The New York Times,* December 8, 1966, p. 1.
15 *Baltimore Sun,* December 9, 1966, p. 1.
16 *Baltimore Sun,* December 16, 1966, p. 1.

would like to see 'some means developed' to limit the arms race and thus avoid the 'wholly new major levels of expenditure' that would be required by deployment of antimissile defense systems by the two major powers."[17] The day after Christmas, the American people were told:

> The Johnson Administration is seriously considering a compromise decision on the Nike-X antimissile system that potentially could mollify both those who favor and those who oppose a quick deployment of such a system. The compromise, high Pentagon officials say, would involve the procurement of some key preliminary items but would not commit the President to go into full scale installation of a missile defense around the country.[18]

For the most part, the implications of the Soviet ABM system were discussed in terms of their domestic impact. As one administrative official expressed it: "If the President did nothing more than continue development of the Nike-X system, he could be crucified politically, and less than two years before the 1968 Presidential election, for sitting on his hands while the Russians provide a defense for their people."[19]

Because many influential members of Congress, key officials in the Defense Department, and the Joint Chiefs of Staff do not fully subscribe to McNamara's strategic doctrine, the U.S. strategic posture for the 1970's will be influenced by more controversy, the introduction of still newer technology, and the assumptions of U.S. policymakers about the shape of world politics for the next decade. The paradox of Rusk's asking the Soviets to refrain from doing something that they have already done suggests that Soviet assumptions differ widely from those of our policy-makers. Many of McNamara's assumptions regarding Soviet capabilities and intentions, which were noted in the first chapter, may prove to be erroneous; yet these assumptions are shaping our future.

The suppositions that guide U.S. strategic planning are freely proffered to the Soviets in the hope that they will emulate them. "To put it another way, McNamara is *the first Secretary* of Defense

[17] *The New York Times,* December 22, 1966, p. 1.
[18] *The New York Times,* December 27, 1966, p. 1.
[19] *Ibid.,* p. 9.

to *prescribe strategies* for this country's *potential enemies* in the hope that they will adopt them for their own sake as well *as ours.*"[20] A primary vehicle for communicating with the Soviet leadership is the annual statement given to Congress on defense policy. In an interview with Richard Starnes of the Scripps-Howard newspapers, McNamara said:

> We also put out an unclassified version that I believe has done more to dispel Soviet misunderstanding of American policy and aims than anything else we've ever done. As soon as the unclassified report is published, the Soviet Embassy grabs dozens of them and ships them home. We don't publish them for their exclusive benefit, of course, but I'm delighted to see them take such an interest in it. I'm as proud of the effect this report is having as anything I've done around here.[21]

However, the Soviets have not yet gotten the message. Does the U.S. failure to achieve a strategic understanding with the Soviets imply a basic failure in American strategy? It could be that the Soviets are not playing the same game with the same rules; it is possible that they may be playing with different rules or attempting to change both the game and the rules.

In his 1967 posture statement,[22] Secretary McNamara admits that in planning our strategic forces, one must take into account their interaction with those of the Soviet Union. In this statement, he assumes that "the general nuclear war policy of the Soviet Union also has as its objective the deterrence of a U.S. first strike."[23] What if it does not? Suppose it is designed to circumscribe the U.S. deterrent? Suppose Soviet nuclear policy encourages the design of a war-winning strategy?

Secretary McNamara believes "that there is a mutuality of interests in limiting the deployment of anti-ballistic missile defense systems."[24] He concludes that "in all probability all we would accomplish by deploying ABM systems against one another would be to increase

---

[20] Norman Moss, "McNamara's ABM Policy: A Failure of Communications," *The Reporter*, February 28, 1967, p. 34.

[21] *Ibid.*, p. 35.

[22] *Statement of Secretary of Defense Robert S. McNamara Before a Joint Session of the Senate Armed Services Committee and the Senate Subcommittee on Department of Defense Appropriations on the Fiscal Year 1968–72 Defense Program and 1968 Defense Budget* (mimeo.), January 23, 1967.

[23] *Ibid.*, p. 35.

[24] *Ibid.*, p. 40.

greatly our respective defense expenditures, without any gain in real security for either side."[25] If one granted his initial assumption and if both sides had refrained from deploying an ABM, this conclusion would be quite true. However, the evidence indicates that the Soviets have been working on large-scale ABM defenses, which seems to invalidate the assumption of mutuality of interests. Ignoring his own assumption, Secretary McNamara stated, "We must base our force planning on the assumption that the Soviets will deploy a reasonably effective ABM defense around their principal cities; and we must be prepared to overwhelm it."[26] Therefore, the decision "to take a number of additional actions to enhance the future capabilities of our Assured Destruction forces" is certainly warranted. The question is when will these improvements in weaponry become available, and how effective will they be against the uncertain effectiveness of a Soviet ABM?

Finally, McNamara suggested:

> The most severe threat we must consider in planning our Assured Destruction forces is an *extensive, effective Soviet ABM deployment combined with a deployment of a substantial ICBM force with a hard-target kill capability*. Such a Soviet offensive force might post a threat to our MINUTEMAN missiles. An extensive, effective Soviet ABM system might then be able to intercept and destroy a significant portion of our residual missile warheads, including those carried by submarine-launched missiles. [The Soviet offensive and defensive threats assumed here are both substantially higher than expected. Italics added].[27]

Yet the U.S. is not preparing against a threat of this magnitude because DOD officials refuse to believe that the Soviets are acquiring such forces. It is illogical to expect U.S. cost-effectiveness analyses or the insights of U.S. game theory to be acceptable to the Soviets—much less to be adopted by them. If they were acceptable, the Soviets would not have deployed an ABM.

U.S. Force Levels and Defense Funding

Although by 1967 the problems of strategic nuclear warfare were apparently better understood than ever before in the United States, discrepancies still existed between the strategic rationale adopted by

[25] *Ibid.*, p. 40.
[26] *Ibid.*, p. 43.
[27] *Ibid.*, p. 45.

the Department of Defense and actual or scheduled U.S. force levels. The organic relationship among strategic retaliatory forces, continental air- and missile-defense forces, and civil defense was clearly perceived, and techniques for determining the appropriate balance of offensive and defensive means had been developed. But funds allocated for strategic offensive forces had substantially declined. (Some increase in funds for these forces is indicated in the fiscal year 1968 budget.) Funds for strategic defensive forces also declined, and those for general-purpose forces rose correspondingly. A prolonged war in Vietnam might further depress the U.S. effort to maintain strategic superiority.

In 1966, U.S. production and development of an ABM defense, which requires at least four years lead time, was deferred:

> U.S. officials say they have no plans to speed development of the Nike-X missile defense system because of Red China's reported missile-launched nuclear success.
> In addition, they said they have no plans to use the added $153.5 million appropriated by Congress this year to begin procurement of the complicated system, which has been under development since 1957 at a cost of more than $2 billion.[28]

Simultaneously, the United States reduced its bomber force at a rapid rate, even though the 200 B-111 bombers that are to replace the B-52 and B-58 bombers currently being phased out have not yet been built. If this trend continues, by 1970 the United States will have only about *one-half* its 1965 megatonnage-delivery capability. This approximation refers to weapons launched and not to those that might reach their targets. The potential effect of an offensive nuclear strike force is the amount of nuclear explosive power that could theoretically be delivered against an adversary, roughly calculated as the total megatonnage that could be carried by the bombers and land- and submarine-launched missiles of the offensive force. Aircraft can carry far greater payloads than can existing missiles, and since the United States has replaced bombers with missiles, its capacity to deliver megatonnage on target has decreased. A more informative picture can be gained by calculating the number of kilo-pounds that could be lifted by a given missile force and, more precisely, by allocating the total lift of warheads and/or penetration aids. Calculations of the exact

[28] *Washington Star*, October 28, 1966, p. 2.

reduction must also take into account the vulnerability, reliability, penetration capability, and accuracy of the various systems comprising the offensive force.

The downward trend of deliverable U.S. megatonnage will probably not be reversed until the United States deploys an improved-capability missile (ICM), which presumably can propel large payloads carrying heavier warheads than those of Minuteman, Polaris, and Poseidon.

The following table on defense allocations indicates a decline in funding for strategic forces and a large increase in funding for general-purpose forces. Research and development funding has remained relatively constant in terms of absolute dollars since 1963; however, the value of the dollar has declined, the cost of R&D has risen, and the percentage of the total defense budget allocated to R&D has dropped.

TABLE I
FUNDING OF UNITED STATES FORCES: 1962–67
(*In billions of dollars*)

	Defense allocations					
Type of force	1962 orig. req.	1962 final req.	1963 act'l rec'd	1964 act'l rec'd	1965 act'l rec'd	1966 est. rec'd	1967 prop.
Strategic offensive	$7.6	$8.9	$8.3	$7.3	$5.3	$5.1	$5.1
Strategic defensive	2.2	2.0	1.8	1.9	1.5	1.6	1.3
Civil defense	—	.3	.1	.1	.1	.1	.1
Total	$9.8	$11.2	$10.2	$9.3	$6.9	$6.8	$6.5
General-purpose	$14.5	$17.5	$17.5	$17.7	$19.0	$30.0	$25.7
R&D		$ 6.8	$ 7.6	$ 7.6	$ 6.9	$ 7.4	$ 7.4

SOURCES: *McNamara 1966 Posture Statement,* pp. 122, 170.

The year 1962 was the high funding period for the research, development, testing, and evaluation of Minuteman and Polaris (including submarines). Since then, strategic forces have been de-emphasized except for penetration aids, for which funding has increased. Minuteman II and III and Poseidon—the advanced versions of Minuteman and Polaris—can be considered qualitative developments. Secretary McNamara has commented:

Three years ago we initiated a program ultimately to replace the Minuteman I with the Minuteman II, which has much greater accuracy, payload, and operational versatility. In addition, its greater targeting capability reduces the number of missiles that need to be earmarked against a given target system to achieve one reliably delivered warhead against each target. . . . We are now making certain further major improvements in the Minuteman which will so increase its performance as to warrant a new designation—Minuteman III.[29]

Table 2 shows some other discernible trends. Since 1955, the defense budget has declined from approximately 60 per cent to 50 per cent of total federal expenditures, and except for an upsurge in 1961–62, the portion of the defense budget devoted to strategic offensive forces and to future weapons for these forces has declined even more rapidly.

A survey of Defense Department weapons choices and funding trends permits two conclusions. First, the Defense Department conveys the impression that it is doing all that needs to be done to maintain a deterrence that will not fail now or in the future. Second, U.S. allocation of funds for strategic offensive and defensive capabilities continued to decrease through 1966, although a small upswing was projected for 1967. Much has been made of the use of so-called cost-effectiveness criteria to bring about defense savings. From the point of view of Moscow, Peking, and Hanoi, the war in Vietnam is a masterpiece of cost effectiveness. The Soviets are helping to induce the United States to spend some $25 billion to $35 billion a year in South Vietnam by furnishing military aid to North Vietnam at a probable cost of about one-twentieth of that amount. Furthermore, there is no evidence that the Soviets are seriously offering their good offices to help permit the United States to disengage with honor from the Vietnamese conflict. According to Crosby S. Noyes, the Russian commitment to Vietnam has deepened.

> That this Russian commitment is growing is beyond question. The recent announcement of a full-scale training program for North Vietnamese pilots in the Soviet Union, the greatly accelerated speed-up of advanced weaponry and above all the public admission that Russian military specialists are in North Viet Nam all suggest a new dimension of Soviet involvement.[30]

[29] *McNamara 1966 Posture Statement*, p. 63.
[30] *Washington Evening Star*, October 11, 1966, p. A-11.

TABLE 2

U.S. DEFENSE ALLOCATIONS, 1954–67

(In billions of dollars)

Fiscal year	Gross national product (GNP)	Federal budget	Defense budget*	Defense budget as percentage of GNP	Defense budget as percentage of federal budget	Strategic-force budget†	Strategic-force budget as percentage of defense budget
1954	$363.1	$ 67.5	$47.0	12.9	69.6	$ 9.3	19.8
1955	397.5	64.4	40.7	10.2	63.3	9.0	22.1
1956	419.2	66.2	40.7	9.7	61.5	8.0	19.7
1957	442.8	69.0	43.4	9.8	62.8	9.9	22.8
1958	444.5	71.4	44.2	9.9	62.0	11.1	25.1
1959	482.7	80.3	46.5	9.6	57.9	10.1	21.7
1960	502.6	76.5	45.7	9.1	59.7	9.6	21.0
1961	518.2	81.5	47.5	9.2	58.3	9.9	20.8
1962	554.9	87.8	51.1	9.2	58.2	9.1	17.8
1963	585.1	92.6	52.8	9.0	57.2	8.4	15.9
1964	623.0	98.4	54.2	8.7	55.0	7.3	13.5
1965	657.0	97.5	52.2	7.9	53.5	5.3	10.2
1966	670.0	99.7	51.1	7.6	51.2	5.7	9.8
1967	722.0	112.8	57.2	7.9	50.6	5.1	8.9

* Defense-budget figures include expenditures for the Department of Defense and other agencies *primarily* related to national defense, including the Atomic Energy Commission.

† These figures include expenditures for strategic retaliatory forces (the major missiles and bombers capable of reaching enemy territory).

SOURCES: U.S. Department of Commerce, Office of Business Economics, *U.S. Income and Output* (GNP figures for 1954–63); *Predicasts* (Cleveland: Economics Index and Surveys, Inc.), No. 18, 4th Quarter, 1964 (GNP figures for 1964 and 1965); U.S. Bureau of the Budget, *U.S. Statistical Abstracts* (federal- and defense-budget figures for 1954–61); *The New York Times*, January 26, 1965 (federal- and defense-budget figures for 1965–66 and strategic-force-budget figure for 1966); *Statement of Secretary of Defense Robert S. McNamara Before the House Armed Services Committee on the Fiscal Year 1965–69 Defense Program and 1965 Defense Budget* (mimeo.), January 27, 1964 (strategic-force-budget figures for 1962–65); text of President's budget message presented to Congress (fiscal year 1967), January 24, 1966, cited by *The New York Times*, January 25, 1966, pp. 21–22.

The Soviet Union signed a new military-assistance and economic-aid program with North Vietnam on October 3, 1966. According to official statements by representatives of both countries, the new allocation represented an increase over the previous annual figure of more than $500 million. Consequently, the conflict in Vietnam may impinge directly on the issue of future U.S. strategic superiority if the Defense Department continues to focus its attention on Asia.[31] In order to redirect our hardware R&D and procurement policies to meet this threat, while at the same time trying to keep the budget reasonably close to previous ones, reductions must be made elsewhere. These cuts may be made at the expense of future U.S. strategic forces and research and development.

As of 1967, U.S. forces appeared to be adequate against the strategic threats of the Soviet Union; the issue is whether they will be adequate in the future. There is evidence that the "Soviet Union is engaged in a massive military research and new weapon development program aimed at achieving a major strategic change in the international balance of power."[32] This Soviet drive comes at a time when our total strategic-forces budget is declining, partially because of the diversion of resources to fight the Vietnam war.

To the extent that the U.S. build-up in Vietnam includes equipment that will have utility a few years from now, it will contribute to future U.S. strategic tactical superiority. At the same time, it is legitimate to question whether the Communist-inspired conflict in Vietnam has already distracted the United States from establishing a sounder set of defense priorities.[33]

[31] *McNamara 1966 Posture Statement*, p. 41. Note that, according to Marquis Childs, "the war in Viet Nam is now costing $2.7 billion a month. Rather than a random figure picked out of the air, this is a careful calculation accepted at the highest level of Government concerned with taxes and debt and the storm cloud of threatened inflation hovering over the economy."—*The Evening Bulletin* (Philadelphia), September 23, 1966, p. B-23.

[32] See *Aviation Week and Space Technology*, March 7, 1966, p. 90. See also Hanson W. Baldwin, "U.S. Lead in ICBM's Said to Be Reduced by Build-up in Soviet Union," *The New York Times*, July 14, 1966, p. 14, where he states: "*Aviation Week and Space Technology*, as well as *Technology Week*, supports the idea of a major segment of the intelligence community that the Soviet Union is engaged in a massive research, development and production program of strategic missiles at the very time that United States programs are 'being slowed and stretched.'"

[33] The author has supported U.S. policy in Vietnam without necessarily endorsing every action taken to execute that policy.

The Soviets, who do not have comparable expenditures for conventional forces, are investing proportionately more than the United States to acquire accurate, high-payload ICBM's and an ABM system.

> The Soviet Government announced [December 15, 1966] that its military spending next year would be increased by 1.1 billion rubles, or 8.2 per cent over this year's arms budget of 13.4 billion rubles ($14.8 billion). Finance Minister Vasily F. Garbuzov declared in a report to the Supreme Soviet that the increase was necessary because "the aggressive monopolist circles of the United States have recently sharpened international tensions and increased the danger of a new world war."[34]

Although this Soviet announcement in effect linked increased military costs to the shipping of Soviet arms to Hanoi, Soviet military spending for North Vietnam is much higher than the publicly stated figure. Furthermore, the real Soviet defense budget is much higher than the official one; and in plain fact, we do not know the specific purposes to which the rising Soviet expenditures will be devoted.

Weapons for the Years of Peak Danger

If the U.S. budget allocation for strategic offense and defense continues to decline and the relative Soviet investment in these forces goes up, U.S. strategic forces soon (even before 1970) may not be able to meet the tasks assigned them.

Analysis of U.S. forces planned for the 1970's and their stated goals and capabilities suggests that, confronted by such Soviet forces, U.S. strategic retaliatory forces might not be able to execute an assured-destruction mission effectively. U.S. capability to deter would be questionable under the "worst possible" conditions of a Soviet first strike.[35]

But the story does not end here. By launching a retaliatory strike against Soviet cities—the task an assured-destruction force would be designed to do—the United States would probably provoke the Soviet Union to counterretaliate in kind with its residual missile force, submarine-launched missiles, orbital warheads, and bomber force. The

[34] *The New York Times,* December 16, 1966, p. 1.
[35] This conclusion is based on the survey of plausible exchange outcomes presented in the Appendix.

United States would be defenseless against either the first or the second wave of a Soviet attack if it lacked a deployed ABM system and the requisite civil-defense shelters.[36]

Future U.S. weapons systems, if they are developed soon enough, could invalidate the pessimistic outcome just suggested. Because of their greater versatility, the Minuteman III missiles, which are to be operational in the early 1970's, may serve as re-entry vehicles carrying several warheads. If equivalent accuracy can be obtained for each separate warhead, the United States would in effect be adding to its offensive missile inventory, which could also be increased by a missile refire capability at each silo.

The United States may also develop an improved-capability missile (ICM), which would be able to lift several times the payload of present Minuteman and Polaris missiles. This weapon is viewed as a long-range answer to the most pessimistic appraisal of what the Soviets may be capable of installing in the way of sophisticated anti-missile missiles several years hence. However, it will take more than five years to perfect such an offensive system. "If the project gets the necessary approval from the Administration and later from Congress as generally expected, it is estimated that the first new missiles could be deployed in 1971 or 1972."[37] This new weapons system would be designed to ensure that the United States could maintain its ability to destroy the Soviet Union even after absorbing a surprise attack. "Such capability is regarded by top Administration leaders as the best deterrence to attack and the key element in maintaining the present precarious strategic balance of power."[38]

[36] According to a Department of Defense release entitled "Current Status of U.S. Civil Defense Program—December 6, 1966": "Civil Defense in the United States has been progressing steadily toward its major objective: fallout shelter for the entire population. A continuing effort is to make maximum use of existing systems and resources rather than propose the implementation of new systems or the procurement of facilities and equipment dedicated solely to civil defense.

"This year, $134.4 million for the fiscal year was requested beginning July 1, 1966. FY 1962–1966 appropriations total $708.8 million. When this is added to the projected program through 1971 approved by the Secretary of Defense, the total is $1.5 billion for a protection system which could save up to 30 million lives in 1970."

[37] *The New York Times*, June 20, 1966, p. 1.
[38] *Ibid.*

If it becomes available soon enough, an improved U.S. offensive-missile would contribute to the preservation of the assured-destruction capability. Mobile land-based missiles are being considered, including both rail- and vehicle-transported versions. There is a possibility that the improved-capability missiles may be mated with existing Minuteman silos; however, these missiles may require completely new and additionally hardened silos. The protection of such missiles might also be achieved by hard-point missile defenses, although the mode of protection will hinge on considerations of cost and strategic trade-off.

Possibilities also exist for major improvements in Soviet ICBM's.[39] If the Soviets were to develop multientry vehicles and achieve comparable accuracy for each warhead, they might come out ahead, since the larger payload of Soviet ICBM's (six times greater than that of the U.S. Minuteman missiles) might permit them to deliver at an earlier date multiple warheads of far greater power than those of U.S. missiles.

In testimony before the Senate, General Earle G. Wheeler, Chairman of the Joint Chiefs of Staff, summarized JCS views regarding the 1967 U.S. strategic situation:

> We believe that the Soviet offensive and defensive buildup does increase the risk of nuclear war because, in the first place, deterrence is a combination of forces in being and state of mind.
>
> Should the Soviets come to believe that their ballistic missile defense, coupled with a nuclear attack on the United States, would limit damage to the Soviet Union to a level acceptable to them, whatever that level is, our forces would no longer deter, and the first principle of our security policy is gone.
>
> I should say here that while I certainly agree—and so do the Joint Chiefs—that the basis of deterrence is the ability to destroy an attacker as a viable nation, as a part of this, there is also the ability of the nation to survive as a nation—in other words, the converse of the first point.
>
> Second, lack of a deployed U.S. ABM increases the possibilities of a nuclear war by accident and by the Nth country triggering.
>
> Third, failure to deploy a U.S. ABM creates a strategic imbalance both within our forces and between the United States and the Soviet

---

[39] According to *Aviation Week and Space Technology*, March 21, 1966, p. 25, there is growing evidence to indicate that the Soviets have made significant progress in developing a multiple, independently targeted re-entry vehicle. This vehicle would scatter warheads well before it reached the target area. See also *Aviation Week and Space Technology*, February 28, 1966, p. 16.

forces. It could lead to Soviet and allied belief that we are interested only in the offensive, that is, a first strike, or that our technology is deficient, or that we will not pay to maintain strategic superiority.[40]

But even with regard to the U.S. offensive assured-destruction capability, concerning which Secretary McNamara and the Joint Chiefs agree, there is much public uncertainty. The public is not advised how much of the U.S. offensive force would be available to destroy residual Soviet strike forces (those not used in the initial attack). Furthermore, we are not told what U.S. offensive forces would be available to deal with Soviet IRBM's posed against the NATO nations. Nor are we told whether any U.S. forces are programmed to attack the logistic support structure and assembly areas of the Soviet Army. However, the impression one obtains from reading the public statements is that in its nuclear-exchange model, the Defense Department pays decreasing attention to Soviet targets outside the restricted assured-destruction–damage-limiting parameters. This, in turn, leaves practically the whole of the Soviets' logistical system and ground-force units untargeted in an ICBM exchange.

The timing of U.S. retaliatory strikes is another subject rarely, if ever, mentioned in the Defense Department's strategic posture statements. One is led to believe, however, that the response would be almost immediate. In reality, due to the time required to assess the situation, to make decisions regarding the scale and character of retaliatory strikes, and to execute the strike by various delivery means, many hours might pass before the full U.S. retaliatory action was consummated. Meanwhile, the United States and its allies—almost completely defenseless against a Soviet missile attack until at least 1970—would continue to be on the receiving end of whatever additional attack the Soviet Union might be able to launch.

One other uncertainty weighs upon the precise technological justification with which Secretary McNamara defends his decisions: Exactly what are the effects of the 1963 test-ban treaty? There is evidence that the Soviet Union, in its 1961 test series, accumulated information about warhead lethality in and above the atmosphere and about the vulnerability of missiles to electromagnetic pulse phe-

[40] Hearings Before the Committee on Armed Services and the Subcommittee on Department of Defense of the Committee on Appropriations, U.S. Senate, 90th Cong., 1st Sess., on S. 666 (Washington, D.C.: Government Printing Office, 1967), p. 251.

nomena—information that the United States has not been able to obtain through large-scale testing. This information may have been particularly useful in the development of the Soviet ABM system.[41]

The United States does have recourse to laboratory analysis and to restricted underground testing and can extrapolate the data thus obtained. But whether it can gain sufficient and conclusive enough knowledge by these means to contend with Soviet methods of exploiting exotic nuclear phenomena (for either offensive or defensive purposes) is to some extent problematical. Secretary McNamara has stated:

> An ABM system employing long range exoatmospheric interceptors in addition to lower altitude interceptors could complicate even a sophisticated attacker's ballistic missile penetration problem. It could also improve overall system performance compared to an equal cost system employing lower altitude interceptors only. However, this conclusion is based on a preliminary analysis and there are still many unresolved questions about the design and performance of a system employing both exoatmospheric and lower altitude interceptors.[42]

Destruction of a nuclear warhead by an ABM could be accomplished in several ways: (1) "exploding" it from blast effect; (2) incinerating it by heat; (3) confusing its electronic brain so that it will not explode; (4) fragmenting its heat shield so that the warhead will burn up on re-entering the atmosphere without exploding; (5) forming a nuclear screen in front of the warhead that would render it useless.[43] The electromagnetic pulse (EMP) effect and other nuclear burst-induced effects are of several types: One involves the

[41] "The most important argument against the test ban is the fact that the Russians seem to have proceeded farther along in the development of a missile defense than the United States. To catch up in this most important field and to introduce a system that is experimentally verified and which is therefore reasonably reliable requires testing. More specifically, it requires testing in the atmosphere. By accepting a limited test ban we have probably accepted a position inferior to the Russians in the important field of missile defense. The disadvantage might possibly be overcome by a great effort which we continue to postpone. A comprehensive test ban would make such an effort all but impossible. It should be understood that if the Russians possess a sufficiently good missile defense while we do not, then our present posture of deterrence will have ceased to operate."—Edward Teller, "Planning for Peace," *Orbis*, Summer, 1966, p. 344.

[42] *McNamara 1966 Posture Statement*, p. 55.

[43] Jules Bergman, "If Zeus Fails, Can Sprint Save Us?", *The New York Times Magazine*, March 20, 1966, p. 26.

actual emission of an electromagnetic pulse of short duration from the explosion itself; another type alters the electrical properties of the atmosphere, causing serious disturbances of the electromagnetic waves used in communications and radar. These disturbances may result in the "blacking out" of radio and radar systems, in the physical degradation of re-entry vehicles, or in warhead ineffectiveness.[44] Physical degradation can take the form of magnetic-tape erasure, fusing of electronic circuitry, or disruption of the solid-state components of the warhead. Because the test-ban treaty has restricted U.S. gathering of data, this country's knowledge about methods three and five is inadequate.

Mention has been made of the significant drop-off in the U.S. capability to deliver megatonnage on Soviet targets. Missile payload can be utilized either for single or multientry warheads or for penetration aids, and, logically, the missile force whose single-delivery units have greater potential payload capability should have far greater flexibility. If employed against targets that were not defended by ABM's, the payload could be used exclusively for guidance and nuclear warheads. Against a sophisticated deployed ABM defense, some of the missile payload could be used to carry penetration aids. The United States has accelerated the development of the Poseidon submarine-launched missile, which presumably will have a superior penetration capability. This advanced submarine-launched missile would, in effect, be the U.S. strategic reserve in the event of a strategic exchange. The capability of a U.S. nuclear-submarine fleet, tegic exchange. The capability of a U.S. nuclear-submarine fleet will be affected by Soviet developments in antisubmarine warfare.

We have no way of knowing how effective the Soviet ABM system would be against either ICBM's or submarine-launched missiles. Secretary McNamara concedes that "the Soviets have placed a different emphasis on defense than we have."[45] But we do not explicitly know the extent to which Soviet defenses would offset a U.S. assured-destruction retaliatory strike. Also, it is impossible to determine what impact, if any, the U.S.–Soviet space competition will have on the strategic military balance. According to James E. Webb, director of

[44] *The Effects of Nuclear Weapons* (Washington: U.S. Atomic Energy Commission, 1962), Chapter 10, "Radio and Radar Effects," pp. 502, 633.
[45] Michael Getler, "McNamara Says Soviets Err on ABM," *Missiles and Rockets,* May 2, 1966, p. 12.

the National Space and Aeronautic Agency, the Soviet Union in 1966 had "a better chance . . . than two years ago" to land a man on the moon ahead of the United States.[46] The 1967 U.S. Apollo disaster obviously improves Soviet chances, even though they afterward suffered a tragic setback.

The dynamics of the situation are crucial. The Defense Department has repeatedly conceded uncertainties in intelligence forcecasting. Under these circumstances, the prudent defense manager would take into account both the dynamic nature of the problem and the uncertainties confronting us and would therefore provide a comfortable margin of superiority rather than, as appears to be the case, balance our strategic superiority on the razor's edge. The most important issue in analyzing U.S. strategic posture for the future is whether a nation committed to a second-strike policy (a policy that the author endorses) can forgo the adoption of a defensive system that would reduce U.S. casualties in the event of a Soviet first strike. McNamara concedes:

> Against likely Soviet postures for the 1970's appropriate mixes of Damage Limiting measures could effect substantial reductions in the maximum damage the Soviets could inflict, but only at substantial cost to the U.S. over and above that required for Assured Destruction. Even so, against a massive and sophisticated Soviet surprise attack on civil targets, there would be little hope of reducing fatalities below 50 or more millions.[47]

This estimate assumes a full civil-defense program (cost $3.4 billion) and a major active-defense program (cost, including ABM, $30.1 billion). "To maintain or improve the postures shown [against an evolving Soviet threat] might involve continuing annual expenditures of $4 to $5 billion."[48]

If the United States relies only on an assured-destruction posture plus a limited civil-defense program, U.S. fatalities resulting from a Soviet first strike would be about 130–135 million. With a full civil-defense program, these estimates would be reduced to about 110–115 American fatalities.[49] A major active-defense program (two variations

---

[46] *The New York Times,* October 11, 1966, p. 22.
[47] *McNamara 1966 Posture Statement,* p. 55.
[48] *Ibid.,* p. 5.
[49] *Ibid.,* p. 53.

were proposed by Secretary McNamara in his 1966 testimony) might reduce U.S. fatalities to 50–95 million people. Damage-limiting-posture A (costing $22.5 billion) might reduce fatalities to 80–90 million and posture B (costing $30.1 billion) to 50–80 million in an early urban attack.[50] These figures indicate that active defense might reduce expected casualties by approximately one-half—a margin that might determine whether the United States would survive as a nation.

In the realm of strategic weaponry, both offensive and defensive, the Soviet Union is forging ahead; whereas the United States is deferring decisions about defensive weapons and is unable to introduce new offensive weapons into its inventory before the early 1970's,[51] even though the Soviet challenge to the strategic balance of power may be made before then. The competition is between two diametrically opposed security philosophies—an all-out U.S. commitment to the offense and the Soviet choice of an offense-defense balance. It is an ironic fact that many of the most informed and perceptive American strategic analysts believe that the Soviet choice is the correct one.

Because of this fundamental difference in posture, the strategic advantage the United States has enjoyed since World War II is no longer assured. With the United States engaged in a protracted struggle in South Vietnam that is commanding its attention, energies, and available funds, the Soviets could well use the opportunity to bridge the strategic gap or even to push ahead. Even prior to 1970, the situation may very well have disastrous ramifications for the United States.

The Countervailing Principle

In choosing an effective strategy for its future security, the United States should "test" possible alternatives in relation to the strategic choices open to the Soviet Union and to Communist China. If the

[50] *Ibid.*, p. 54.

[51] "A rapid increase in the Soviet ICBM force is causing concern among some officers in the Pentagon. . . . The hard facts about the looming challenge to our strategic superiority in the nuclear delivery field are sufficient to make it likely that a new debate about a potential 'missile gap' may develop in the months to come."—Hanson W. Baldwin, "U.S. Lead in ICBM's Said to Be Reduced by Buildup in Soviet Union," p. 14.

problem were essentially a static one, it would be comparatively easy to design a U.S. strategic posture capable of coping with a known Soviet strategic force. But the security problems facing the United States are intrinsically dynamic, and probable interactions among the United States, the Soviet Union, and Communist China are difficult to predict.

In recent years, the Pentagon's usual pattern in making military choices has involved assessing the existing and projected enemy threat and then adjusting U.S. weapons selection and procurement levels accordingly. This practice of opposing a given threat with appropriate power might be called the *countervailing principle*. In the face of a comparatively low Soviet threat, the United States can choose to embrace a relatively low yet adequate strategic posture. A major difficulty in applying the countervailing principle, however, is the difficulty of assessing with precise accuracy the adversary's present or projected forces. The Department of Defense is particularly aware of the uncertainties of strategic planning and of the probabilities of error in its intelligence estimates of Soviet strategic offensive and defensive forces.[52] Yet, in spite of this awareness, the

---

[52] In 1965, Secretary McNamara stated: "Pervading the entire Damage Limiting problem is the factor of uncertainty of which there are at least three major types—technical, operational and strategic. Technical uncertainties stem from the question of whether a given system can be developed with the performance characteristics specified. Operational uncertainties stem from the question of whether a given system will actually perform as planned in the operational environment.

"The third type, strategic uncertainty, is perhaps the most troublesome since it stems from the question of what our opponent or opponents will actually do—what kind of force they will actually build, what kind of attack they will actually launch, and how effective their weapons will actually be."—*Statement of Secretary of Defense Robert McNamara Before the House Armed Services Committee on the Fiscal Year 1966–70 Defense Program and 1966 Defense Budget* (mimeo.), February 18, 1965, pp. 40–41.

In 1966, McNamara reiterated this point by stating that "in order to assess the capabilities of our general nuclear war forces over the next several years, we must take into account the size and character of the forces the Soviets are likely to have during the same period. While we have reasonably high confidence in our estimates for the near future, our estimates for the latter part of this decade and the early part of the next are subject to great uncertainties. As I pointed out in past appearances before this Committee, such projections are, at best, only informed estimates, particularly since they deal with a period beyond the production and deployment lead-times of the weapon systems involved."—*McNamara 1966 Posture Statement*, p. 3.

Department of Defense at times acts as if it can estimate exactly what Soviet capabilities will be and what risks they will pose to the United States.

Realistically, we can never be absolutely certain of our estimates on future Soviet capabilities. The consequence for the United States is that it may inadvertently overrate its own speed and accuracy in detecting and reacting to marked changes in Soviet capabilities and shifts in Soviet strategy. For example, suppose the Soviets' increased intercontinental-missiles inventory is matched by their acquisition of a penetration capability. The United States has probably been able to discover the former in time to take appropriate countermeasures; but because of the complexities of missile penetration, we might not learn at all of the latter. Also, there is the distinct possibility that the Soviets will succeed in deploying a new weapons system in space without immediate discovery by the United States.

It is easy to ignore these possibilities, yet the failure of the United States to anticipate the Soviet missile gambit in Cuba is a matter of record and should serve as a warning against this kind of euphoria. While the U.S. intelligence system provides some guarantee against surprises, it cannot be relied upon as our *only* protection.

U.S. R&D programs are not especially geared to counter possible Soviet weapons surprises rapidly or to provide the weapons that might be needed to execute a wider range of strategic options. To take account of the full spectrum of technological threats and counters, the U.S. R&D effort would have to be reoriented and its scope enlarged. Let us assume, for example, that the United States continues to judge an ABM system provocative, infeasible, or too costly and that the Pentagon decides not to deploy the system that it has already developed. Since the Soviet Union is in the process of deploying its ABM system or systems, a strategic imbalance will naturally arise as the Soviets proceed to round out their deployment. If the United States wished to discourage the Soviet ABM deployment, it could inform the Soviets that ABM's would be deployed around Washington and New York to match Soviet ABM deployment around Leningrad and Moscow. To take this action, however, the United States would need production facilities, which it presently does not have, for making and deploying these weapons quickly.

If the United States wishes to apply the countervailing principle more effectively, it must (1) devote greater intelligence efforts to obtaining information on Soviet technological developments and (2) devise mechanisms to ensure that when such information is received, it is headed more promptly than has sometimes been the case in the past. In addition, the United States must drastically reduce the production time of long-load-time weapons that it may need in the future. Given the uncertainties of long-range technological intelligence estimates, U.S. R&D programs, for maximum security effectiveness, must not only develop counters to expected adversary capabilities but also innovate technological developments that promise future strategic *advantages* to the United States. If such a dynamic approach toward tomorrow's security is to operate effectively, the United States must rely less on imprecise evaluations of future intentions and more on hard estimates of our adversary's growing weapons capabilities.

There are two principal problems involved in intelligence forecasting. The first is the availability of precise information regarding the adversary's capabilities. The second concerns policy-makers' manipulation of intelligence to match the subjective desires of key officials—in keeping with the saying that the "wish is father to the thought." In recent years, the latter tendency has become too common. The U.S. intelligence community has forecast most developments clearly and accurately. The problem is that the political authorities refused to accept or recognize them until they became so obvious that they could not be ignored. The Soviet ABM development is a classic example.

Intelligence about technology is hard to obtain, not only because the work is hidden in laboratories and closed facilities, but also because the end purpose of research and development is never obvious. The information that an adversary is working on a hypersonic aircraft does not invariably indicate that the end product will be put to military use. Some will argue that the adversary is developing hypersonic vehicles for commercial transport purposes, and no one can prove that they are wrong. The fact that developments can be undertaken for a multiplicity of purposes complicates the task of intelligence forecasting.

Lead Time for Survival

History is strewn with accounts of sincere, brilliant men of good will who have failed to meet the political, social, and economic responsibilities entrusted to them by their societies. Bitter, bloody, and irrevocable tragedy has often followed. Affluent and technically advanced nations have sometimes been cruelly dismantled by poor and technically inferior tyrannies because the advanced nations lacked the will to use their resources and knowledge to survive and were beaten at their own game.

Sparta conquered Athens when it mastered the superior naval technology that had been the sinew of Athenian power. When the Romans finally surpassed the Carthaginians in their ability to fight on the sea, Carthage was destroyed. Germany did not invent the airplane, nor did it leapfrog England and France in aircraft and armored-tank technology, which was available to any of the Western powers; but it breached the Maginot Line and drove the British to the sea at Dunkirk. Since World War II, the Soviet Union, once a predominantly land-based power, has sought mastery in missile warfare and space.

A thousand years ago, it took but a few hours to forge a sword and perhaps six months to equip a slow-moving army, which might travel ten miles a day. During World War II, it took some three to five years to design, build, and deploy a fighter plane or a tank. Now, to take full advantage of technical knowledge and to keep pace with the technological advances of other nations, it takes even longer to design and build strategic weapons. In modern security management, *lead time* has consequently become a critical factor for weapons development and national survival.

Currently, it can take from ten to fifteen years to conceive and develop a radically new ICBM. If we are to face realistically the alternatives before us, we must recognize that our weapons systems and corresponding strategic posture for the 1970's will come from yesterday's and today's work. To wait until 1970 to alter our strategic posture for 1975 will be too late for translating our technology into advanced deployed weapons systems.

Growing lead times pose other problems that are not generally understood. Individuals currently responsible for U.S. security, including the Secretary of Defense and overseas commanders, become concerned about a new threat when they learn about a new weapon being tested by an adversary. Unless the weapon is completely unanticipated or novel, they may have three to five years to develop a counter to it. On the other hand, the total lead time from the Soviet Union's current basic research to an achieved operational capability exceeds the period in which any Secretary of Defense is likely to be responsible for U.S. security, particularly for analyzing hostile threats and choosing compensating weapons. Under these circumstances, if the United States is unwilling to start work on long-lead-time systems in the absence of a clear military threat, its forces cannot hope to get these systems *in time* if a threat appears in the future. For this reason, the weapons slow-down during the past five years will confront the next few U.S. Presidents with almost insuperable strategic problems.

The surging technological revolution is forcing us to question the permanence of such conceptual conditions as nuclear stalemate, deterrence, or *détente*. Is there any way of judging the Soviet approach to these problems? In estimating an adversary's potential, relatively little effort should be devoted to divining his future intentions, for these are rarely predictable. What we can do is assess his capabilities and then visualize the range of actions he might take, given certain kinds and levels of forces. Motivations and intentions can be judged retrospectively, however, since the capabilities that exist today reflect the past intentions that created them. If one looks at evolving Soviet strategic capability from this perspective, the most salient feature of Soviet military planning has been the *continuing search for decisive advantage.*

A comparison of the 1967 weapons programs of the United States and the Soviet Union, in both offensive and defensive aspects, uncovers the possibility that the United States may be rapidly moving into a lead-time cul-de-sac.

The Military Coin: Offense and Defense

The Soviet Union already possesses a massive air-defense system, including warning, surface-to-air missiles, and interceptor aircraft that might be able to blunt a retaliatory attack by the dwindling number of manned aircraft of the U.S. Strategic Air Command. For the near future, the major portion of the U.S. strategic retaliatory forces will consist of Polaris and Minuteman missiles possessing a relatively low payload and hence relatively low-yield warheads and a minimal capacity for penetration. Only if their penetration could be assured would these missile forces be suitable for both a damage-limiting and a counterforce strategy.

Perhaps the most conclusive public evidence that the Soviets have already deployed a strong antiballistic-missile system was expressed by Senator Albert Gore, chairman of the Senate Disarmament Subcommittee:

> Gore expressed these views in an interview following the first series of disarmament subcommittee hearings on how the U.S. should respond to Russia's deployment of a missile defense. His subcommittee has heard testimony from both military and Central Intelligence Agency leaders on Russian ABM progress. Gore said Russia is installing a missile defense for Moscow and 26 other areas. The defensive missiles outside Moscow have a dual role of intercepting high altitude bombers as well as missiles, according to the intelligence leaders.[53]

By extrapolating from their past deployment record for other major weapons, we should have anticipated the progressive build-up of the Soviet antiballistic-missile system, particularly since the Soviets had tested operational offensive and defensive missiles armed with nuclear warheads prior to the test-ban treaty.

A prudent U.S. planner would credit the Soviet antiballistic-missile system with an effectiveness at least comparable to most U.S. development. While some U.S. offensive missiles could probably penetrate this system, many of them might not reach their targets.[54] On the U.S. side, even if the decision to deploy an ABM were made now, a minimum of four to five years would be required to make the system operational and thus to provide protection for large urban complexes in the United States or hard-point defense of its missile silos.

---

[53] George C. Wilson, "Gore Proposes U.N. Supervision of American and Soviet ABMs," *Washington Post*, February 13, 1967, p. 7.

[54] The counter argument, baldly stated, is that "since the Soviet defense will be ineffective against our steadily improving offensive panoply, a reasonable response would be cynical satisfaction at their waste of resources, and relief that Moscow continues to prefer defensive expenditures to offensive ones. The only real concern, escalated arms competition, should be allayed by the recognition that there is no compelling reason for us to join it."—Jeremy J. Stone, "The Anti-Missile Folly," *The New Leader*, January 2, 1967, p. 13.

Mention has been made of the stress that Soviet doctrinal writings place on the value of pre-emptive first strike. The accurate, high-yield Soviet missiles would provide an effective counterforce weapon against existing and projected land-based U.S. defensive missile forces that were undefended. If the Soviets could destroy a high percentage of U.S. Minuteman missiles in their silos, then the Soviet ABM system would have to defend only against the residual land-based U.S. missile forces and Polaris missiles launched from the sea. Unfortunately, because of their trajectory, the Polaris offers a Soviet ABM system an easier target than an incoming intercontinental ballistic missile.

A technological lead-time cul-de-sac is not hypothetical, for the offensive and defensive forces that both the United States and the Soviet Union have been acquiring may soon fit the model just described. The longer the United States delays in the deployment of an antiballistic-missile defense system or in the procurement and deployment of ICBM's with much larger payloads than those it now possesses—or, far worse still, puts off both these actions—the faster the deterrent value of the U.S. strategic force will decline. In fact, only by constant improvement of both the sword (offense) and the shield (defense) of its strategic forces can this decline be avoided. Today, as in previous periods of history, there is a never-ending contest between the offense and the defense, occurring not only in tactical weaponry and warfare—for example, in Vietnam—but also in the field of strategic bombers and ICBM's—for example, in surface-to-air missiles and antiballistic-missile systems. In this cyclical struggle between offense and defense, developments in one area promote improvements in the other. This reciprocal feedback mechanism is the most constant aspect of military preparations.

Until the middle of 1963, manned SAC bombers constituted the mainstay of U.S. strategic offensive forces. The first defense against this form of attack was radar-controlled antiaircraft guns and fighter interceptors. The Soviet air-defense system entered its main period of growth after the Korean War, when the U.S. bomber force was being greatly strengthened. In 1955, the Soviets began to add a surface-to-air antiaircraft missile to their air-defense forces. This missile was designed for use against aircraft flying as high as 60,000 feet. Together with guns and fighter aircraft, these first-generation missiles were incorporated into a separate command—the PVO air-defense forces.[55]

During this same period—the middle and late 1950's—as the Soviet SAM's were being deployed, the U.S. was beginning to deploy its Nike-Ajax air-defense missile, followed by its second-generation successor, the Nike-Hercules system. The deployment of SAM's led many military people both here and in the Soviet Union to believe that these missiles spelled the end of manned combat aircraft.

The massive, rapid deployment of Soviet SA-2 missiles forced SAC to modify its aircraft structurally for low-altitude penetration. These bombers were formerly designed for high-altitude penetration, but the strengthening of tail and wing surfaces, the provision of more powerful engines, and increased fuel capacity would allow them to penetrate below the minimum altitude (3000–5000 feet) of Soviet radar systems and SA-2 arming devices. In addition, stand-off nuclear-armed missiles (air-to-surface), decoys, electronic countermeasure systems, and terrain-avoidance radar systems were added to further ensure successful penetration.[56] Without these additions, improvements, and modifications, SAC's ability to penetrate Soviet SAM defenses might have decreased considerably.

The war in Vietnam has demonstrated inadequacies in the SA-2's, which are deployed throughout North Vietnam. In fact, only 5 per cent of the SA-2's fired have hit and downed U.S. aircraft. To counter the threat, U.S. fighter-bombers have adopted a variety of countermeasures, including new evasive tactics, air controllers and directors,

[55] PVO, Protivo-Vozdushnaya Oborona, literally means Anti-Air Defense. *The Dictionary of Basic Military Terms* (Moscow, 1965), p. 181, defines PVO thus: "Defense from an air enemy. It is divided into: (1) PVO of the troops; (2) National PVO; and (3) PVO of the Navy.

"*PVO of the Troops* represents a complex of military actions of different forces and means of PVO, carried out with the aim of repelling enemy aviation and rocket strikes on troops and rear objects in mutual support with troops of National PVO.

"*National PVO* is the totality of general government measures securing the active defense of the vitality of important regions and objects in the territory of the country from actions on them from the air. National PVO is carried out first of all by the troops of National PVO, fulfilling missions in defeating the enemy in the air in mutual action with all services of the armed forces.

"In contemporary conditions, PVO includes anti-airplane, anti-rocket, and anti-cosmic defense."

[56] Leon H. Dulberger, "Advanced Strategic Bombers," *Space/Aeronautics*, June, 1966, *passim*.

and low-altitude penetration and defense suppression.[57] Nevertheless, the presence of the Soviet SAM's in North Vietnam has forced the U.S. aircraft to attack at lower altitude, where conventional radar-directed automatic guns have taken a considerable toll.[58]

Ironically, although one could conjecture about the accuracy of the SA-2 against high-altitude B-52's before the latter were modified to attack at low altitude, Secretary McNamara adduced the supposed SA-2 effectiveness (which is now known to have been exaggerated) as justification for terminating manned-bomber production in 1962 and delaying the start of production of a new manned bomber. Meanwhile, the Soviets have introduced SAM's, which presumably are effective at low altitudes.[59]

As this brief history suggests, in the recurrent battle between defense and offense, air defenses do not have the upper hand when offensive penetration capabilities work as they should. With regard to the tug of war between offensive and defensive missiles, the defensive technology of the ABM seems to be catching up, even though only ten years ago any defense against an ICBM was deemed impossible.

In light of the evidence that the Soviets are deploying an ABM, the need for qualitative improvement for the U.S. ICBM force should not be (and is not being) neglected, and the capability of U.S. offensive forces to carry out an assured-destruction mission must be constantly improved. Conversely, once defense against any form of attack becomes feasible, the outcome of a hypothetical nuclear exchange—and hence the deterrent credibility of a given strategic force —will favor the side possessing the optimum mix of offensive and defensive weapons.

Air attack and defense in Vietnam is a lesson in the uncertainty associated with sophisticated weapons development and deployment, for the performance of a given weapon may exceed or fall below ex-

[57] *Aviation Week and Space Technology,* "Special Report: The War in Vietnam," 1966, p. 17; and Sam Butz, "Our Pilots Call Hanoi 'Dodge City,'" *The New York Times Magazine,* September 16, 1966, p. 66.

[58] Butz, *op. cit.,* pp. 64, 72; Hanson Baldwin, "Air Missiles in Vietnam," *The New York Times,* July 15, 1966; and Neil Sheehan, "Hanoi Bolstering Air Raid Defenses," *The New York Times,* September 28, 1966, p. 1.

[59] Butz, *op. cit.,* p. 68; and *Aviation Week and Space Technology,* "Special Report," p. 20. See *Technology Week,* "World Missile/Space Encyclopedia Issue," July 25, 1966, pp. 133–35 for Soviet SAM data and code names.

pectations—either to the advantage or to the disadvantage of the offense. In Vietnam, the air offense has gained the edge, though at considerable cost. As for missiles, we do not know what the interaction of U.S. ICBM's and the Soviet ABM would be. The Defense Department appears to underestimate the possible effectiveness of the Soviet ABM. If its analysis should be wrong, the lack of either the Poseidon or an improved-capability missile may mean a lengthy period (1967–71) during which U.S. offensive forces may not be as effective as they are credited with being.

It is important to keep in mind the dynamic and reciprocal relations (offensive and defensive) of the technological battle. In dialectical fashion, the offensive and defensive tend to catch up with each other. Consequently, military superiority is dependent on simultaneous efforts to maximize the effectiveness of both offensive and defensive systems.

As of 1967, the United States was not vigorously engaged in efforts to improve the two components of its strategic forces. Although there may still be sufficient time to reverse this trend, the day may come when it will be impossible. At a certain stage in the development of a Soviet offensive-defensive posture, when the U.S.S.R. is capable of successfully launching a first strike against the United States and of subsequently defending the Soviet heartland, the Soviet Union may one day inform the United States through diplomatic channels that it will not tolerate the deployment of a U.S. antiballistic system or any improvement in U.S. offensive missile systems. If the United States were to acquiesce to such an ultimatum, its world position would crumble.

In 1966, the United States was devoting much of its energies to the struggle in Vietnam. Some of the U.S. defense efforts in Vietnam (desirable though the author believes them to be) were made at the expense of the future strength of U.S. strategic offensive and defensive systems. Although there has been no noticeable build-up of conventional forces in the Soviet Union, there has been a steady increase in the power of Soviet striking forces, in the efficiency of Soviet defenses against strategic attack, and in the production of fissionable material.

The pendulum swings back and forth in many areas of human endeavor. President Eisenhower's 1954 "New Look" placed primary reliance on nuclear weapons for the security of the United States. Since 1961, the emphasis has been in the other direction: U.S. conventional and tactical forces have been expanded, while the operational role of nuclear weapons has been deliberately played down as a matter of policy. The human desire to diminish the potential role of nuclear weapons is understandable, but it is debatable whether this is a practical course for the United States to follow in relation to an adversary who appears to be placing increasing stress on such weapons. Whatever the reason, the Department of Defense has not acted on the logic of its own offensive-defensive strategic analysis. One should, therefore, distinguish sharply between Defense Department rhetoric and the weapons it buys or the strategic forces it maintains or creates.

Between Strategic Superiority and Arms Control: Some Suggested Actions

Despite tendencies to overlook Soviet capabilities and to stress Soviet peaceful intentions, both the President of the United States and the Secretary of Defense have pledged themselves to maintain U.S. strategic superiority until an effective arms control agreement can be reached with the Soviet Union. These pledges notwithstanding, the crucial issue, as I have pointed out, is whether the Soviet Union may be on the verge of gaining an irreversible lead-time advantage over the United States in critical weapons systems.

I do not wish to impugn the sincerity of either the President or his Defense Secretary. In making pledges to maintain U.S. strategic superiority, they mean what they say. But day-to-day actions and decisions—carried out for reasons of efficiency, economy, or the demands of social programs, arms control,[60] or the war in Vietnam—are undermining their pledges.

I have sought to demonstrate that the Soviet Union is contesting

[60] A ranking Soviet diplomatic official, participating in a conference on arms control and related matters in October, 1966, made it clear that the Soviet Union considers it perfectly natural to acquire all possible means of defense, including antimissile missiles. In reply to a question about possible Soviet reactions to a U.S. missile defense program, he said that his country would not find this particularly disturbing. In fact, he added, Russian observers often find it difficult to understand why there is such a heated debate about the "destabilizing" effects of missile defense in the United States.—James E. Dougherty (conference participant) memorandum to William R. Kintner, November 4, 1966.

U.S. strategic superiority by deploying both an antiballistic-missile system and a rapidly expanding force of ICBM's. I have concluded that the United States is moving into a technological cul-de-sac that might enable the Soviet Union to reverse the existing world balance of power. The uncertainties associated with this conclusion relate to the effectiveness of the ABM system now being deployed by the Soviet Union, which, in turn, is related to the technical proficiency of the penetration aids carried by U.S. missiles. In spite of these uncertainties, it is apparent that if present U.S. policies toward procuring strategic offensive and defensive forces remain unchanged, the Soviet Union could in the near future achieve a significant first-strike advantage over the United States. This development, with all its attendent risks to the survival of this nation, may yet be avoided— provided the United States immediately takes the following priority actions:

1. Begins the immediate deployment of an ABM system.

2. Procures from existing production facilities and deploys several hundred additional Minutemen. (This action should ensure offensive superiority during years of peak danger—that is, before follow-on missiles can be added to the U.S. inventory.)[61]

3. Accelerates production of Minuteman III and Poseidon missiles and initiates rapid development of the improved-capability missile.

4. Retains in inventory all available B-52 and B-58 bombers (providing an alternative attack mode) until advanced follow-on manned bombers are available.

5. Accelerates development and production of an advanced manned bomber. (If the FB-III proves effective, it should be pressed into service sooner.)

6. Speeds up the civil-defense shelter program.

7. Increases its program of underground testing so as to improve its ABM capability as well as its offensive re-entry vehicles.

[61] The only action Defense Secretary McNamara decided to take after conceding that there was "considerable evidence" that the Soviet Union was building and deploying an antiballistic-missile system was the accelerated development and deployment of the Poseidon missile. "Deployment of the Poseidon would mean complete re-engineering of the firing tubes on this country's fleet of Polaris submarines from which the missiles would be launched if necessary.

"The Secretary said that this and other 'refitting' changes would cost 'somewhat in excess' of 60 per cent of the initial cost of the Polaris submarines."— *The New York Times,* November 11, 1966, p. 1.

The measures just listed will compensate for some of the mistakes made in the past. Assuming the United States passes through the years of peak danger, it is fundamentally imperative that it adopt a basic policy of technological innovation to stay ahead of, rather than respond defensively to, Soviet developments. For example, the failure of the United States to possess a MRBM should be rectified immediately. As the foregoing actions are taken, the United States should publish internationally (as much as intelligence security permits) its official estimates of Soviet ABM complexes and launchers and Soviet offensive missiles. Simultaneously it should reiterate its efforts to induce the Soviet Union to forgo an ABM deployment as well as to place a "freeze" on offensive forces. The United States should indicate its willingness to enter into around-the-clock disarmament talks on the basis of reciprocal inspection of all arms reduction. At the same time, U.S. leaders should convey to the Soviet leadership by concrete actions a determination to maintain strategic superiority, at whatever cost, until such agreements are reached. These are the steps that need to be taken if American security and world peace are to be preserved.

A Doctrine of Selective Response

To maintain order—the basic prerequisite for any civilized society —justice needs to be supported by appropriate degrees of physical power. The issues raised by the advent of nuclear weapons revolve around the kind of power that can appropriately be used to defend the international order against its would-be disturbers.

The fact that nuclear weapons can, by their very existence, deter what might otherwise be serious threats to the peace has enabled many people to escape Communist subjugation. The maintenance of the nuclear deterrent has been a formidable task. No one would argue that the U.S. nuclear deterrent is entirely free of all dangers; no course of action in world politics is entirely safe. Yet, thus far, the Western world, under U.S. leadership, has managed both to contain most Communist efforts toward expansion and to persuade its adversaries to refrain from resorting to nuclear conflict. At the same time, the United States has sought with patience and imagination to find a doctrine for nuclear war that is morally defensible. It has moved from the doctrine of massive retaliation against population centers to the doctrine of a deliberate, selective, and controlled response, which insofar as it is possible, seeks to avoid the destruction of nonmilitary targets.

The President of the United States has at his disposal the nuclear arsenal that safeguards the freedom and security of this country and many other nations and supports U.S. commitments and political prestige. Both the President and the American people bear immense responsibilities for world peace. They cannot treat the issues of nuclear strategy as simplistically as some of those who live in countries that have little or no nuclear power.

To a considerable extent, the reduction of unnecessary casualties is implicit in the doctrine of deliberate, selective, and controlled response as well in the strategic concept called counterforce. The counterforce concept was first seriously considered by the United States in 1961 but subsequently abandoned. U.S. officials had concluded that the difficulty of pinpointing target locations, plus the combination of relatively inaccurate missiles and the high-yield weapons they were carrying, would make it impossible to conduct a counterforce attack that would differ fundamentally from the attacks that would be launched against cities. Technological developments, particularly in the last several years, may again make it possible for the United States to pursue a second-strike policy that would not necessarily result in the indiscriminate destruction of the adversary's population. Conceivably, a damage-limiting strategy or a quantitatively superior counterforce posture could meet the requirements. If the United States held the strategic posture that such a policy demanded, the likelihood of nuclear war might be greatly diminished.

Within the past several years, an effective antiballistic defense system appears to have become technically feasible at a cost that is within U.S. means. If it is desirable to lessen the indiscriminate damage that might be inflicted on the populations of other nations, it is also an obligation of a government to attempt to protect its own population from the attacks of nations whose leaders may be less restrained by moral strictures. At the very least, the United States should develop a ballistic-missile defense (BMD) to combat any blackmail that China might attempt against our population after acquiring long-range delivery means in the 1970's. But even beyond this purpose, the acquisition of a BMD would help to guarantee the maintenance of that margin of U.S. strategic superiority which has rendered the Soviets noticeably less belligerent since the Cuban missile crisis.

Beyond building up its defenses, the United States should also develop strike forces that can destroy opposing offensive forces with the least possible collateral damage to civilian populations. Again, there are developments in reconnaissance capabilities and guidance systems and reductions in weight-to-yield ratios of nuclear warheads that could permit a discriminating, selective, and deliberately phased counterattack. Even though it may be impossible to insulate all civilian populations from the collateral damage of a nuclear conflict, the United States, which has the resources to develop discriminating strategic forces, should be under some compulsion to do so.

During World War II, moral nihilism was manifest in the bombing of Rotterdam, London, and Hamburg; in the indiscriminate attacks on Leipzig and Dresden; and in the atomic strikes against Hiroshima and Nagasaki. Technical limitations and an inadequate understanding of strategic targeting may have justified these raids. However, such indiscriminate attacks may no longer be militarily useful except when all other means of breaking the enemy's will have failed. Consequently, either the resort to force must be ruled out as an instrument of policy under any circumstances or means must be sought to make war in the nuclear age a more rational instrument of national policy than it has thus far been conceived to be. By these criteria, finite deterrence must be rejected as a concept and a strategy; it approaches the epitome of moral nihilism, since it is clearly based on achieving the maximum destruction of populations.

Since there is no possibility of repealing the nuclear age, humanity must learn to live with the immense destructive power than can result from either nuclear fission or nuclear fusion. Modern technology is forcing all peoples into a new world community and is creating a mutuality of interests among nations. The earth is everyone's home and neighborhood. No longer is it possible for one nation to inflict great destruction upon peoples at a distance without inviting retaliation from some corner. Nuclear pacifism is not a way out of our dilemma. The balance must be struck between world peace and the defense of values and of life—not only life itself but also the quality of life. Indiscriminate destruction of mankind would be a debasement of man's humanity. Hence, the need for strategic forces that can be employed with discrimination and restraint confronts the leaders of the West with a moral obligation from which they cannot escape.

Superior forces designed in accordance with such criteria will enable the United States to reap political gain from its present and potential nuclear advantage. The resultant strengthening of the strategic link between North America and Western Europe would ease the task of coping with Communist pressures in many parts of the globe. A credible U.S. superiority might also favorably influence the United States–Soviet dialogue on arms control. As a precondition, however, U.S. military research and development must be of such magnitude and quality as to neutralize single or multiple Soviet technological break-throughs. Perhaps the U.S. combination of superior forces-in-being and potentially superior forces-in-prospect might eventually convince the Soviets that a continuation of the arms race would be an unjustified diversion of their resources.

The Soviets cannot be expected to reach such a decision in the near future. In the interim, the United States should develop new monitoring and surveillance techniques that would warn not only against nuclear developments in the U.S.S.R. but also against any hostile build-up that might lead to conflict elsewhere. A combination of superior power and more effective intelligence about Communist capabilities and activities can assist us in keeping the peace until Communist leaders abandon whatever hopes they may have of imposing their system upon people by coercion.

9

Power and Persuasion

The relationship between power and values has always posed one of mankind's most vexing philosophical problems. The advent of nuclear weapons has magnified the problem, but the essential question remains unresolved: What are the appropriate objectives for which power should be used?

Although power is always usable, at least in the psychological sense of influencing human behavior, it is commonly assumed that neither the United States nor the Soviet Union can consider resort to general nuclear war, or even the risk of such a conflict, a rational instrument of foreign policy. Nevertheless, both the United States and the Soviet Union, as well as other nations, continue to produce nuclear weapons and to develop related military capabilities. The Soviet Union is apparently striving for technological military superiority; likewise, the United States—despite the assertions of those who hold that a technological stalemate exists between the two leading nuclear powers—is officially committed to maintaining a technological military lead over the Soviets.

Each side's nuclear posture will influence the other's actions in confrontations between them or with Communist China. Because nuclear weapons and delivery systems, whether they are used or not, are the core of the military strength of both sides, the power best equipped to use them in ways that can yield military advantage will be able to act with greater assurance and enjoy greater psychological confidence in periods of international crisis.

The United States cannot contemplate using nuclear forces the way Marxism-Leninism permits Communist leaders to consider such a contingency. As General Gavin has suggested: "The thought still persists in many minds that the ultimate in sophistication and usefulness in weapons systems is the high-yield megaton bomb delivered by missile or aircraft. By its very nature it is believed that it should be able to cope with almost any threat to our survival."[1] Obviously, we can solve few political problems by just projecting our superior nuclear posture. Our hydrogen bombs cannot prevent Egyptians, Indonesians, or South Vietnamese Buddhists from burning USIA libraries. However, the possession of strategic superiority, together with the threat that its possible use implies to Communist leaders, will put a restraint on the Soviet's instigation and exploitation of crises. Thus, nuclear weapons can provide a protective mantle under which, with other means, the United States can safely oppose Communist incursions into various parts of the world.

U.S. support of its foreign policy by means of peaceful persuasion would be lost, however, if Soviet leaders were ever able to gain what they seek: comprehensive strategic superiority over the United States. The Soviet drive to achieve such superiority issues from the well-spring of Marxism-Leninism, which asserts that mastery of physical things precedes mastery of the political order. Elsewhere I predicted:

> It is conceivable that in time political warfare . . . will completely replace military warfare between nations and become the primary weapon in international struggles for power. It is also likely that the political warfare of the future will not be based on the philosophical rhetoric of today. The class warfare source of communist ideological motivation is probably too narrow to serve much longer as a base for conflict strategy. Man may abandon general military warfare, for its growing destructiveness may make it altogether irrational; but, unless man completely abandons conflict, he will engage in variations of political warfare. For the present, military and political warfare are likely to exist side by side. It is probable that those most capable of their combined use will achieve victory.[2]

Unfortunately, the Western world in general and the United States in particular have not been very adroit in political warfare and other forms of unconventional conflict. From time to time, the United States has resorted to the ultimate threat of nuclear war to compensate for its failure to anticipate and prevent political defeat. Castro's take-over of Cuba and the resultant missile crisis provides the classic

[1] James M. Gavin, "Military Power: The Limits of Persuasion," *Saturday Review*, July 30, 1966, p. 20.
[2] William R. Kintner and Joseph Z. Kornfeder, *The New Frontier of War* (Chicago: Henry Regnery, 1963), p. xix.

example of strategic superiority snatching a partial victory from the jaws of political disaster. Yet many Americans advocate that the United States give up its strategic advantage before the American people and their government acquire greater competence and sophistication in combating the subtler forms of expansion.

Windows for Strategic Choice

What leaders perceive about the future and their adversaries' behavior in that future influences their choice of strategic weapons today. These perceptions are affected, in turn, by their separate environments. The cultural milieu and the prevalent values guiding conduct often determine the choices of strategy by individual leaders. For this reason, the differences in philosophical beliefs prevalent in American and Soviet society directly influence attitudes in Washington and Moscow toward the utility of nuclear weapons, delivery means, and defensive measures.

Commenting on the interplay of arms control measures, inspection, and the basic conflict of U.S.–U.S.S.R. objectives, Charles Burton Marshall wrote:

> The mode of thought underlying the U.S. approach, whether or not recognized and acknowledged, rests on ideas of natural law. A Unified Creation, with a pattern of right reason inherent, is postulated. Good is identified with it. Principles are held as reflections of this good. What opposes good is ascribed to aberrant free will. Interests are seen as colored with such aberrant imperfections associated with misguided free will. Principles thus transcend interests.[3]

On the other hand:

> The U.S.S.R. view is different. The U.S.S.R. asserts a total claim on the future, based on its dialectic concepts of history. An essential aspect of this claim is that history progresses by inherent momentum toward a final perfection perceivable only through Communist doctrine. Concepts of legitimacy are derived from the law of history which ordains eventual universal triumph for Communist interests and purposes. All other interests and purposes are deemed deviant and devoid of legitimacy.[4]

[3] Charles Burton Marshall, *Cuba: Thoughts Prompted by the Crisis* (Washington, D.C.: Washington Center of Foreign Policy Research, 1963), p. 17.
[4] *Ibid.*, p. 18.

The influence that these respective sets of philosophical principles have on U.S. and Soviet strategy differs markedly. Communist ideology has always stressed the inevitability of conflict and its progressive role in human and social development. This attitude helps to shape the Soviet approach toward technology and weapons development. As one Soviet military author wrote:

> Throughout the entire history of wars a contradiction has existed and continues to exist between the means of destruction and the means of defense. . . . It is well known that the law of unity and struggle of opposites reflects the fact that inner contradictions are inherent in all phenomena of nature, society and human thought, and that the resolution of these contradictions constitutes the sources of any development.[5]

Western leaders believe that conflict is destructive and should be avoided whenever possible. The idea that conflict may be the result of aggressive drives inherent in human beings is only reluctantly being accepted. Concerned over the mounting threat to the survival of the human species from the combination of uncontrolled primitive instincts and highly elaborate destructive weapons, Konrad Lorenz wrote:

> Looking upon man as he is today, in his hand the atom bomb, the product of his intelligence, in his heart the aggression drive inherited from his anthropoid ancestors—this seems like a bad dream, and it is hard to believe that aggression is anything but the pathological product of our disjointed cultural and social life.
>
> And one could wish it were no more than that! Knowledge of the fact that the aggression drive is a true, primarily species-preserving instinct enables us to recognize its full danger: it is the spontaneity of the instinct that makes it so dangerous. If it were merely a reaction to certain external factors, as many sociologists and psychologists maintain, the state of mankind would not be as perilous as it really is, for, in that case, the reaction-eliciting factors could be eliminated with some hope of success. . . .
>
> The completely erroneous view that animal and human behavior is predominantly reactive and that, even if it contains any innate elements at all, it can be altered, to an unlimited extent, by learning, comes from a radical misunderstanding of certain democratic principles:

[5] Lieutenant Colonel V. Alekseyev, "The True Compass of the Assimilation and Practical Application of Knowledge," *Krasnaya zvezda* (*Red Star*), January 28, 1964.

it is utterly at variance with these principles to admit that human beings are not born equal and that not all have equal chances of becoming ideal citizens.[6]

It is equally difficult for many Americans to admit that the Western idea of resolving differences through reasonable give-and-take has not taken deep root in many parts of the world. The Soviet leaders, certain that conflict will continue as long as capitalism exists, will naturally prepare for conflict at every level. U.S. leaders will prepare to engage in conflict only when they judge such actions absolutely unavoidable.

These considerations indicate the various roles that nuclear weapons might play in a philosophically and geographically divided world. The Soviets' abrogation of the three-year moratorium on nuclear testing in 1961 and their covert introduction of missiles into Cuba in 1962 were both in keeping with a philosophy that inspires the search for predominant military power.

There has been a constant effort to sell the notion that the Soviets are throttling their atomic development and weapons production in response to our arms control views. There is no evidence to support this notion but much evidence to the contrary. For one thing, the Soviets philosophically reject the technological-plateau theory, which seems to bemuse many American scientists. Peter L. Kapitza, the distinguished Soviet physicist, after reviewing some of the history of great theoretical insights into the nature of matter, asked this question:

Will such discoveries be made in the future? Have the secrets of nature been exhausted? It is typical of these discoveries that their significance is recognized only after twenty or thirty years, when their theoretical importance is understood and when their conflict with contemporary views is resolved. We ask whether there are still fundamental laws of nature waiting to be found.

If we honestly extrapolate this curve, we see that it does not have any tendency toward saturation and that in the very near future many discoveries will be made which will increase our control over nature and put new strength in our hands.

[6] Konrad Lorenz, *On Aggression* (New York: Harcourt, Brace & World, 1963), pp. 50–51. Lorenz is director of the Max-Planck Institute for Behavioral Physiology.

Continuing in this vein, Kapitza stated:

> In seeking new discoveries there is much that awaits us, and here
> Hamlet's words are relevant: "There are more things in heaven and
> earth, Horatio, than are dreamt of in your philosophy." Just as it was
> in Shakespeare's time, so it is today and so it will always be. In essence,
> nothing more or less involved than the law of dialectical development
> of nature.[7]

Such positive attitudes toward fundamental discovery are matched
by Soviet determination to translate discovery into technological military superiority. The following revealing excerpts on this theme are
from an article published in *Communist of the Armed Forces:*

> The achievement of quantitative and qualitative superiority over the
> enemy usually demands long industrial efforts. At the same time, the
> creation of a weapon that is new in principle, secretly nurtured in
> scientific research bureaus and constructors' collectives, can in a short
> time sharply change the relationship of forces.
>
> The *surprise* appearance of one or another new type of weapon is
> coming forward as an essential factor, especially in contemporary cir-
> cumstances. Surprise in this area not only demoralizes the enemy, it
> also deprives him of the possibility of using effective means of protec-
> tion from the new weapon for a long time.[8]

The history of oft-invaded Russia also influences the security decisions of the present masters of the Kremlin. Except for the Civil War,
the United States has never known armed conflict within its borders.
Because they have drunk tragedy's cup to the full, nothing is more
natural for the Russians than to do everything in their power to prevent a recurrence of military disaster. It is just as natural for American leaders, accustomed to a heritage of success and an environment
of affluence and material power, to disregard warnings of potential
tragedy. Thus, the Soviets may overensure and the Americans under-
ensure against the respective risks they pose to each other.

The Debates Around Détente

U.S. strategic nuclear decisions have been greatly influenced if
not actually based on intuitive political judgments. In the normal

[7] *Bulletin of the Atomic Scientists,* April, 1962, p. 4.
[8] Lieutenant Colonel V. Bondarenko, "Military-Technical Superiority: The
Most Important Factor of the Reliable Defense of the Country," *Kommunist
vooruzhennykh sil* (*Communist of the Armed Forces*), September, 1966, p. 10;
unpublished English translation by Harriet Fast Scott.

course of affairs, this is the way it should be. The problem concerns the nature of the informing insights by which these judgments are made. In 1965, a number of former government officials tried to promote a three-year Soviet–United States moratorium on the production of antimissile-missile systems. Jerome B. Wiesner, scientific adviser to President Kennedy, first opposed the ABM as technically infeasible and subsequently argued against building it on the grounds that any attempt to construct a defense against missiles would trigger a United States–Soviet arms race in offensive as well as defensive missiles. Furthermore, he felt that a U.S. decision to build an ABM would "destabilize" the existing strategic balance and disrupt the emerging U.S.–U.S.S.R. *détente.* Apparently, the opponents of the ABM do not believe that the present stability is a function of U.S. strategic superiority and national will power.

The arguments *against* a U.S. ABM defense and a NATO nuclear force and *for* an antiproliferation treaty with the Soviet Union are based on essentially the same political rationale. In a programmatic statement, one of the leading spokesmen for this point of view, Eugene Rabinowitch, set forth reasons why, above all other policy goals, the United States should pursue a policy of *détente* with the Soviet Union.[9] In summary, he argued that because of the U.S.S.R.'s technological and economic growth, the Soviets' interest in self-preservation now takes priority over ideological expansion. "Peaceful coexistence," initially a tactical expedient, has become the primary aim of Soviet policy. China has emerged as a "third world power" and as the ideological leader in the fight against the "capitalist" West and "revisionist" Communism. In fifty years, if not sooner, China is likely to rank with the U.S. and U.S.S.R. as an industrial and military power. Our chance of avoiding a disastrous conflict with a "nuclearized" China lies in ending the Cold War with the U.S.S.R. and in the immediate cooperation of both countries in establishing a stable and economically progressive system "in all areas under their control." Ultimately, China, once she becomes a first-class military and technological power, will have no reasonable alternative but to take her place as a peaceful member in the international community. U.S. policy should aim at closer cooperation with the U.S.S.R. in ensuring

[9] Eugene Rabinowitch, "The New Perspective," *Bulletin of the Atomic Scientists,* November, 1965, pp. 2–3.

stability and in facilitating China's acceptance of peaceful coexistence with the rest of the world. Eventually, the United States and the Soviet Union should form an alliance against Communist China until that nation achieves equivalent rank and is ready to join a three-power world rule.

This kind of rationale focuses on the comparatively remote menace posed by Communist China and ignores the fact that Soviet nuclear power is clearly the more immediate threat to the United States and will remain so for decades to come. It does not allow for the probability that Europe could emerge as a "third power" long before China. In a sense, Europe already qualifies.

Eventually, cooperative relations may develop between the United States and the Soviet Union that will not jeopardize vital Free World interests. But until incipient transformations within the Soviet system take deep root, the prerequisite for termination of the conflict is the maintenance of U.S. superiority. Presumably, the United States, by hewing to a policy of superiority and by applying its technology intelligently, may remain superior indefinitely vis-à-vis the Soviet Union. Yet the advocates of a *détente* oppose indefinitely maintaining U.S. superiority on several grounds.

Superiority is said to lead to instability. The ideas of Lewis F. Richardson have found a ready hearing in this country. He concluded that the more a nation arms itself (even granting that its leaders sincerely desire to preserve peace), the greater are the chances of war:

> What nowadays is euphemistically called national "defense" in fact always includes preparations for attack, and thus constitutes a threat to some other group of people. This type of "defense" is based on the assumption that threats directed toward other people will produce in them either submission or negotiation, or avoidance, and it neglects the possibility that contempt or retaliation may be produced instead. Yet, in fact, the usual effect between comparable nations is retaliation by counterpreparations, thus leading on by way of an arms race toward another way.[10]

[10] Lewis F. Richardson, "Mathematics of War and Foreign Politics," in *The World of Mathematics*, ed. James R. Newman (New York: Simon and Schuster, 1956), II, 1243. See also his *Arms and Insecurity* (Chicago: Quadrangle, 1960). Richardson based this conclusion largely on his analysis of the arms race preceding World War I. He argued that a competitive arms

Others deprecate strategic superiority by concluding that "any attempt, however ingenious and forward-looking, at assimilating nuclear power to the purposes and instrumentalities of the nation-state is negated by the enormity of nuclear destructiveness."[11]

Some students of conflict and international order, however, have suggested that superiority may promote peace and stability in international politics.[12] Particularly, when a revolutionary power aims to upset the *status quo,* the loss of superiority by the defensive powers encourages instability. Inis Claude has maintained that "a potential aggressor is likely to be deterred more effectively by confrontation with preponderant rather than merely equal power."[13] This logic is rejected, however, by those so obsessed by the fear of nuclear weapons that they see no linkage between preponderant strategic power and political advantage. Simultaneously, the Soviets have discovered how to exploit, both actively and passively, Western fears of nuclear war in order to weaken the resolve of their opponents and thus to use nuclear threats of their own for attaining their political goals: "In a sense, the Soviet leaders seem to have grasped what may be the salient strategic truth of our times: That men's minds are by far the most profitable and perhaps the only suitable target system for the new weapons of the nuclear age."[14]

Soviet leaders now discern the possibility, remote as it may seem, that the leading powers of the Free World may in time decide to disarm themselves. In not a few of their international dealings, the

---

race made that war inevitable. The British, however, barely maintained sufficient naval supremacy, nor did they openly assert their secret understandings with France. World War II was made possible by the one-sided German arms race. See *The World of Mathematics,* II, 1246, for Richardson's charts showing the 1909–14 arms race.

[11] Hans Morgenthau, "Four Paradoxes of Nuclear Strategy," *American Political Science Review,* March, 1964, p. 35.

[12] See, for example, A. F. K. Organski, *World Politics* (New York: Knopf, 1958); and Inis L. Claude, Jr., *Power and International Relations* (New York: Random House, 1962).

[13] Claude, *op. cit.,* p. 56. As another writer noted: "The relationship between peace and the balance of power appears to be exactly the opposite of what has been claimed. The periods of balance, real or imagined, are periods of warfare, while the periods of known preponderance are periods of peace."— Organski, *op. cit.,* p. 292.

[14] Thomas W. Wolfe, *Soviet Strategy at the Crossroads* (Cambridge, Mass.: Harvard University Press, 1964), p. 23.

Soviets are acting as if the world had already moved into the post-nuclear age.

> It is not at all inconceivable that the most important result of a continuing arms race in the modern era may be our emergence from the age of "nucleophobia" into what one might term the post-nuclear age. Although the basic conflicts in the world would remain, the post-nuclear age would mark the end of the fear of nuclear war as a dominant motivating force in foreign and domestic policies around the world. This, however, is precisely what the Soviets hope to avoid. Although the Soviets have already lost their fear of nuclear war, they hope to be able to continue exploiting the fear of nuclear war to manipulate the thinking and actions of their opponents.[15]

There is some evidence that the Soviet Union is conducting its foreign policy as if the West had already destroyed its nuclear arsenal or at least a good part of it. The U.S. effort to contain Communism from 1947 to the Cuban missile crisis was generally successful. Subsequently, the West has found it difficult to select any political-military alternatives to nuclear weapons that will halt Communist expansion. Lesser powers, in both the Communist and the non-Communist worlds, appear to believe that a genuine nuclear stalemate exists. For this reason, the nuclear confrontation between the United States and the Soviet Union is held to be of relatively little importance in contemporary world politics—a condition partly responsible for the pursuit of more nationalistic foreign policies in Western Europe and elsewhere.

Bridge Building

Many of those who oppose U.S. efforts to maintain strategic superiority do so on the grounds that American superiority is a prime source of world tensions and must somehow be whittled down if a genuine *détente* with the Soviet Union is to be achieved. Yet global peace is threatened not by nuclear arms that might go off spontaneously but rather by Communist efforts to fuel the many local conflagrations that now dot the globe. According to President Kennedy:

[15] Robert Dickson Crane, "Some Basic Strategies of Arms Control," in *The Prospects for Arms Control*, ed. James E. Dougherty, with John F. Lehman, Jr. (New York: Macfadden-Bartell, 1965), p. 122.

"The communist drive to impose their political and economic system
on others is the primary cause of world tension today."[16]

In recent years, this appraisal has rarely been used by Washington
officials in evaluating the implications of Soviet deployments of an
ABM system and accelerated Soviet production of ICBM's. In 1967,
President Johnson conceded:

> The Soviet Union has in the past year increased its long range missile
> capabilities. It has begun to place near Moscow a limited anti-missile
> defense. My first responsibility to our people is to assure that no nation
> can ever find it rational to launch a nuclear attack or to use its nuclear
> power as a credible threat against us or our allies.[17]

One would hope that this statement would imply a commitment on
the part of the government to reassess its security programs "to assure
that no nation can ever find it rational to launch a nuclear attack."
Instead we were told:

> That is why an important link between Russia and the United States
> is our common interest in arms control and disarmament. We have
> the duty to slow down the arms race between us, in both conventional
> and nuclear weapons and defenses. Any additional race would impose
> on our peoples, and on all mankind, an additional waste of resources
> with no gain in security to either side.[18]

In his 1967 budget message to Congress, President Johnson stated:

> In 1968, we will continue intensive development of Nike-X but take
> no action now to deploy an antiballistic missile (ABM) defense; ini-
> tiate discussions with the Soviet Union on the limitation of ABM de-
> ployments; in the event these discussions prove unsuccessful, we will
> reconsider our deployment decision. To provide for actions that may
> be required at that time, approximately $375 million has been included

[16] John F. Kennedy, "Toward a Strategy of Peace," a speech made at commencement exercises at American University, Washington, D.C., June 10,
1963, *Department of State Bulletin*, July 1, 1963, p. 5.

[17] State of the Union Message, *Philadelphia Inquirer*, January 11, 1967,
p. 4.

[18] *Ibid.* However, in his 1967 budget statement, the President requested substantial stand-by funds for the possible start on the production of the Nike-X
missile. By so doing, the President "served notice on Soviet officials that the
United States was taking serious steps to prepare for production of antimissile
missiles if a no-deployment agreement is not reached. This should give his
negotiators additional leverage with the Russians."—*The New York Times*,
January 25, 1967, p. 17.

in the 1968 budget for the production of Nike-X for such purposes as defense of our offensive weapon systems.

Maintain our decisive strategic superiority by initiating procurement of the advance Poseidon submarine-launched missile, improving our present strategic missiles, and further safeguarding our capacity to direct our forces in the event of attack.[19]

Despite substantial evidence that the Soviet Union is again preparing to challenge U.S. strategic superiority, the United States continues to adhere to a one-sided military doctrine. Although for the past several years the United States has sought to dissuade the Soviet Union from deploying an ABM system, it seems highly unlikely that Soviet leaders can now be induced to dismantle the ABM system they have already deployed. U.S. repetition of this diplomatic overture in 1967 belied an underlying apprehension that all is not well with our strategic posture. The rationale for this diplomacy was candidly stated by Roswell L. Gilpatric.

At worst, Soviet intentions regarding a renewed arms race should be treated as ambivalent and unclear rather than entirely negative. *Their ABM deployment can be accounted for otherwise than as indicating a desire to alter the strategic power balance.* It not only is in keeping with the ultimate in defensive postures but also has resulted from military pressures within the Soviet regime rather than from a far-reaching decision to abandon the détente objective [italics added].[20]

Having surmised that the Soviets may want a *détente*, Gilpatric stated that any 1967 U.S. decision to proceed with major new weapons will jeopardize the *détente* so ardently sought by Washington. He therefore concluded:

If a third world war is to be avoided the United States, as the most advanced of the superpowers, must take the lead in demonstrating a willingness to practice self-discipline both in the use of force and in providing itself with the power to apply force. The present situation puts to a critical test our national determination not to be swerved from the rightness and sanity of that course.[21]

In the 1967 State of the Union Message, in which President Johnson advocated disarmament talks to ease the Soviet strategic threat,

[19] *The New York Times,* January 25, 1967, p. 20.
[20] Roswell L. Gilpatric, "Are We on the Brink of Another Arms Race?", *The New York Times Magazine,* January 15, 1967, p. 84.
[21] *Ibid.*

the President also told the American people: "We have chosen to fight a limited war in Vietnam in order to prevent a larger war—a war almost certain to follow if the communists succeed in taking over South Vietnam by force. If they are not checked now, the world can expect to pay a far greater price to check them later."[22]

Just which Communists the President had in mind is not clear. For without the immense aid and diplomatic support the North Vietnamese are receiving from the Soviet Union, as well as from Communist China, the war in Vietnam would probably be over. According to Harrison E. Salisbury, "North Vietnam's fighting ability is almost completely dependent upon the aid and support of both China and the Soviet Union."[23] It should be obvious that only one or the other or both of the Communist giants could promote a larger war. Paradoxically, Washington officials regard Communist China, which in 1967 was in the throes of a cultural revolution, as far more menacing than the stabler and more powerful Soviet Union. Toward the latter nation, "our objective is not to continue the cold war, but to end it."[24]

The advocates of peaceful engagement and "bridge building" with the East claim that the Cuban missile crisis marked the high tide of Soviet aggression. Subsequently, the United States joined with the Soviet Union in the test-ban and hot-line agreements and traded wheat for Soviet gold. Despite the stepped-up tempo of the war in Vietnam, the Johnson Administration has been accelerating its efforts to improve relations with the Kremlin. President Johnson set the tone for a campaign of peaceful engagement in a major policy speech made on October 7, 1966. In this speech, he said: "We do not intend to let the differences on Vietnam or elsewhere prevent us from exploring all opportunities for reconciliation with the East." Subsequently, the United States and the Soviet Union agreed on the terms for a space treaty and authorized the initiation of direct airline flights between Moscow and New York. Other agreements proposed by Washington in 1966 were an East-West trade-relations bill that would extend most-favored-nation treatment to several Eastern European Communist nations and a United States–Soviet consular

---

[22] State of the Union Message, *loc. cit.*
[23] *The New York Times*, January 17, 1967, p. 1.
[24] State of the Union Message, *loc. cit.*

treaty. Also in the wind was the U.S. plan to open all but two or three ports in the United States to ships from European Communist countries. All these measures were advanced as reasonable marginal steps designed to ensure that the *détente* will continue to blossom.

A few dark clouds marred the vision of the United States and the Soviet Union marching arm in arm toward the sunset of a durable peace. In January, 1966, the Soviet Union participated in a tricontinental conference in Havana and proclaimed its support of Communist wars of national liberation in Latin America, Africa, and Asia. Large quantities of Soviet arms were shipped to Algeria in 1966 to aid in its conflict with Western-oriented Moroccans. Under Egyptian auspices, the Soviets were simultaneously building naval bases in Alexandria and Yemen. They also supported, with arms and advice, Egyptian and Syrian endeavors to fan Arab hostilities against Israel, which culminated in the 1967 Arab-Israeli war. In December, 1966, Soviet Premier Kosygin discussed with President de Gaulle a pan-European conference that would be convened to bring about an all-European peace settlement from which the United States would be excluded. Earlier, Kosygin had visited Turkey to try to wean that once-staunch ally further away from the United States. Also in 1966, a distinguished American scholar of Soviet affairs, Marshall Shulman, was peremptorily asked to leave the Soviet Union.

In December, 1966, the Soviet Union announced that its military spending would be increased by 8.2 per cent, primarily because "the aggressive, monopolist circles of the United States have recently sharpened international tensions and increased the dangers of a new world war."[25] In a message to Hanoi, Soviet Defense Minister Malinovsky stated that "the fighters of the Soviet Army and Navy energetically condemn the bloody crimes of the United States militarists in Vietnam."

The Soviets have repeatedly called for the unity of Vietnam and the expulsion of the American aggressor. They have boasted about the excellent quality of the missiles, antiaircraft guns, and planes they have sent to support North Vietnam. North Vietnamese pilots have been trained both in the Soviet Union and in North Korea. When all the facts are added up, it appears that in Vietnam the United States has been as much at war with Moscow as it has with Ho Chi

[25] *The New York Times,* December 16, 1966, p. 1.

Minh. Nevertheless, the United States has repeatedly implored Moscow's good offices to end the conflict in Vietnam, but to no avail.

From the record, it is logical to conclude that the Soviet Union is more interested in promoting Western disunity and in weakening American influence than it is in achieving a genuine *détente*. To one unattuned to the arcane logic of "bridge building," it remains difficult to reconcile Soviet action with official American interpretations of Soviet intentions.

The Soviets profess to be the leaders of a world revolutionary force, and their main criticism of the Chinese Communists has been that Chinese polemics against Moscow imperil the over-all Communist cause. As *Pravda* expressed it: "The policy of subverting unity of action, of intensifying attacks on the Marxist-Leninist parties is harmful to the entire international Communist and liberation movement."[26] The leaders in Moscow, however, have attempted to build a reputation for being less adventuresome than their counterparts in Peking—a reputation not entirely deserved. Both the Chinese- and the Soviet-led revolutionary forces, like bicycle riders, can maintain equilibrium only by moving forward.

No matter how many difficulties the Communist world may experience internally, the United States can ill afford to subscribe to policies based on the sanguine assumption that the Communist strategic threat to U.S. security has diminished. The total destructive power at the disposal of the Soviet Union is becoming greater with each passing year. The size, diversity, and technical sophistication of the Soviet economic system and the absolute volume of resources that the Soviets are able to allocate to the military sector are quite sufficient to present a threat of great magnitude and indefinite duration to the United States and its allies.

Since advanced offensive and defensive weapons are becoming increasingly costly and technologically complex, the Soviets, beset by internal economic troubles, may desire temporarily to relax political tensions and even the technological military competition with the United States. The Soviets know that the United States is far better able than they to bear the expense of continued competition in armaments technology.

[26] *The New York Times,* November 21, 1965, p. 5.

Since the Cuban missile crisis, the world has experienced a precarious nuclear *détente* between the Soviet Union and the United States. Two interpretations of the motivation behind the *détente* are possible: The Soviet Union is simply playing for time until the constellation of forces is more favorable and until Soviet strategic capabilities can be increased; or the Soviets have found their previous course too risky and sincerely desire a *rapprochement* with the United States. In the short term, these motivations may coincide. As a matter of fact, it is in the U.S. interest to see to it that they do.

If the Soviets desire a settlement, they will undoubtedly seek to achieve it as cheaply as possible. A too easily won period of relaxation of tensions may tempt the Soviets, whatever their present intentions, into a more intransigent future course. Until the Kremlin abandons its conflict doctrine and practices, the United States, while keeping the door open to a real accommodation, must conduct its policy on the assumption that the Soviets are playing for time. The United States, while selling time as dearly as possible, should test the sincerity of the Soviets' desire for a *détente* by determining the extent to which they are willing to resolve major outstanding political issues. Unless real progress is made on issues threatening the peace, the United States must be wary of chasing after the semblance of harmony rather than its substance and must reject the appealing notion that a *détente* is an end in itself. Americans would do well to heed Leonid Brezhnev:

> . . . the "cold war" and the confrontation of military blocs, the atmosphere of military threats, seriously hamper the activity of revolutionary, democratic forces. . . . And, conversely, the past few years have shown quite clearly that in conditions of slackened international tension the pointer of the political barometer moves left.[27]

In Defense of Values

The U.S. nuclear arsenal reinforces and sustains U.S. conventional power and is a strength that can be used to influence human behavior. The growing belief that the tremendous destructive power of

[27] Speech by Leonid I. Brezhnev, April 24, 1967, at Karlovy Vary, Czechoslovakia, cited in U.S. Congress, Senate, Subcommittee on National Security and International Operations of the Committee on Government Operations, *The Soviet View of NATO,* 90th Cong., 1st Sess., 1967, p. 14.

nuclear weapons renders these weapons useless as a rational instrument of policy[28] confronts the United States with a basic dilemma: The security of the United States and its allies throughout the Free World is ultimately dependent on weapons that many people assert will never be used. Since Soviet acquisition of a major nuclear arsenal, the notion that peace—rather than peace with justice and freedom—should be the basic aim of American policy has gained new advocates.

As nuclear capabilities have grown in destructive potential, policymakers have become less certain of the values in defense of which force can be justifiably used. Some students of American social history in the twentieth century contend that Americans have, in general, become less certain than their forefathers of the values that should guide them in their dealings with other peoples. War has been one of the most persistent scourges of the human race. Now that the excessive destructive power of atomic weapons has been added to the historical disorders of war, it has become proper to ask how the idea of a "just war" can be defended.

The values we are committed to defend find expression only in living human beings; hence, the beliefs and hopes that make human existence worthwhile might themselves disappear in a general nuclear exchange. On the other hand, submitting to an aggressor who is not squeamish about the use of nuclear weapons might ultimately bring about equally massive liquidation of human beings and their values. A peace cult that places human survival above every other value could, if it became a universal doctrine, destroy what is purposeful and challenging in human existence. What would the quality of life be like in Western Europe today if Hitler had been met everywhere in the West with passivity and pacifism?

Many students of contemporary world politics tend to overlook the intrinsic philosophical conflict between Communist-controlled states and those societies governed by some form of representative democracy. The philosophical gulf between Western pluralistic societies and Communist-controlled societies is strikingly revealed in the following:

[28] In one sense, force can never be a rational instrument of policy. Yet the possession of force may be required to make an adversary behave more rationally.

Cybernetics is a new science which is being used progressively more frequently. It aspires to the study of processes of *control occurring in nature, industry and human society,* that is, to the coverage of practically all of human activity and, for this reason, we rightfully demand that the ideological basis on which this science develops in the Soviet Union be impeccable. As has been pointed out above, since the first days of the Revolution V. I. Lenin was very much *absorbed in the science of control.* During all the years of existence of the Soviet regime considerable attention has been given to these matters in the USSR [italics added].[29]

Basic philosophical divergence on the nature of man and the political order does not necessarily imply an inevitable resort to armed conflict by either side. For the most part, and for very practical reasons, the Communist-controlled states have chosen to coexist with their adversaries during the nuclear age. They have chosen coexistence because unless they achieve decisive superiority, the destruction wrought by nuclear arms would be entirely disproportionate to the goals they are committed to pursue. The contrary might prove to be the case if they do achieve superiority. Nevertheless, many Western students of contemporary international relations turn to disarmament, whether achieved through unilateral U.S. initiatives or through international agreements, as the only logical alternative to the present dependence on nuclear weapons as the ultimate arbiter of conflict.

A mutual agreement to disarm, if actually carried out, would probably give rise to new means of conflict, which could ultimately be as destructive to political institutions and human values as the outlawed weapons systems. In fact, many strategists contend that the existence of nuclear weapons has forced the superpowers to proceed with great caution and to raise their competition to a higher plane of rationality, characterized by subtler moves and limited violence. Such analysts fear that if nuclear weapons should be done away with, the more primitive tendency toward the full-scale use of brute force might very well reappear. This could lead to conditions of grave instability and, sooner or later, to general war, which, paradoxically, would be likely to become nuclear.

[29] U.S. Department of Commerce, Office of Technical Services, Joint Publications Research Service, *Cybernetics at the Service of Communism: USSR* (Washington, D.C.: Joint Publications Research Service, 1962), translated from the Russian *Kibernetica na sluzhbu kommunizma,* ed. A. I. Berg (Moscow and Leningrad, 1961), 1, 7.

Nor can we readily assume that each side in the global confrontation is equally interested in the removal of nuclear weapons from the conflict arena. Despite many advances that have been made in the protection of strategic offensive forces, by either hardening or concealment, and despite the advances that have been made in the potential protection of heavily populated urban areas, there may be circumstances under which a calculated first strike could give an expansionist power unsurpassed military advantages.

The United States has properly rejected the launching of a first nuclear strike as a morally and politically indefensible act. Yet, it is not always recognized that the renunciation of a first strike in the nuclear age demands enormous additional defense expenditures. A nation that deliberately chooses to support the principles of international morality in the nuclear age must be willing to pay a high price. Thus far, the United States has shown itself willing to pay this price for a stable, nonprovocative strategic-weapons system and for safeguards against its accidental, premature, or uncontrolled use.

There is no easy way out of the dilemma posed by the threat of nuclear weapons. Nuclear pacifists have the easiest position to defend, at least superficially. They assert that all resort to force is immoral, yet every society maintains forces for the purpose of ensuring domestic order. Unless steps are taken to curb international as well as domestic anarchy, the survival of the individual citizen, even of the avowed pacifist, is threatened just as much as the lives of those who assume the obligation for maintaining external order.

Thorny problems such as these have prompted a widening debate in the United States on the subject of war and peace in the nuclear age. Unfortunately, outside of professional circles, there is almost no counterpart to this debate taking place inside the Soviet Union. Public debate over foreign policy is nonexistent in the Soviet Union and all other Communist states, since politics, in such countries, is the preserve of the elite—an exceedingly small group of dedicated conflict-oriented individuals.

Any effort to establish some kind of *modus vivendi* with the individuals who rule the Soviet Union is based upon the assumption that trustworthy agreements can be reached with them. The presumed trustworthiness of the Soviet Government cannot be based on an identity of political interests between that government and the

United States, for Communist doctrine espouses conflict between classes and between states, that is, between "socialist" and "imperialist" states. Throughout Soviet history, pronouncements from the Kremlin have been designed to serve a political purpose. The Soviet Government, by every means of propaganda, makes a deliberate and constant effort to shape the thought of the Soviet people. Soviet leaders have frequently practiced deception toward their own people and in their relations with the peoples and governments of other countries.

When Premier Khrushchev was installing MRBM's in Cuba, he used every means of communication within his reach to convey to Washington the impression that these missiles were purely defensive. From his point of view, they were, since by their own doctrine the Soviets cannot fight an unjust or aggressive war or possess offensive weapons. In November, 1965, Senator Henry M. Jackson declared that the Soviet Union had reneged on a promise to reduce production of nuclear-weapons material. The senator concluded that "contrary to a widespread impression that Moscow is cutting its strategic military capability, in truth Moscow is diligently expanding both its offensive and defensive capacity—including ballistic missile and nuclear warhead development and production."[30]

The totalitarian government of the Soviet Union is generally able to provide itself with the security and secrecy required to prevent the dissemination of information it desires to withhold. We simply do not know what experiments Soviet scientists are conducting behind the walls of their many laboratories. Even under conditions of complete disarmament, on a bilateral or multilateral basis but without adequate inspection, the knowledge and ingenuity of the Soviet scientists could be marshaled anew to seek a decisive military advantage over the Free World. Consequently, the assumptions underlying "experimentalist" plans for the United States unilaterally reversing the arms competition may be altogether fallacious.

If it is an aim of the Soviet Union to gain an exploitable strategic superiority over the United States, then the experimentalist approach

[30] Quoted in Chalmers Roberts, *Washington Post*, November 24, 1965, p. 7. (Senator Jackson is chairman of the Joint Atomic Energy Committee's Military Applications Subcommittee and is a member of the Senate Preparedness Subcommittee of the Armed Services.)

of unilateral initiative will be fraught with extreme danger. The Soviets might use a strategic advantage for the attainment of political objectives, such as the withdrawal of the Western powers from West Berlin and other outposts on the periphery of the Free World. The United States, having started down the experimentalist path to peace, may have gambled away its strategic superiority while still possessing a considerable force. Under these circumstances, the United States might refuse Soviet demands and threaten to fight; yet the strategic inferiority of the United States might lead the Soviets to misinterpret these threats as a bluff. The result could be the very war that the unilateralists, as well as the author, wish to avoid.

Some observers hold that the societies of the Soviet Union and the United States are slowly converging to the point where fundamental differences will become blurred. The Soviets, however, reject this thesis:

> In circles of bourgeois ideologists, the perspective of so-called convergence of capitalism and socialism is widely discussed, again on the basis of the conception "a single industrial society."
>
> Preaching "convergence," as a matter of fact, is the expression of the unrealizable hopes of the restoration of capitalism in socialist countries so long as the socio-economic basis, in quality, of the forthcoming alleged "synthesis" of capitalism and socialism proposes the notorious system of "free ownership," that is, private ownership. . . . The thesis of a common "industrialism" for socialism and capitalism undoubtedly signifies an attempt to castrate the specifics of socialist development, to hide the basic qualitative difference between capitalism and socialism, speculating on the similar features of their technical development but consequently distorting the true nature of socialism and its future perspective.[31]

Convergence, if it ever takes place, will be an exceedingly slow process. Both societies are changing, for no society is static. In the Soviet Union, the present trend appears to be toward "liberalization," yet the Soviet Government seems determined to control and manipulate this trend and to forestall East-West convergence at any but a "safe" price. In any case, the Western construct of a safer world should not be based on *a priori* propositions that have not yet been borne out by empirical evidence.

[31] Yelena Nodrshinskaya, "The Heralds and Henchmen of Reaction," *Pravda*, February 4, 1966, translation by Harriet Fast Scott.

Many of the current assumptions about the Soviet Union, on which recommendations for U.S. policy are based, are derived either explicitly or implicitly from perceptions of the Sino-Soviet dispute and the progressive disintegration of the Soviet bloc. The fact is that, all along, the global power of the United States has been a factor in forcing the split-up of the Communist world. Were it not for this factor, the Soviet Union, holding a near monopoly of weapons of mass destruction, might be able to assert and maintain its unquestioned supremacy over all Communist nations.

The Use of Influence

In the years since the death of Stalin, there has emerged in the Soviet Union a "reformist" element that is presumably opposed to the doctrine of. Communist expansion through war. An opposing faction of radical "adventurists" is said to advocate world revolution even at the risk of nuclear war. Between these two groups stands the Party leadership, allegedly steering a middle course but willing to threaten the gravest consequences when the United States acts to defend its commitments. Although both Soviet groups continue to strive for world Communism, it has proven more difficult for the United States to cope with those favoring coexistence than with the Communist "war hawks." The split in NATO today must be attributed in significant part to the "soft" Khrushchev line, even though the former Soviet Premier's commitment to genuine permanent coexistence need not have been deeper than, for example, Stalin's commitment to a *détente* in the 1930's.

The issue is whether the United States can or should try to influence these Soviet groups. If we should, the ability of the United States to manipulate Communist means might ultimately influence Communist ends. Substantial Western superiority might strengthen the hand of the reformists, whereas the unwillingness of the West to maintain superiority might abet the radicals. The converse might also occur. Substantial Western superiority might provide the radicals with an argument for augmented Soviet force levels. Sustained U.S. superiority, however, would likely render futile any attempt by either a reformist or a radical Soviet faction to expand the Communist world. In sum, U.S. military superiority in support of sound policies and backed by an adroit ideological offensive would be one realistic circumstance for inducing fundamental transformations in Communist-controlled societies.

The West's power need not be increased to such provocative proportions as to incite a desperate Soviet response. Even while maintaining or, if need be, building capabilities, the United States should communicate a willingness to proceed by careful stages toward genuine disarmament and arms control. The Soviets, for their part, would have to signal their intention to abandon expansionist policies. They might, for example, raze the Berlin Wall and withdraw from Cuba just as the Western European nations have withdrawn from most of Asia and Africa. None of these measures would lessen the essential security of the Soviet Union or even the integrity of Communist institutions.

One day, the Soviets may demonstrate an increasing and genuine interest in rational negotiations and accommodations. Yet a society in whose institutional fabric militant goals and conspiratoral conflict methods have been inextricably woven cannot be expected to turn to moderation and respectability, even if it wishes to do so, except over a long period of time.

The Pursuit of Peace

For the past ten years, the United States has tried to reduce tensions with the Soviet Union in order to create a world in which the risk of nuclear war can be sharply reduced. President Eisenhower's "Open Skies" proposal, made at the 1955 Geneva summit meeting, was an unprecedented offer to conduct reciprocal aerial inspection of the military installations of the two major powers and thus to reduce the chances of a nuclear conflict. At the height of the Hungarian uprising, John Foster Dulles, the principal exponent of the "liberation" doctrine, gave the Soviets an indication that the United States appreciated their concern for the security of their western borders.

In our desire for peace, we have responded to Soviet peace moves with unflagging eagerness. Many times we have hoped; many times we have been disappointed. The Soviets have broken the monotony of the Cold War with an occasional Berlin crisis and threatened the United States and its allies with nuclear blackmail. The U.S. response has been measured and restrained, and successive U.S. administrations have continued the quest for peace. President Kennedy declared in his speech at American University on June 10, 1963:

> World peace, like community peace, does not require that each man love his neighbor: it requires only that they live together in mutual tolerance, submitting their disputes to a just and peaceful settlement. And history teaches us that enmities between nations, as between individuals, do not last forever.[32]

Paradoxically, the goal of the Communists is also peace—but for their kind of peace, the precondition is the elimination or conversion of non-Communist political systems. Since few non-Communists want peace on these terms, what approach is feasible? Practically all persons who seek an alternative to the Cold War and the ensuing military preparedness at least share the belief that evolutionary changes will have to take place within the Communist system if the basis for a more peaceful world is to be created. The issue dividing the advocates of differing paths toward peace is really one of means: What means or combination of means can best persuade the Soviet Union and Communist China to abandon their expansionist efforts?

It is often said that there are no absolutes in the world of politics, that all things are relative. There is certainly no absolute guarantee against war, but there is almost a moral certainty that if we remain strong, there will be no nuclear holocaust in the indefinite future. The best that man can do is to make this world as safe as possible under presently prevailing circumstances.

It is a cardinal rule of Communist strategy to move forward when the enemy's resistance is weak, to stand fast when his resistance is strong, and to retreat in the face of overwhelming force. Had Moscow known beforehand of the U.S. determination to defend South Korea, Americans might not have had to fight there at all. Similarly, when Khrushchev arranged to place Soviet missiles on launching pads in Cuba, he apparently did not believe that the United States would become aware of them before they became operational; or else he expected the Kennedy Administration to temporize until their deployment was a *fait accompli*. Both the Korean War and the Cuban crisis were the result of the Soviet leaders' miscalculations of U.S. intent and vigilance. In this sense, the United States must shoulder

[32] *Department of State Bulletin*, July 1, 1963, p. 3.

part of the blame for those major crises, since whenever there was no doubt about U.S. strategic superiority and determination to back up its commitments and policy objectives, the Soviets avoided a direct confrontation.

The world struggle is a dispute over political and philosophical values. Since under Communist conflict doctrine it is permissible for Communists to impose their system by force and coercion, those who reject Communist values must have the power to prevent their own forced conversion. Thus, for the West, military power serves the purpose of ensuring that the political and philosophical dialogue with the Communist leadership can continue.

Obviously, changes cannot be imposed on the Soviet Union from without. Indeed, any attempt to do so would probably bring about the nuclear disaster we seek to avoid. But changes within nations do not occur in a vacuum; invariably they are in some measure influenced from the outside. The Bolshevik Revolution of 1917, for instance, had its origins in ideas introduced from Western Europe. Many wars of the past have been caused by regimes that could either disregard or manipulate public opinion. A democracy finds it difficult, if not impossible, to pursue a policy of aggression. The process by which some kind of representative government can be introduced into the Soviet system is difficult to perceive. The Communist Party of the Soviet Union seeks to mold human destiny in accordance with its leaders' ideas of what the future ought to be. This concept of rule allows the leadership to disregard present shortcomings in their system. According to one astute observer: "The people of the U.S.S.R. may starve under Lenin; they may be worked to death in Stalin's concentration camps; they may live cramped and meager lives even under the milder principate of Khrushchev. These in-between things hardly matter—so long as all comes right in the end."[33]

A fundamental Western goal should be to induce Soviet leaders to be more concerned with the present needs of their subjects and less concerned with the "utopia" of the distant future. The discrepancies between the present conditions and those promised for the future in Communist countries are intrinsic contradictions that make Com-

[33] Oscar Gauss, "Soviet Economic Developments," *Commentary*, February, 1964, p. 68.

munist systems vulnerable to political persuasion by the West.[34] There is much evidence that Communist leaders are vulnerable to systematic critiques of Communism's inescapable contradictions.[35] If the West employs all the arts of communication to undermine the faith of Communist leaders, the props that support Communist power may eventually crumble. Isolated efforts are not enough. We must conduct a dialogue with the Communists in every sphere of philosophical and social activity, both behind the Iron Curtain and in the West. Throughout the period of the Cold War and even in periods of *détente,* the Soviets and the West have been engaged in debate rather than dialogue. For the most part, neither side has listened very attentively to the other. The Western mind, imbued with a liberal tradition, has been somewhat more willing to hear what the other side had to say, but it has often been repelled by the inflexible dogmatism of nineteenth-century Marxist ideology, on which Soviet statements have usually been based.

A sizable segment of the Western intellectual community has always been favorably disposed to at least some of the analytical categories that characterize the Marxist theoretical system; for this reason, the West has been more willing than the Communists to conduct an authentic dialogue. The Communists have sometimes acted as if they were afraid to enter into two-way communication, lest they be corrupted by what they regard as a decadent culture. If both sides are to make contributions for their mutual benefit, they must engage in an intellectual exchange—an exchange about the kind of world

[34] On Communist contradictions, see H. B. Acton, *The Illusion of the Epoch: Marxism-Leninism as a Philosophical Creed* (London: Cohen & West, 1955); John Robinson Beal, *The Secret Speech* (New York: Duell, Sloan & Pearce, 1961); Bertram D. Wolfe, "Communist Vulnerabilities," *The New Leader,* September 7, 1959, reprinted in *American Strategy for the Nuclear Age,* eds. Walter F. Hahn and John C. Neff (Garden City, N.Y.: Doubleday, 1960), pp. 89–102.

[35] For an interesting personal account of the effect of the realization of Communist contradictions on the minds of professional Communists, see Wolfgang Leonhard, *Child of the Revolution* (Chicago: Henry Regnery, 1958), pp. 380–86. Leonhard, a former Communist who defected to the West (1949–50), describes his personal reactions to the Western press, of which he was an avid reader from 1945 on. He states that an occasional article that described Communism in the Soviet Union or Eastern Europe in its true light often led to some serious soul-searching by Communist Party members. The rest of the Western press was regarded as propaganda and therefore made no impact.

order that they would like to see emerge; about the role of science and technology, of the spiritual and cultural values inherited from the past, in the solution of human problems; and about optimum forms of national, regional, and international organization in a dangerously complex world. There are some signs that this kind of dialogue is beginning.

The dialogue must continue until Soviet leaders acquire the "rational temper of mind" that is the prerequisite for a just solution of the issues dividing us. The United States and its allies must maintain sufficient military power to prevent the Communists from resorting to nuclear war to escape from their self-created dilemma.

Successful timing is the key to successful politics. In foreign policy, timing must be related to the hierarchy of threats confronting a nation. The first concern of the United States, therefore, must be Soviet nuclear power and, to a far lesser extent, Communist China. Many voices proclaim that the time has come to arrange a *détente* with the Soviet Union. President de Gaulle's vision of a "Europe from the Atlantic to the Urals" is based on what he sees as a need to prepare the Western world against an impending Chinese drive across Asia. Raymond Aron, the well-known political writer, interpreted de Gaulle's aims in this fashion: "The Unity of the Greater Europe—from the Atlantic to the Urals, even if impossible today—would seem to be from now on the ultimate objective of Western Politics."[36] Almost simultaneously came the report that "President Johnson ordered his senior consultants on the North Atlantic Treaty Organization to start thinking more in terms of a long-range easing of tension with Eastern Europe and less in terms of the static anti-Soviet defense of the last 17 years."[37]

To help shift Western apprehension from Moscow to Peking, Soviet spokesmen have been promoting the specter of the yellow peril. After attending the 1964 Afro-Asian Solidarity Conference in Algiers, B. G. Gafurov, the leader of the Soviet delegation and Asian-affairs expert, declared in Paris: "Don't you French see that the Chinese are trying to unify the yellow and black races against the whites? Don't you see that the nature of socialist propaganda of the Chinese is dan-

---

[36] *Figaro*, May 7–8, 1966, p. 3.
[37] *The New York Times*, May 18, 1966, p. 1, report by Benjamin Wells.

gerous, not only for the Soviet Union, but for the nations of Europe as well?"[38]

If the Chinese become a serious threat to the Soviet Union and indirectly to Western Europe, an East-West *rapprochement* can be effected. Meanwhile, the Soviets are capitalizing on the Sino-Soviet split as part of their endeavor to gain hegemony over whatever form of Europe emerges if NATO disintegrates.

The United States "welcomes the desire of most of the governments in Eastern Europe for more normal relations with the nations of the West."[39] At the same time, it recognizes that Communist "wars of liberation are supported by Moscow and Peking"[40] and that both "principal Communist nations are committed to promotion of the Communist world revolution—even while they disagree bitterly on tactics."[41] Yet the U.S. government seems concerned primarily with Peking's role in supporting aggression and little with the scale of Soviet aid to Hanoi and Cairo or the subtle tactics the Soviets are using to dismantle NATO. Instead, the United States, Great Britain, and France seem to be competing with one another to establish an accord with Moscow. Meanwhile, the Soviets applaud Rumania for asking for a revision in the Warsaw Pact that signals further erosion in NATO. The fact that the Soviet Union has always sought the elimination of NATO is virtually overlooked.

It can be argued that the Soviets have maneuvered the United States into a corner by engaging us in negotiations concerning a moratorium on developing further ABM defenses. U.S. officials have reported that the Soviet Union had indicated "it preferred to broaden discussion of a proposed limitation of antimissile defenses. Moscow, according to these officials, has suggested that the talks take up the even more complex problem of limiting offensive missile systems."[42]

There is a possibility that the Soviets will widen the talks even further to include Vietnam, the antiproliferation treaty, and Germany. The Soviet Union has increased its aid to Hanoi and will probably do nothing to try to stop the war in Vietnam until the U.S.

[38] *Frankfurt Algemeine Zeitung,* April 6, 1964.
[39] Secretary of State Dean Rusk, in a speech delivered to the Council on Foreign Relations, New York, May 24, 1966.
[40] *The New York Times,* May 25, 1966, p. 8.
[41] *Ibid.*
[42] *The New York Times,* February 22, 1967, p. 1.

agrees to omit the "European option" from the text of the antiproliferation treaty. The Soviets seek to exploit the growing opposition in
the United States to the war in Vietnam. There seems to be little
doubt that the administration in Washington would like to have this
conflict resolved well in advance of the 1968 elections. A primary
aim of Soviet foreign policy has been the neutralization and/or demilitarization of West Germany. Early in 1967, Premier Kosygin
issued several statements from London that pointedly linked Vietnam
and Germany. The Soviet negotiation formula for U.S.–U.S.S.R.
issues might be reduced to the following: No U.S. ABM plus no
"European option" in the antiproliferation treaty equals peace in
Vietnam. It is possible that the Soviets are making their difficulties
with Communist China look worse than they really are in order to
induce the United States to settle with Moscow. The Soviets want
Americans to perceive the Soviet Union as a staid, *status quo* power,
one that is worried about the belligerent and irrational Chinese. Increasingly, the American people are being led to believe that the
problems of Europe and of NATO are a nuisance and stand in the
way of world peace in general and peace in the Far East in particular. This line of reasoning is plausible—it also demonstrates how the
Soviets exploit their military programs for diplomatic gain.

If the Soviets are patient enough, Western unity and hence Western strength may disintegrate. The past gives some counsel to the future: "It is a melancholy fact that both what we believe about ourselves and what we believe about the Russians militated against our
ever having been able to negotiate from strength, and militates in
favor of their being able to do so."[43] In the decade ahead, the Soviet
Union is likely to grow stronger in relation to the United States than
it is today. If we have often fared poorly when stronger, how shall
we fare when relatively weaker? The U.S. phobia concerning Peking
ignores the possibility that during the next decade Communist China
may never become the threat that many experts predict. Herman
Kahn, for example, stated in 1966 that Japan rather than Communist
China, will be the leading power in the Far East by the mid-1970's.[44]
McGeorge Bundy, national security adviser to Presidents Kennedy

[43] Coral Mary Bell, *Negotiation from Strength: A Study in the Politics of
Power* (New York: Alfred A. Knopf, 1963), p. 239.
[44] Third International Arms Symposium, Philadelphia, April, 1966.

and Johnson asserted in Tokyo:

> The real power of Communist China remains quite limited. I would hold, for example, that the whole future of Asia depends more upon the policy and purpose of the people and government of Japan, because of the great economic, social and political strength of modern Japan, than it does on mainland China.
>
> I do not think that mainland China constitutes a power or will constitute a power of size and effectiveness to make its doctrine real over a very long period of time.[45]

But even if Communist China becomes the strong, implacably hostile power that many persons fear, the United States will have time to deal with that problem. Perhaps the Soviet Union will change so that a cooperative relationship between the United States and the Soviet Union will become feasible as a restraint to Chinese Communist ambitions. But we cannot wish such cooperation into existence before the seeds of change within the Soviet system have pushed further through the harsh soil of Communist control.

Many of the tragedies of this century can be attributed to the lack of democratic institutions in Communist countries. John Strachey analyzed the structural failure of Communism in the brilliant essay "The Challenge of Democracy."[46] Few men are better qualified than Strachey, who knew Communism from the inside, to diagnose the implications of totalitarian rule for world order. As Strachey saw it, only representative government could avoid the crimes and disorders associated with totalitarianism:

> Representative government is the all important core of democracy as a whole. All the other, and in themselves equally valuable, features of democracy depend on this central feature: how freedom of speech, freedom of assembly, freedom of association, the rule of law, etc., are dependent in the long run for their very existence on representative government.
>
> No government in any one of the Western democracies can depart too far from the general point of view of the majority of its population. If it does, it gets dismissed, and another, more amenable, government is put in its place.[47]

[45] *The New York Times,* May 22, 1966, p. 16.
[46] John Strachey, "The Challenge of Democracy," in *The Great Ideas Today* (Chicago: Encyclopædia Britannica, Inc., 1965), pp. 520–90; originally published in *Encounter,* Pamphlet No. 10, 1963.
[47] *Ibid.,* p. 554.

Turning to the Communist system of rule, Strachey contended:

> The endowment of "the Party" with divine right has become a genuine historical monstrosity. It has led, and still leads, to crimes and disasters seemingly without end. . . .
> But what has all this got to do with democracy? It has got this to do with it: the policies of super concentration on heavy industry and armaments would have been totally impossible in a democracy.[48]

The issue of world peace is far broader than the United States–Soviet confrontation. Nuclear weapons exist in a politically divided world of international anarchy. If the human race, beset by many problems,[49] is to live with nuclear weapons, new political arrangements will have to be devised for their control.

This development, in turn, will depend on the advent of genuine cooperation between the Soviet Union and the United States and its Western allies. Communist China, too, may be persuaded to live in nuclear peace with the rest of the world. But the first and essential stage, Western-Soviet cooperation, can emerge only from a continuing exchange of ideas among Moscow, Washington, Paris, London, and Bonn.

For some time to come, however, the continuation of such an exchange will be a function of strategic superiority in the West. International communication of this sort might shift the value system and perception of the Soviet elite from an orientation toward conflict and revolution to a genuine dedication to human dignity and conflict resolution. This is likely to be a long, painful process of evolution, of alternating "thaws" and "freezes," of progressive assertion of the individual over totalitarian rule. For Americans, this is likely to be a period of alternating hope and disappointment, of uncertainty, and, if we are wise, of hard work for the cause of freedom, justice, and human progress.

For all mankind, the closing decades of this century will be a perilous passage into the third millennium. The character of the coming age will, in large measure, be determined by the extent to which Western values and the institutions of representative government can be communicated—and communicated speedily—to the leaders

[48] *Ibid.*, pp. 557, 568.
[49] Aldous Huxley catalogues many of these, particularly overpopulation, in *Brave New World Revisited* (New York: Harper & Row, 1965).

of the Soviet Union. The United States, as the leader of the West, will have a major voice in the shaping of the future world. President Kennedy expressed the universality of America's mission: "Our nation is commissioned by history to be either an observer of freedom's failure or the cause of its success." A measure of that success would be the reacceptance by the Russian people of the humanist, democratic traditions of the West. The task confronting the United States is to utilize, prudently, its power and persuasion in the making of the world of the future. In this formidable undertaking, the character of U.S. strategic forces, as well as the values they defend, will play a role of decisive importance.

Appendix

*Analysis of the Capability of Projected 1970 U.S.
Offensive and Defensive Forces to Execute Assured-
destruction and Damage-limiting Missions
Against Projected 1970 Soviet Forces*

The official projection of U.S. strategic offensive forces from 1962
through 1970 contrasts with the uncertainty that beclouds the future
of our strategic defensive forces.[1] This contrast reflected the greater
emphasis being placed on offensive strategic forces in comparison
with defensive forces, which, in turn, indicates that the U.S. policy
is to invest in penetration capability to overcome any Soviet ABM
system. These two components—the assured-destruction forces and the
damage-limiting forces—together comprise the U.S. strategic posture.
According to Secretary of Defense Robert S. McNamara:

> The requirement for strategic forces lends itself rather well to reason-
> ably precise calculation. A major mission of these forces is to deter war
> by their capability to destroy the enemy's warmaking capabilities. With
> the kinds of weapons available to us, this task presents a problem of
> reasonably finite dimensions, which are measurable in terms of the
> number and type of targets or aiming points which must be destroyed
> and the number and types of weapon delivery systems required to do
> the job under various sets of conditions.
>
> The first step in such a calculation is to *determine* the number,
> types, and locations of the *aiming points in the target system.*
>
> The second step is to *determine* the numbers and explosive yields
> of *weapons* which must be delivered on the aiming points *to insure the
> destruction of the target system.*

[1] These forces were projected in the *Statement of Secretary of Defense Robert S. McNamara Before the House Subcommittee on Defense Appropriations
for Fiscal Year 1967–71 Defense Program and 1967 Defense Budget* (mimeo.),
February 23, 1966. (Subsequently referred to as the *McNamara 1966 Posture
Statement.*)

The third step involves a *determination* of the size and character *of the forces best suited to deliver these weapons,* taking into account such factors as:

1. The number and weight of warheads that each type of vehicle can deliver.
2. The ability of each type of vehicle to penetrate enemy defenses.
3. The degree of accuracy that can be expected of each system, i.e., the CEP.
4. The degree of reliability of each system, i.e., the proportion of the ready operational inventory that we can count on getting off successfully within the prescribed time.
5. The cost effectiveness of each system, i.e., the combat effectiveness per dollar of outlay [italics added].[2]

Since the United States needs a capability to retaliate after being attacked, the number of strategic offensive weapons that would be destroyed by enemy attack must be taken into account. According to Secretary McNamara, an estimate should be made of the following:

The size, weight, and effectiveness of a possible enemy attack—based on estimates of the size and character of the enemy's long-range strategic offensive forces and their warhead yields, reliability and accuracy of their weapons system.

The degree of vulnerability of our own strategic weapon systems to such an attack.

Clearly, each of these crucial factors involves various degrees of uncertainty. But these uncertainties are not completely unmanageable. By postulating various sets of assumptions, ranging from optimistic to pessimistic, it is possible to introduce into our calculations reasonable allowances for these uncertainties.[3]

Once the number of weapons to be delivered on particular targets has been determined, choices are then made of the means of delivery —missiles or bombers. These choices are made, in principle, on a cost-effectiveness basis: All else being equal, what is the cheapest way of doing the job?

Although the United States has not yet invested in an operational ABM or adequate civil-defense system, the Defense Department recognizes that a sound strategic posture requires some optimum com-

[2] U.S. Congress, House Subcommittee of the Committee on Appropriations, *Department of Defense Appropriations for 1963,* 87th Cong., 2nd Sess., 1962, Part 2, p. 13.
[3] *Ibid.*

bination of strategic offensive and defensive forces. Secretary Mc-
Namara has said:

> Closely allied to the strategic retaliatory forces are the continental air
> and missile defense forces, i.e., those forces specifically designed to de-
> fend the North American continent from enemy attack. . . .
>   In contrast to the offensive mission, the defensive mission does not
> lend itself to even a reasonably close calculation of requirements. Fur-
> ther, we must bear in mind that no matter how much we spend, we
> simply cannot in this day and age provide an absolute defense for the
> continental United States.[4]

In his 1966 testimony, McNamara reiterated that general nuclear-
war forces should consist of two basic capabilities: the one to deter
a deliberate nuclear surprise attack (assured destruction), the second
to limit damage to population and industry by reducing the destruction that could be delivered by the adversary's offensive forces (damage limiting) in the event deterrence[5] should fail. It is calculated
that under the worst possible conditions—a Soviet surprise first strike
—a high proportion of the assured-destruction forces would survive
and that the effective delivery of even one-fifth of those surviving
assured-destruction forces on Soviet cities would be sufficient to destroy one-third of the Soviet urban-industrial population targets.[6]
Except inferentially, the published posture statements of the Secretary of Defense do not specify the mission and targets of the offensive
damage-limiting forces.

The outcome of a nuclear strike would change drastically if the
U.S. offensive damage-limiting forces could not fulfill their presumed
mission, that is, the destruction of the residual Soviet strike forces.
The Soviets not only would be able to utilize their ICBM's, bombers,
and command and control centers, which would otherwise be attacked by the damage-limiting forces, but also would be able to preserve their capability for killing tens of millions more Americans. In-
terestingly, it was reported following a White House briefing that
Secretary McNamara believes that "the country which attacks first
is likely to get hurt the worst."[7] His reasoning is that once the Soviets

[4] *Ibid.,* p. 42.
[5] See *McNamara 1966 Posture Statement,* p. 45.
[6] *Ibid.,* p. 48.
[7] *The Evening Bulletin* (Philadelphia), February 16, 1967, p. 58.

have expended their offensive capability, the United States would aim at everything, including population centers. This strategy would break down if a Soviet first strike simultaneously hit U.S. missile silos and undefended American cities.

The following projections may approximate the U.S. and Soviet strategic forces for the beginning of the 1970's:

TABLE I

U.S.S.R. 1970 strategic force	U.S. 1970 strategic force
1,000 ICBM's	1,020 ICBM's
20–40 orbital bombs	656 Polaris
800 IRBM's used against Eurasia	465 bombers
200 bombers	No ABM
200 submarine launch missiles	
An operational ABM system	
More extensive air-defense system	Air-defense system

With respect to the foregoing projections, the consequences of a calculated Soviet counterforce strike designed to knock out U.S. offensive forces in 1970 can be estimated: If the Soviets fired 1,000 (estimated) ICBM's—keeping in reserve all reload missiles, bombers, and submarine launch missiles—a significant proportion of the U.S. alert forces (exact quantity unknown) would survive. Under the worst conditions postulated by the Defense Department— that is, survival of only one-fifth of the assured-destruction forces (assuming 75 per cent reliability for Soviet ICBM's), which would be sufficient to destroy one-third of the Soviet urban-industrial complex—between one-fourth and one-fifth of the U.S. land-based missiles may survive (about 200–250). Given 75 per cent reliability, some (150–190; average 170) residual ICBM's would impact on Soviet targets. Because ICBM's are a relatively new weapons system and relatively few of them have been tested, there are insufficient data to determine their exact reliability. Seventy-five per cent appears to be a reasonable reliability figure, taking into account the complexity of the system. Assume that two-thirds of Polaris are on alert (27 boats) and that more than one-quarter of them are neutralized by Soviet ASW forces, leaving a total of 20 boats capable of firing 16 missiles each (320). Again, assuming one-quarter (80) are unreliable, 240 Polaris would impact. Consequently, about 410 U.S. missiles (the sum total of impacting land- and sea-based missiles) would theoretically be able to deliver their warheads to the Soviet target area. However, these would then encounter the deployed Soviet ABM system. Table 2 indicates a plausible range of U.S. land- and sea-based missiles that would reach Soviet territory:

TABLE 2

U.S. MISSILE IMPACT AS A FUNCTION OF U.S.
MISSILES SURVIVING A SOVIET FIRST STRIKE

No. of U.S. missiles surviving Soviet first strike	Impact, 75 per cent reliability*	Polaris addition†	Total Impact†
200	150	240	390
250	188	240	428
300	225	240	465
350	262	240	502
400	300	240	540
450	338	240	578
500	375	240	615
550	412	240	652
600	450	240	690

* This figure could vary as much as 20 per cent on the low side and 15 per cent on the high side, that is, between 55 and 90 per cent.
† Errors due to rounding.

Table 3 indicates the total number of missiles that could impact (last column of Table 2) if a Soviet ABM system is taken into account, with various kill probabilities postulated.

For the most adverse exchange model—that is, if the Soviet ABM force were to destroy some 75 per cent of an incoming U.S. strike that consisted of 410 Minutemen and Polaris missiles—only about 103 missiles would impact on their targets. But to achieve the assured-destruction mission of destroying 150 Soviet urban complexes, at least 150 missiles, or one per target, would have to impact. Under the postulated conditions, it is possible that not all 150 complexes would be destroyed. In fact, the ones attacked might not suffer severe damage, owing to the limited size of U.S. warheads. Furthermore, unless retargeting were effectively accomplished, some preplanned

TABLE 3

SOVIET ABM KILL POTENTIAL (KP)

U.S. impact	Remaining U.S. missiles after Soviet ABM Kp is included								
	35% Kp	40% Kp	45% Kp	50% Kp	55% Kp	60% Kp	65% Kp	70% Kp	75% Kp
390	253	234	214	195	176	156	137	117	98
420	273	252	231	210	189	168	147	126	105
465	302	279	256	232	209	186	163	140	117
502	326	301	276	251	226	201	176	151	126
540	351	324	297	270	243	216	189	162	135
578	376	345	317	289	261	233	202	173	145
615	400	369	338	308	277	246	215	184	154
652	425	392	359	326	293	261	227	196	163
690	448	415	380	345	310	276	242	207	173

targets might not be struck and others might be hit by more than one missile.

The value of a Soviet ABM depends in part on what it is protecting. To assign a high kill potential to a Soviet ABM that protects only a few cities or targets from a few U.S. missiles might not devaluate U.S. missile-penetration capability significantly. Alternatively, a full Soviet deployment of ABM's before 1970 might significantly alter the military balance, especially if the ABM's provide defense for both cities and military sites located in the Soviet heartland—the Moscow-Leningrad-Kiev triangle. In addition, an area-defense capability might also reduce U.S. missile capabilities. To see how such a situation would affect our missile-penetration capability, we have assumed an over-all attrition rate as the result of a Soviet area-defense system.

The reader should note that this primitive exchange model is illustrative only. No one now knows the actual number of Soviet ICBM's that could be launched against U.S. missile silos by 1970; nor can anyone know the survivability and reliability of U.S. missiles employed in an assured-destruction mission. But several plausible outcomes have been suggested.

This admittedly crude analysis of the forces planned for 1970, their stated goals, and their projected capabilities suggests that the

U.S. strategic retaliatory forces may not be able to execute the assured-destruction mission effectively under every circumstance. At the very least, the analysis shows that the U.S. capability to deter is questionable under the "worst possible" conditions postulated in Secretary McNamara's testimony—that is, if only about 200 U.S. missiles struck Soviet targets.

Several variables are crucial to the measure of effectiveness of strategic forces. For strategic offensive forces, these variables are: (1) survivability, (2) reliability, (3) penetrability, (4) CEP, and (5) yield. Each of these variables is interrelated and in some cases affects all the others. For the strategic defensive forces, the variables are: (1) reliability, (2) accuracy, and (3) kill potential.

Secretary McNamara has pointed out on many occasions that the effectiveness of strategic offensive forces is dependent on the ability of the surviving defensive forces to retaliate. In diverse ways, each of the variables mentioned above would reduce the absolute number of missiles exploding on target.

Because of the high-yield Soviet warheads and their unknown effect on hardened missile silos, it can be expected that a certain number of U.S. missiles would be made inoperable by EMP effects, such as target tape erasures, by blast-silo door malfunctions, or by command and control problems. Attrition of the surviving force would result from unreliable systems components (either delivery or weapon). The attrition rate might vary from 15 to 40 per cent as a result of guidance-control problems, booster-separation difficulties, or detonation malfunctions, for example.

Unknowns related to enemy air and missile defenses might also reduce a retaliatory attacking force. A high kill potential for a Soviet ABM, ineffective U.S. penetration aids or decoys, and so on, would affect the number of offensive weapons exploding on target.

As an expression of the accuracy of a missile, the CEP helps to determine the missile's ability to destroy a particular target. The nature of the target and the yield of the weapons-system warhead also determine how many warheads would be allocated to destroy the objective. Missiles propelled by large boosters have considerable payload capability; and because they can carry more warhead yield and decoys, they have significant advantages over lower-payload systems. For larger payloads, targeting options are greater and achievable with fewer missiles. In the case of lower payloads, several missiles may be needed to destroy one target.

Unless U.S. intelligence can reduce the uncertainties associated with Soviet strategic capabilities, fewer U.S. missiles might arrive on target than anticipated. With fewer missiles arriving on target (owing to the interplay of variables discussed above), Secretary McNamara's calculations may be too optimistic. Because of the unexpected, especially in a nuclear attack, it seems prudent to take measures that not only will enhance the U.S. retaliatory force (for example, more or improved missiles or alternative forms of penetration such as a new bomber) but also will provide some degree of damage limiting (for example, shelters and ABM defenses).

Index

Antiballistic missiles, 67, 72–74; Chinese and, 157, 218; in coercive strategy, 131; damage limiting and, 55; and deployment, case against, 155, 227; destabilization and, 157–58; developments in, Soviet, 62, 117; Dyson on, 156; R. B. Foster on, 155–56; freeze on, 155, 157; Kosygin on, 158–59; Nike-X, 72; Nike-Zeus, 72, 117; and nondeployment, criticism of, 155–56, 218; in persistent strategy, 122–23; Project Defender and, 68; in restrained strategy, 126; Stone on, 155–56; Talenskii on, 158; technical problems associated with, 200–202; and U.S. action, recommended, 218; U.S. strategy and, 157, 189–91, 213–15, 253–60; White House Conference on International Cooperation on, 155, 227

Antisatellite system, 151

Arms control: ABM moratorium, 8; and bombs in orbit, U.N. resolution prohibiting, 149, 151; Deutsch on, 144; fissionable material and, 8, 149; hot line and, 149, 233; inspection, 149, 151; NATO and, 171–72, 174–75; and negotiations, political, 149–54; nonproliferation treaty, 8, 16, 17, 227; nuclear strategy and, 138; Nuclear Test Ban Treaty, 8, 149, 233; plutonium reduction and, 149; positions on, 144, 147; proposals for, 139–40; prospects for, 159–62; Soviet interest in, 149–50; in space, treaty on peaceful use of, 152–53; strategic weapons freeze and, 154, 217

British deterrent, 92–93, 166
Bundy, McGeorge: on U.S. strategic superiority during Cuban missile crisis, 5

China: demography of, 106; economy of, 107; military power of, 107; nuclear development of, 136; nuclear potential of, 93, 107; nuclear strategy of, 108–9; "people's war," doctrine of, 108; Soviet relations with, 104
Command and control, 76
Conflict doctrine: Communists and, 100–101; Western ideas of, 101–3
Counterforce, 34, 45–47, 181, 218
Credibility, 38
Cuban missile crisis, 5, 7, 17, 22, 47, 55, 60, 62, 176, 233, 236; John F. Kennedy on, 5

Damage limiting, 45, 47, 181–83, 187
Decision-making: in the Communist system, 103–4; role of rationality in, 103; in the West, 103
Defense; see Nuclear strategy
Détente, 12, 112–13, 227–30; ABM and, 227, 232; deterrence and, 236–41; nonproliferation and, 227; U.S. and, 137, 233–35; U.S.S.R. and, 124–28, 134, 233–35, 236
Deterrence: Hook on, 144; problems of, 236–41; in U.S. strategy, 183–91
Deutsch, Morton: on arms control, 144
Dulles, John Foster: on massive retaliation, 27, 30–31; on SEATO, 29
Dyson, Freeman J., on the ABM, 156